THE

TO☠IC

STATES

OF

AMERICA

And How Spirituality Can Foster a National
Nervous Breakthrough
By Matt Socha

*This book is dedicated to my mother
and all my loved ones in Spirit.*

*And to the victims of the attacks on September 11, 2001 and their loves ones.
And to all of the casualties of wars and combat which have emerged since and their loved ones.*

*And to all those I have hurt or harmed in any way,
I sincerely apologize and hope you will forgive me.*

*And to all those who have hurt or harmed me,
I want you to know that I forgive you.
That does not mean you will be given another chance to do so.
Nor does it mean that I like you.*

And, above all, this book is dedicated to Spirit...

Contents:

Introduction

*"The price good men pay for indifference to public affairs
is to be ruled by evil men."*

- Plato

Ponzi schemes. Insider trading. Bullying on the rise. Molestation and child pornography scandals. Internet, marketing, and employment scams. An increase in hostile, toxic work environments. Hidden fees. Higher rents, taxes, and cost of living. Bursting housing bubbles and market crashes. Derivative and insider trading. Predatory lending. Soaring gas prices. New, endless, unconstitutional, and privatized wars for profit. Corrupt politicians representing corporate and foreign rather than constituent interest. Super Political Action Committees. Bickering political parties that act the same. Searing national debt. Increasing surveillance. The TSA. Customer service representative are more blasé and cavalier, customers are more demanding and abusive. Narcissistic, entitled, and domineering behavior on the rise. False flag operations. A pill-popping population. The rich get richer as the poor get poorer as the middle class disappears. Worst of all, the Golden Rule appears to be endangered.

There are so many symptoms of an empire in decline, Ancient Rome looks utopian in comparison. And many of us are appropriately worried.

Why is all this happening? As this book will explore, it's all due to one thing: *Our response to fear.*

Many of us feel that most, if not all, of the afflictions our country is facing (if not the world) is due to a poor economy, limited resources, an inept government, each other or, most specifically and what I had perceived to be, a corrupt ruling class. While these are likely to have some validity, a deeper examination reveals that all the maladies our country is currently facing could not have manifested without a foundation of mismanaged fear.

The original concept for this book was, like this version, divided into two parts. The first was to explore the toxic manifestations in American politics, media, economy, and culture and how it has spread as a fear epidemic. Specifically, it was to examine the ways and means by which a psychologically (and spiritually) malignant source of this toxicity, or "the power elite," spread fear and stress downward to the general population, causing it to become politically, economically, vocationally, and socio-culturally toxic as well. By doing so, this privileged minority usurped power in the form of money and control. In the second part of the book, various methods geared at spiritually cleansing and protecting ourselves, others, and - ultimately - our population from this toxicity would be explored.

However, a dream I had one night after ninety pages into the first draft changed my perspective.

In this dream, I was showing a retail vacancy to a woman who was planning on using the space to open a restaurant. She accepted the lease, but with the condition that I make some adjustments to the decor. In the space were two adjacent wall-sized murals connected at ninety-degree angles, both of which had dark brown trimming going across the top and the bottom. The one on the left had an earth-toned tapestry motif whereas the one on the right had very light, pale, pastel colors. Both were beautiful, we thought, but the buyer wanted to make some changes. The buyer liked the pale one on the right, but wanted the trimming painted pure white. She liked the one on the left, but wanted its earth-toned designs to be covered with a layer of white while keeping its trimming dark brown. I was a bit surprised by this, but I got to work covering this mural with white paint.

Initially confused by this dream when I woke up, it soon made sense later in the day. This dream was about the book, and I had received a message to modify it. The mural on the right represented the second, spiritual-based half of the book. Instead of the main body (the mural) being in the context of "dark" (the dark brown color of the trimming), it should be in the framework of Spirituality, unconditional love, and the Greatest Good (the white paint.)

The earth-toned mural on the left represented the first half of the book describing human dynamics, or it's "tapestry" in the framework of "dark." The white coat represented a thorough, uniform, and neutral perspective on this elaborate design - covering this "earthy" part with a perspective of non-judgement and truth, even though it was to be kept in the context of the "dark," or fear.

After interpreting this dream, it became clear to me: the source of the toxicity did not originate from a "privileged elite" per se. Rather, the source I had presumed to be dark was actually fear itself. The pyramid model was still applicable, yet the perspective had shifted: the fear "trickling-down" didn't just start at the top; it was the top: not in the sense that "the top" is "evil," yet they are deep down the most fear-motivated out of all of us. Those of us who seemed to have "the most" had the least in terms of secure, self-referential, unconditional love. I came to understand that their toxicity was not just due to the fact that they are fearful but, more importantly, how they have reacted to this fear. Yet, the fear that they harbored was being spread outward from its epicenter- seemingly with intention.

Like many of us, I had grown angry and frustrated at many of the "leaders" within the legislative, corporate, and financial sectors and was not impervious to the extent of the atrocities committed against the very constituents they were supposed to serve and protect. Yet, what previously appeared to be selfish, greedy, and self-serving acts at the expense of others' wellbeing were revealed as outcroppings of unresolved fear. Consequently, the harm that was inflicted on others as well as their true selves revealed them to be not just spiritually deficient in self-love and conscience, but "spiritually bankrupt." The contempt that I felt now accompanied with compassion and pity. Because of this, I ask that you read the following pages with an open mind free of judgement. It is not the objective of this book to lambaste, judge, or condemn anyone or to favor a particular "side." I do not and will not subscribe to any specific political affiliation, nor is the content of the following pages meant to represent a particular group of any sort.

Yet the effects of the elite's actions and decisions have caused many of us to feel undue stress and fear which, depending on our own capacity, have led many of us to engage in self-inflicting and/or unethical behavior. In doing so, many of us have lessened contact with our own conscience and true self, which is one of love. This has led to the overall degradation of our willingness to abide by The Golden Rule: "Do unto others as you would have them do unto you." If you haven't noticed, less and less of us are following it.

Many of us (if not, all of us) are hopeless, furious, scared, frustrated, depressed, and confused about our current state of circumstances - and understandably so. Most of us are concerned about the future - for our children, our grandchildren, and ourselves. Yet all of us want solutions, and it clearly does not appear to be coming from our elected officials. Neither, for a variety of reasons, have many solutions come from those within us who have been proactive. Perhaps these solutions do not even exist, or perhaps they lie within - perhaps we need to change ourselves.

As the first part of this book will illustrate, many of the problems we currently face have arisen from our own mishandling of fear, its infectious properties, and being exposed to more fear. Provided this is the case, many solutions can be found in modifying our reactions and assisting others with this as well. This will be the focus of the second part of this book: the ways we can manage and even transmute our fears and the fears of others by love, specifically using various spiritual practices to detox from fear.

To begin, we must first take a look at how many of us have been conditioned to handle fear.

☆

Part I:
One Nation, Under Stress

1

Origins of Defense Mechanisms: Schemas and their Reactions

"The only thing we have to fear is fear itself."

- Franklin Delano Roosevelt

Have you ever met a malevolent baby? One who scams, deceives, controls, manipulates, or tortures someone else? Of course not. Outside of crying to vocalize a need, babies are affectionate, emotionally honest, and loving. Have you ever met one who was depressed, addicted, or suicidal? I hope not. Babies are energetic, curious, and vivacious. All of us as human beings start our lives loving and trusting, fascinated and exploring, readily stating our needs and emotionally honest. Each one of us was born as a spiritual tabula rasa: we knew nothing but to love and be loved. We started out as little beings of pure love, as this was our true nature.

Yet, as we matured into adulthood, many of us faced various circumstances which challenged our true nature. Most of us faced these challenges in our earlier developmental stages, often in the form of neglect, mistreatment, trauma, or abuse, causing us to face instances of fear rather than love. If we did not have a secure, consistent, loving, and supportive presence in our lives throughout our developmental stages, we were not equipped to effectively cope with such fearful experiences yet had to find a way.

Such emotionally charged episodes during developmental stages tend to imprint ten anxiety inducing emotional patterns known as "schemas" which, although usually manifested in early life, continue to afflict the person during the course of their adulthood. Being vulnerable, the ego of the child subjected to these powerful sets of negative thoughts and feelings is prone to adopt defense mechanisms as a means of emotional and psychological protection. Yet, as they mature, these defense mechanisms become counterproductive and vestigial in their protection; instead, these "issues" generate unnecessary angst and negative feedback in their adult selves. The following is a brief description of the ten schemas:

Table 1:

1. **Abandonment:** Fear of being left alone
2. **Deprivation:** Fears around one's needs being ignored or not met or not being understood or cared for
3. **Subjugation:** Fear that another's will will override precedence one's own
4. **Mistrust:** Fear of being violated, or that people cannot be trusted
5. **Unlovability:** Fear that one is not lovable for who they are; that they are defective or flawed
6. **Exclusion:** Fear that one will not be accepted by or does not belong in a group
7. **Vulnerability:** Fear of catastrophe
8. **Failure:** Fear that one will not succeed or will never be successful
9. **Perfectionism:** Fear that one must be perfect
10. **Entitlement:** Belief that rules do not apply to oneself

The first five of these schemas pertain to early experiences with our parents and family, while the last five manifest as we interact with the world beyond our home.

"Entitlement" may be difficult for some to grasp as a schema yet, although it may not reflect a type of fear in itself, a person (as a child or later in life) who is conditioned to believe that the rules do not apply to himself will eventually experience some sort of anxiety later on upon learning that this isn't the case. Whether the child was spoiled, made to feel "special," or exonerated from ethical, behavioral, social, and interpersonal codes, he will learn they hard way that he is not special or above personal responsibility. The little kid who is given anything he or she wants without working for it stands a high chance of accruing debt as an adult. The child who is raised as "the little man," "princess," "the boss," or "papi" will not be tolerated as an adult with exaggerated sense of importance and entitlement. Such children may grow up trying to find others - willfully or not - to provide money, material goods, limited boundaries, and excessive adulation and attention (known as "narcissistic supply"), yet will be eschewed by others who have genuine self-esteem. Narcissism (outside of Narcissistic Personality Disorder, which will be discussed later) is therefore an typical byproduct of entitlement, since the belief (or the rule) that everyone is unique but not special is not self-applicable. Also, entitlement itself can appear as a reaction to a subjugation schema: a person may compensate for his fear of his will's being dominated by being overly assertive and violating the rule(s.) Overall, if there is a fear associated with entitlement, it is usually the "fear of not being special."

It should be noted that, although these schemas and their respective defense mechanisms tend to manifest at an early age, environmental factors experienced later in life can also foster such maladaptive pattens. Also, it is not always the case that one schema is experienced at one particular time. It is oftentimes the case that certain maladaptive patterns arise from a group of schemas, or a *schema cluster.* A certain behavior linked to negative feelings and defense mechanisms, for example, may have a basis in unlovability, abandonment, and deprivation schemas. Such clusters can make it more difficult to elucidate the root fears behind a maladaptive pattern. More still, a schema which had its roots in childhood may evolve to take the form of a different schema. A child who felt unloved, for instance, may feel compelled to appease her parents at any cost. In order to gain her parents' approval and attempt to build self-worth, she may barter her will to cater to the wishes of her parents. Thus, her unlovability schema evolves into one of subjugation.

The characteristic of the manifested maladaptive pattern is likely due to the nature of the parent-child (or, teacher-child, peer-child, etc.) dynamic itself. A child may develop an abandonment schema from a parent who was largely withdrawn and emotionally unavailable (due to the parent's own schemas.) Such a child may lash out at the parent for not being emotionally present. Or, a parent who is consistently domineering may cause their child to develop a subjugation schema where their defense is to passively succumb to others' needs and wishes and never their own.

With regard to these schemas, the responsive maladaptive patterns take different forms which vary among different individuals. For example, an unlovability schema in one person may manifest a deep sense of sadness in the form of shame, worthlessness, and lack of self-confidence, causing them to become reclusive, shy, self-pitying, or hard to get to know. In a different person, they may turn to consuming food, drugs, or alcohol to "cover-up" these negative feelings. Another person may masquerade it behind an arrogant, plumped-up ego or bravado or an air of self-importance, desperately presenting to the outside world a person who appears much better than they actually feel about themselves as they seek out excessive adulation or approval as compensation. In another, they may "take out" the negative emotions linked to feeling defective on others, thus externalizing their own lack of self-worth by means of emotional scapegoatism.

For each schema, the maladaptive reactions appear to manifest four different types of defense mechanisms: *internalization, avoidance, overcompensation, and projection*.

A defense mechanism of internalization involves the person incorporating the fear-based messages into their own persona or reality; that is, the person absorbs the negative emotional content of the schema into their self-concept as a means of protection. As illustrated in the previous example, an internalized mechanism for an unlovability schema could cause a person to become withdrawn since, "you wouldn't love me anyway if you got to know me." With respect to a subjugation schema, this type of mechanism might cause a person to become quiet, docile, and unassertive since "nobody listens to me or cares about what I want anyway." The mechanism can take the form of seclusion, as the reaction to an exclusion schema will be one of avoidance, "since I don't belong." The internalized mechanism can also serve as a passive, codependent means of compensation as person adopts a "poor me" role. Here, the person puts their negative emotions on display in order to inspire pity from others. In the case of person who feels she is unattractive, she will go about imparting a sullen, forlorn, and despondent demeanor around others with the hope that they will "feel sorry for her" and take on and mend her lack of self-worth. The avoidance defense operates in avoiding, numbing, or diverting awareness of the negative feelings associated with the schema. This tends to involve anesthetizing the negative feelings associated with the schema by means of a substance or an activity. The fears that arise from issues of mistrust can cause someone to chain smoke as a means of coping. Someone with fears of being abandoned may turn to consuming alcohol or drug use. A person with fears of needing to be perfect may become a workaholic. Another with an unlovability schema may try to drown out their emotional pain with food or sex. Or, the person's mechanism be simply be that they "shut down," in that being distant and aloof itself provides protection. This can take the form of being physically or emotionally withholding as in the case of "not rocking the boat" or "biting one's tongue." The purpose of this mechanism is to manage the negative feelings through emotional repression, oftentimes involving some sort of anesthetization.

Overcompensation as a defense mechanism occurs when a person subscribes to an alternate reality that counteracts the emotional pain they experience. At its core, overcompensation functions by denying the existence of negative emotions: the ego protects its host by ignoring the emotional pain altogether. This mechanism escalates when it subsequently adopts a contrary and bogus concept. Here, despite being an delusion, a fabricated perception is preferred over reality since fit is not just less painful, but preferable and even pleasurable. Like the initial example involving the unlovability schema, this mechanism can take the form of manufactured self-importance or narcissism. Yet this defense mechanism often involves convincing others of this alternate reality as well, such as the reaction to an exclusion schema which involves developing an entourage or "being the life of the party." The motto of this mechanism would be, "Not only is the fear (and the schema) nonexistent, it is completely untrue." The purpose of this mechanism is to avoid confronting negative feelings by denying their existence and/ or replacing reality with a contrary, manufactured version.

The defense mechanism of projection superimposes the negative feelings on others. A form of emotional scapegoatism, projection is a means of forced empathy, as "misery loves company." A person who feels subjugated and deprived will seek to make others in his company "feel his pain" by subjugating and depriving them. When coupled with overcompensation, projection simultaneously superimposes the negative feelings as the person feels better about themselves, resulting in an emotional scapegoatism which provides the person a sense of feeling more powerful, superior, and worthwhile at the expense of others' wellbeing. Someone with an unlovability schema rooted in her personal appearance will find gratification in calling another person ugly. Another with a failure schema will take delight in seeing someone else fail or making them feel like a failure. The motto for this mechanism would be, "You feel and deal with my pain because I don't want to feel or deal with it (or be the only one who does)" or "It's you, not me."

Looking closely at these four different types of maladaptive responses, a certain duality appears. The emotional distress ensuing from a triggered schema can be either self-oriented (internalization and avoidance) or outward-oriented (overcompensation and projection.) With self-oriented mechanisms, the emotional pains tend to stay with the person having the schema reaction. With outward-oriented mechanisms, the emotional pain is to be accommodated and/or absorbed by others.

It is less likely for the negative feelings of an internalizer to impact others as they are the person experiencing the emotional pain of their schema the most. Here, it is the person calling themselves ugly, not others. Although it can be draining to be in the company of an internalizer feeling sorry for themselves, the negative emotions behind this passive mechanism tend to lie mostly with that person. If the internalization of their pain is so strong, the person may even harm themselves, which will surely be felt by others. However, although internalization sometimes places negative emotions on display, it is the person with the schema who feels them the most.

Similarly, it can be draining to be around someone who diverts their issues by numbing themselves with drugs or alcohol or is emotionally unavailable due to being self-absorbed or absent minded. It can also be quite draining to be given the cold shoulder for a period of time. Yet, since it is the person's own awareness to their emotional pain that is being diverted rather than others', it is usually the person himself who is most affected by this defense mechanism.

Overcompensation, unlike the previous two, is much more likely to affect others and harm them as a consequence. Since its basis is denial and creating an alternate reality or self-concept, it generates narcissism and self-exoneration/entitlement (since self-accountability and accurate self-awareness is both denied and overcompensated for.) This can result in ethical and moral compensation, justification or rationalization of misdeeds, exploitation, various forms of lying, and manipulation, since all involve denying accountability and truth, an expectation to be exonerated, and an inflated sense of self. Thus, an "overcompensator" who has, say, deprived or violated others is likely to reinvent history, deny the mistreatment, and expect to be let off the hook. In such cases, others will bear the brunt of this of this type of mechanism by enabling, being coerced into providing excessive adulation or attention as narcissistic supply, or being violated in some manner, all of which they may or may not be willing to go along with.

Projection is certain to affect another person or party. By superimposing the negative feelings associated with the schema - making others feel unlovable, deprived, subjugated, mistrusting, etc. - other persons will endure unwarranted hurt, shame, accountability, distress, and emotional or physical abuse.

Whether a person self or outwardly orients may be due to a variety of factors. This could be due to some sort of inherent predisposition; that is, perhaps some children possess an innate emotional threshold allowing them to be more capable in acknowledging their negative feelings, while other children not possessing this wherewithal turn to mechanisms of projection, overcompensation, and/or "alternate realities" as a mean of coping. Perhaps this is due to the degree of the trauma itself from which the schema originated.

Whatever the case, the deciding factor determining whether or not a mechanism is self or outwardly expressed is apparently the degree of acknowledgement of the negative emotions - *with the dividing line being denial*. Those who tend to have self-oriented defense mechanisms of internalization and avoidance are prone to manifest disorders involving depression, addiction, seclusion, and/or low self-worth, since the person has identified with negative emotions associated with the schema to some extent. In essence, they identify with or anesthetize the negative emotional content of their fears because they do not deny them; rather, they come into direct contact with them. For example, a person with a deprivation schema may have encountered frequent episodes as a child when they were not listened to. This carries over into their adulthood the established belief that "no one listens to me." Since they believe that no one listens to them - or at least feel that is the case - they do not speak up or vocalize their needs since they believe no one will listen. As a result, they are not listened to and their prophecy is self-fulfilled.

Those who harbor outward-oriented defense mechanisms, on the other hand, react to their "issues" by denying their existence and believing an alternate reality or self-concept and/or projecting the negative feelings onto someone or something else. In short, these reactions attempt to deny the schema's existence by replacing it with a manufactured egoic construct. Someone with the same deprivation schema previously described may overcompensate for their fear of not being listened to by being overtly loud and unrelenting in speaking their mind, wants, or needs, perhaps even dominating and overriding the ability for others to speak theirs. The emotional wound is still the same: "No one listens to me." Instead of recognizing this, the ego takes over to ensure that "EVERYONE LISTENS TO ME ALL OF THE TIME." The wound is still there, yet it has been drowned out and covered up by a mental construct. Just because it has been covered up does not mean the wound has healed; in fact, it is still very much there and is not going anywhere until it is acknowledged - only then can the wound be dressed. Alternatively (or additionally), this individual may lash out at others even when they are being attentive and may be a horrible listener himself.

As such, there appears to be decrease in emotional awareness of the mechanisms in the following order: internalization, avoidance, overcompensation, projection. An internalizer readily and consistently comes face-to-face with the negative emotional content of their fears whereas the avoider knows they're there, but tries to "cover it up." The overcompensator, at the very least, denies the negative emotional content while the projector places the negative content onto something or someone outside of him.

Because of this, people who tend to have self-oriented mechanisms are prone to perceive themselves as victims whereas those with outwardly-directed mechanisms *will not* perceive themselves as criminals. This may explain why those of us who have developed "dis-orders" of depression, anxiety, substance abuse, avoidance, panic, and suicidal tendencies are more likely to seek recovery than those with dis-orders based in entitlement and narcissism, particularly Narcissistic Personality Disorder (NPD), Anti-Social Personality Disorder, and psychopathy. The latter group rarely acknowledge they have a problem or seek help since their mechanisms involve the denial and/or projection of the emotional anguish behind the disorder. This may also explain why inwardly manifested dis-orders are more likely to heal: denial is not (or less of an) obstacle. It is also important to mention that an individual may grow accustomed to depending on *both* self and outward oriented mechanisms to manage their fears. Such persons are considered to be "passive-aggressive." The propensity to rely on both types of mechanisms is likely the causality behind dis-orders such as Bipolar (or Manic-depressive) Disorder.

However, this presence or absence of denial suggests another factor responsible in the manifestation of defense mechanisms: the faculty of *conscience*. Because those who internalize or divert their negative feelings avoid directly harming others by keeping their issues "on their side of the fence," their clean conscience tends to remains intact. Those who overcompensate or project, by creating an alternate, self-exonerating reality or superimposing the negative feelings onto others, are more likely to harm others and thus violate their own conscience. Thus, *the defense mechanisms of overcompensation and projection are more aptly termed "offense mechanisms."* The fact that the negative feelings behind such mechanisms are left disregarded and unhealed guarantees repeat offenses. Moreover, the fact that they have now violated their consciences - *in addition* to having unhealed emotional wounds - escalates both the mechanisms' frequency and intensity *since the pain now associated with the guilty conscience (or remorse) must also be denied, anesthetized, overcompensated for, and/or projected by the ego.* Thus, their conscience continues to erode causing spiritual debt to accrue. The personality emerging from this negative-feedback mechanism is often considered to be "toxic" or "malignant." This downward spiral most likely accounts for the symptoms of narcissism, anti-social behavior, and other malignant personality manifestations worsening over time.

An eroding conscience and the accrual of spiritual debt are not the only byproducts of repeat offense mechanisms. Since the malignant personality understands on a deeper, subconscious level that they have harmed someone else, they will fear repercussions from the victim. If the amount of unresolved transgressions has reached a certain level, the fear of reprisal will take on the form of paranoia. The paranoia, then, will act as powerfully as a schema itself, requiring the malignant personality to employ more offense mechanisms to hold at bay, thus expediting a negative feedback mechanism:

Figure 1: The Downward Spiral

Schema/Remorse/Paranoia

↘

↑   Reaction/Offense mechanism =
Self-exoneration/negative affect on others
Violated Conscience/Spiritual Debt ↵

An example of this would be a person who projects their negative feelings of being deprived by stealing. Fearing they will not have enough, they steal from others. Stealing from others violates their conscience, accrues spiritual debt, and generates remorse, joining the repressed emotions of the pre-existing deprivation schema. To buffer both the remorse and the schema, they steal more from others, leading to more conscience violation and accrual of spiritual debt, leading to more remorse, and so on. To maintain this cycle, the ego is likely to rationalize or justify this behavior. However, the "downward spiral" results in amassing spiritual debt, eroding the conscience and, as will be described later, spiritual bankruptcy.

Unfortunately, this negative-feedback mechanism does not only affect the person reacting to their schema. Since others will be recipients of mistreatment, they will, in turn, be required to face fear in the form of stress as well. If they can react in a healthy manner, the buck will stop with them. If they react in a self-oriented manner, they absorb and harbor the negative, toxic energy. If they react in an outward-oriented manner, the fear spreads. If the latter is the case, it is highly likely that those of us accustomed to outwardly orienting our fear will act as an emotional epicenter, spreading out our negative emotions outward for others to react to, which leads to an epidemic of fear.

And it must be noted that these emotional epicenters could be calmed if someone - anyone - taught these souls to address their fears with love.

Yet if these epicenters aren't calmed, how devastating can their wake of destruction be?

X

2

Dangerous Dynamics: Offense and Defense Mechanisms

Epicenters of Fear

"Forgive them, Father, for they know not what they do."

- Jesus Christ

In order to understand how harmful the effects of a person who has been solely dependent on offense mechanisms to manage their fears can be, let's look again at the schemas and observe the negative emotional effects of the corresponding fear:

Table 2:

1) **Abandonment:** Feelings of panic, sadness, loneliness, anger, and anxiety at times of aloneness and separation.
2) **Deprivation:** Feelings of panic, loneliness, despair, hopelessness, anxiety, sadness, anger, or resentment when emotional, physical, or psychological needs are not met or disregarded.
3) **Subjugation:** Feelings of sadness, anxiety, frustration, anger, and resentment, perhaps surrender when will is overridden.
4) **Mistrust:** Feelings of suspicion, panic, or anxiety; a fear of intimacy; shies away from trust.
5) **Unlovability:** Feelings of shame, lack of self-worth, and unworthiness.
6) **Exclusion:** Feelings of anxiety and deep sadness in group settings.
7) **Vulnerability:** Feelings of fear of disaster, incessant worry over one's wellbeing.
8) **Failure:** Feelings of fear of failure. Sadness and hopelessness that one will never succeed.
9) **Perfectionism:** Feelings of anxiety that one must be perfect. Fear that performance must be flawless.
10) **Entitlement:** Anxiety when rules/regulations are imposed or upon realization that one is not special.

Now, what kind of person would appear if all the schemas were affecting and mismanaged with overcompensation and/or projection? What if their responses were extreme and/or worsened over time? In order to obtain a profile of an individual who over-compensates for (involving denial and adherence to an alternate, contrary "reality") and/or projects the negative thoughts and feelings in response to these schemas, consider the following:

Table 3:

1) Abandonment: Overly demanding of others' company. Despotically controlling others' whereabouts, up to and including enslavement, imprisonment, or captivity. Abandons others interpersonally, emotionally, or physically for little or no reason or cause. Disregard/disinterest for interpersonal relationships and intimacy. Emotionally or physically aloof, ungiving, or absent. Prone to being overly upset at or retaliating against another after feeling abandoned, despite little to no evidence that abandonment initially transpired.

2) Deprivation: Steals and/or cons possessions, finances and other resources from others overtly or insidiously. Projects false persona of mental/emotional health and stability. Highly materialistic, self-focused, entitled, and greedy; possesses substantially more than one needs. Complete disregard for others' emotional, physical, and psychological needs and well-being. Lacks empathy for others' emotional, physical, financial, and psychological strife. Devoid of genuine emotion/displays shallow effect or contrived feelings. Deprives others without compunction.

3) Subjugation: Over-assertion of one's will. Complete disregard for others' wills, wishes, and desires. Despotic and tyrannical. Insatiable need for power and control.

4) Mistrust: Highly secretive; engages in covert activity. Claims to be trustworthy or a victim yet exhibits criminal behavior. Manipulative and conning. Frequent and extreme violator of others' rights, such as privacy, personal boundaries, personal property. Frequently engages in spying, extortion, interrogation, or blackmail. Sexual deviance and infidelity. Highly paranoid and indiscernibly mistrusting. Falsely accusatory of innocent others.

5) Unlovability: Grandiose persona/grossly inflated sense of self. Projects air of self-importance. Self-involved/self-absorbed. Perceives self as flawless/perfect and expects others to as well. Requires excessive adulation and narcissistic supply/ "Napoleon Complex." Verbally deprecating and abusive toward others. Obsessed with personal appearance. Incapable of human attachment and employing empathy. Contemptuous toward others. Devoid of compassion. Blames others for misdeeds and flaws; scapegoatism.

6) Exclusion: Need for despotic control on a group regardless of size. Requires to be center of attention within a group (or a community or the world.) Possesses an entourage, "toadies," or collection of sycophantic subordinates. Excludes/ostracizes others. Ostracizes or retaliates against those who fall out of favor.

7) Vulnerability: Highly obsessed with self-protection; lifestyle is insular, exclusive, clandestine, and well-guarded. Feeling of invincibility and immortality. Impulsive and/or self-destructive behavior. Highly manipulative and paranoid. Frequent and extreme violator of others' wellbeing. An insatiable need for power and control. Disregard/disdain for human well-being and life.

8) Failure: An insatiable need to succeed or appear successful. Refusal to accept shortcomings/ blames others for faults. Regards other as inferior/worthless.

9) Perfectionism: Unaccountable for actions, poor-performance, shortcomings, and lack of aptitude; self-exonerating. Perfect public persona and personal appearance. Resorts to scapegoatism/ superimposes faults and shortcomings on others. Finds fault in everyone, even if the faults are inaccurate or invented. Perceives themselves - and no one else - as perfect.

10) Entitlement: Devoid of conscience and self-accountability; absence or lack of remorse. Megalomania/extreme narcissism. Pathological lying. Parasitic/oppressive lifestyle. Believes in being above rules and the law yet strictly enforces on others/draconian. Pursues self-gratification regardless of any amoral, harmful, or conscionable repercussions experienced by others as a consequence.

The above traits, admittedly extreme, provide an accurate portrayal of a personality type whose responses to the various schemas consisted of overcompensation and projection at their most malignant, especially if reinforced and relied upon over time. Despite the extremity, this profile, unfortunately, is not unrealistic. These qualities may remind you of a highly abusive spouse or parent, a highly toxic boss, a morally corrupt politician, or a tyrannical despot.

Most people, of course, do not react to their schemas and behave in such a manner, since they usually have a combination of both defense and offense mechanisms; or, their behaviors is not as extreme.

However, this profile ably reflects the condition commonly known as "psychopathy." Although the criteria for analysis and diagnosis has been (and still is) subject to some discord, the most commonly used diagnostic tool in modern practice is the Psychopathy Checklist Revised (PCL-R), a rating scale assessment developed by Dr. Robert D. Hare which focuses on the following twenty-one criteria presented below. [1] These criteria are divided into three groups or "factors" and are as follows:

Table 4:

Factor 1: Personality Aggressive Narcissism:

- Glib and superficial charm
- Grandiose (exaggeratedly high) estimation of self
- Need for stimulation
- Pathological lying
- Cunning and manipulativeness
- Lack of remorse or guilt
- Shallow affect (superficial emotional responsiveness)
- Callousness and lack of empathy

- Failure to accept responsibility for own actions

Factor 2: Case History "Socially Deviant Lifestyle"

- Parasitic lifestyle
- Poor behavioral controls
- Need for stimulation/proneness to boredom
- Early behavior problems
- Lack of realistic long-term goals
- Impulsivity
- Irresponsibility

Traits not correlated with either factor:

- Many short-term marital relationships
- Juvenile delinquency
- Revocation of conditional release
- Criminal versatility
- (Recently added:) Acquired behavioral sociopathy/sociological conditioning (i.e. a person relying on sociological strategies and tricks to deceive)

The first group, Personality Aggressive Narcissism - also known as the "selfish, callous, and remorseless use of others" group - involves traits such as grandiosity or an inflated sense of self (narcissism), a strong sense of entitlement, lack of empathy and remorse, pathological lying, a need to be the center of attention or draw attention to oneself, arrogance, and a inflated yet inaccurate and distorted perception of one's own talents, aptitudes, and accomplishments. The second group, Socially Deviant Lifestyle, includes such traits as failure to conform to societal norms with respect to lawful behavior, deception or repeated lying, impulsiveness or failure to plan ahead, reckless regard for safety of self and others, poor impulse control, chronic irresponsibility, lack of remorse as indicated by being indifferent to or rationalizing the mistreatment of another.

Dr. Hare summarizes psychopaths as *"intraspecies predators who use charm, manipulation, intimidation, and violence to control others and to satisfy their own selfish needs. Lacking in conscience and in feelings for others, they take what they want and do as they please, violating social norms and expectations without guilt or remorse."* [2] Most, like Dr.Hare, will recognize psychopaths as being without integrity, empathy, accountability, compassion, and remorse: in short, a conscience.

Many believe that a requirement of psychopathy is violent behavior, such as in the extreme cases of serial killers. While it is not uncommon (and oftentimes likely) for a psychopath to resort to violence, many leave a wake of destruction without inflicting any sort of physical harm. Instead, the resulting damage may be financial, emotional, or psychological in nature - the effects of which can manifest itself physically post-trauma. It is therefore not necessary for someone to be violent in order to be diagnosed as a psychopath.

Another misconception is that psychopaths are insane or afflicted with some sort of psychosis; that is, that they are prone to irrational thinking or are out of touch with reality. Although psychopathic and psychotic traits are not mutually exclusive, psychopathic individuals are generally capable of logical and rational thinking, free of delusions, and very much in touch with reality. Indeed, the success of the psychopath relies heavily on accurate awareness of reality and the ability to manipulate it.

Much debate and research has centered on the nature of psychopathy; that is, whether it exists inherently in the individual or develops as a result of environmental factors. Although the above alludes to the probability that psychopathy and other malignant personality disorders have a basis in maladaptive schema reactions, some research has determined some physiological differences between the brains psychopaths and non-psychopaths. A study at the University of Wisconsin-Madison found that psychopaths have reduced connectivity between the ventromedial pre-frontal cortex of the brain (the area responsible for empathy and guilt) and the amygdala (the region responsible for fear and anxiety.) [3] Similarly, another study at King's College London's Institute of Psychiatry found that the brains of psychopaths had significantly less grey matter in the anterior rostral pre-frontal cortex and temporal lobes.[4] Still another, conducted by James Fallon at the University of California Irvine, found abnormalities in the orbital pre-frontal cortex (believed to be involved with ethical behavior, moral decision-making, and impulse control) and its relationship to the amygdala.[5] It is worth noting that the ventromedial, the anterior rostral, and the orbital pre-frontal cortices are located in the Brodmann areas 10,11, and 47 of the prefrontal cortex, which are located just behind and above the eyes and directly above the sinus cavity.

Although similar physiological brain abnormalities have been observed in those diagnosed as psychopaths, the question as to whether or not psychopathy exists as a result of structural dysfunction is still left unanswered. For instance, Fallon found that his own orbital pre-frontal cortex bears the same inactivity as those of psychopaths, yet he himself is not a psychopath. Moreover, the question surrounding whether or not these physical abnormalities are congenital or develop over time is still unanswered. Similar to an physically inert person who develops atrophied muscle tissue over time, perhaps a person who does not allow the experience of fear, accountability, or remorse develops similar atrophy in brain tissue. If this is the case, expecting a psychopath to exercise their conscience would be akin to expecting a atrophied individual to bench press two-hundred pounds. And, if this is the case, it would suggest that at some point the individual "stopped exercising." That is, through denial and projection, they stopped acknowledging the negative feelings of fear, anxiety, sadness, etc. for such an appreciable amount of time that they can no longer handle their weight.

Interestingly, new research is confirming such neuroplasticity of the brain and that environmental effects and mental/emotional states do have an affect on its physiology. One study has found that participation in Mindfulness-Based Stress Reduction (or MBSR, a meditative technique) increases grey matter density in regions of the brain associated with learning and memory processes, emotion regulation, self-referential processing, and perspective taking.[6] Another has found that meditation "strengthens" the brain by increasing the amount of gyrification or "folding" of the cortex, which may allow the brain to process information faster. [7]

As you can see, the nature of psychopathy and other malignant personality disorders - whether they are environmental or inherent - is still in the process of being fully understood. Yet, as more studies are conducted and therapeutic advancements are made, I believe both "nature" and "nurture" will be seen as co-factors. Could it be that psychopaths exist due to their maladaptive methods of handling trauma? Could an overactive ego be responsible for preventing authentic healing due to the lack of attention to their inner-anxiety and emotional wounds? As previously mentioned, I do not believe that anyone is "born evil," yet I do believe it is possible that each of us differ in our innate capacity to withstand, transmute, and recover from trauma and fear. However, I strongly believe that there is a conditional component to this.

Because of this, the goal of this book is not to brand or diagnose anyone as a "psychopath" or with another psychological personality disorder. Whether you choose to assign such terminology is entirely your prerogative. I refer to those who consistently deny and impose their fears and negative emotions onto others as "spiritually malignant." If the frequency, duration, and intensity of this behavior escalates to the degree to which their conscience is divorced, such persons will be referred to as "spiritually bankrupt."

Clearly, the previous offense mechanism schema profile and the PCL-R checklist depict persons who are highly malignant to the point of being spiritually bankrupt. While most of us do not resort to externalized behavior this extreme, these profiles will be used as reference points going forward. Others who resemble these profiles to a lesser extent will be referred to as "toxic" or "malignant personalities." They often leave others who come into contact with them feeling drained, "sapped," frustrated, upset, angered, fearful, and anxious. Specific offense mechanisms behind this will be explored later.

For now, it is imperative to emphasize that *the objectives of "managing" issues with offense mechanisms are the following:* ***to dominate and control others, to establish narcissism (or an inflated, fantasy sense of self), and to reinforce entitlement in order to be exempt from rules and accountability.*** Specifically, ***they are used to avoid any sort of acknowledgement of the negative emotional distress associated with fear and remorse by inflicting such distress on others or denying it altogether.***

However, in order for toxic, malignant, or psychopathic personality types to exist, others must be willing to bear the brunt of their overcompensation and projection. If a personal boundary is not created, the recipient will absorb the negative feelings associated with the malignant personality's offense mechanism and, more specifically, its underlying fears. Those who have self-directed defense mechanisms will be most susceptible to this.

Fear Receptacles

"It takes two to tango."

- American proverb

Since malignant personalities mismanage their fears through overcompensation and/or projection, they require others to enable such offense mechanisms. It is therefore necessary for malignant personalities to find reliable, unchallenging targets - ones who will cooperate in absorbing their negative feelings. The most convenient targets are those who have pre-established self-oriented defense mechanisms, since they are already accustomed to incorporating their fears into their persona (internalization) or anesthetizing the fears after taking them on (avoidance.)

Malignant personalities seek out those who will enable them based on noticeable personality characteristics born out of self-oriented defense mechanisms. To understand how malignant personalities make this assessment, let us first revisit the schemas from Table 1:

1.   **Abandonment:** Fear of being left alone
2.   **Deprivation:** Fears around one's needs not being met or ignored
3.   **Subjugation:** Belief that another's will takes precedence of one's own
4.   **Mistrust:** Fear of being violated
5.   **Unlovability:** Fear that one is not lovable for who they are; that they are defective
6.   **Exclusion:** Fear that one will not be accepted by or does not belong in a group
7.   **Vulnerability:** Fear of catastrophe
8.   **Failure:** Fear that one will not succeed or will never be successful
9.   **Perfectionism:** Fear that one must be perfect
10. **Entitlement:** Belief that rules do not apply to oneself

In order to gain understanding into the personality types sought out by malignant personalities to project or overcompensate for their fears, it is necessary to assign self-oriented defense behavior to each schema:

Table 5:

1) Abandonment: Withdrawn and reclusive. Depressed and/or anxious when alone. Overly accommodating to and enables others' excessive demands for company. Engages in substance abuse (alcohol, food, drug, etc.) or diversionary activity when alone.

2) Deprivation: Does not vocalize one's needs. Does not stand up for one's rights. Takes care of others and/or little for self. Martyrdom; tends to others' needs while sacrificing own. Wallows in hurt, anger, and resentment, and engages in aloofness and sulking when one's needs are not met. Turns to substance abuse or activity (physical or mental) when needs are not met.

3) Subjugation: Acquiesces to others' wills and demands. Unassertiveness, resignation, and consistent feeling of defeat. Taken advantage of; overly accommodating and agreeable. Turns to substance abuse or activity (physical or mental) when will is ignored.

4) Mistrust: Isolation and avoidance of intimate/close relationships or social interaction out of fear. Naive and overly trusting; susceptible to being victimized. Lax in personal boundaries. History of being abused.

5) Unlovability: Depressed, even suicidal. Low self-esteem and self-worth. Hypersensitive. Lacking in self-care. Shy, withdrawn, and hard to get to know. Lacking in social skills. Unobjectionable toward mean-spiritedness, toxicity, or abuse. Excessively/indiscriminately kind, friendly, and adulating. Anesthetizes feelings of low self-worth with food, drugs, alcohol, shopping, and obsession with personal appearance.

6) Exclusion: Avoids group/social settings. Distant and aloof with others. Engages in substance abuse (alcohol, food, drug, etc.) or diversionary activity when feeling shunned. Tries to "fit in" with others who shun.

7) Vulnerability: Hypochondriac. Highly nervous and anxious in general; excessive and constant worry. Panic attacks in distressing situations. Frequently ill or injured. Turns to substance or activity to buffer feelings of anxiety.

8) Failure: Unassertive and devoid of goals. Avoids challenges or projects out of fear and panic. Resorts to mindless activity or substance abuse to counter fears associated with lack of achievement.

9) Perfectionism: Fear, panic, and anxiety over flaws being noticeable or underperformance. Resorts to mindless activity or substance abuse to counter fears associated with achievement.

10) Entitlement: Anxiety and fear associated with the realization that one is ordinary, average, or substandard. Anxiety experienced when one does not get their way or rules are applied.

You may come up with your own behavioral assignments to self-oriented schema defense, yet the personality profile becomes clear: those reliant on self-oriented defense mechanisms tend to be passive, unassertive, docile, withdrawn, overly accommodating, fearful, anxious, hypersensitive, depressed, aloof, addicted, self-destructive, and low in self-worth.

Looking again at the extreme malignant schema profile, the traits assessed by the PCL-R (Tables 3 and 4, respectively), and the malignant objectives of dominating/controlling others, establishing narcissism, and reinforcing entitlement, we see how those with self-directed defense mechanisms make "lock and key" yet highly dysfunctional companions for those with offense mechanisms. Acquiescing to the malignant goals, *those with self-directed defense mechanisms are willing/docile victims, provide narcissistic supply, and enable entitlement.* "Narcissistic supply" specifically refers to a source or reservoir of excessive admiration, adulation (such as "ass kissing" or "brown-nosing"), attention, appeasement, interpersonal support, or sustenance.

Malignant personalities can easily realize their objectives of dominating others and reinforcing entitlement with those who have a fear-based, pre-conceived notion of being powerless. Likewise, malignant personalities can readily derive narcissistic supply from those who self-direct their fears since they already have the built-in perception that others are more lovable, talented, successful, empowered etc. than they are. For them, at least having something or someone to love, adulate, or adore is better than nothing or no one at all (even themselves); vicarious "self-love" is better than none at all. However, as will be explored later, the malignant personality will actively maintain their source of narcissistic supply by ensuring that her self-worth is kept low.

Most people who mismanage their unresolved issues do not resemble personalities as polarized as those portrayed in the previous two profiles. Rather, they tend to oscillate between defense and offense mechanisms in order to "manage" the negative energy they encounter. This is noticeable in any type of organization where a "chain of command" exists. If the top of the chain is malignant, subordinates directly beneath are likely to project any negative emotional energy they inherited onto *their* subordinates rather than hold their "superiors" accountable for their behavior.

Regardless, this "offense-defense" dynamic is anything but symbiotic. As we will see, if this cycle of fear transfer is not broken, the end result can be not only irreparable damage, but an epidemic of fear.

⊕

3

"Spiritual Malignancy": A Holistic Perspective on Toxicity

*"There's too much tendency to attribute to God
the evils that man does of his own free will."*

- Agatha Christie

Many psychotherapists propose the concept of "mindfulness" as a means of schema therapy. The purpose of mindfulness is to dissolve our reactions to disturbing emotions while being careful not to reject the emotion itself. The process involves stilling the mind and thus allowing for a more present, aware, and objective mindset to observe the emotions which arise during episodes of schema reactions. In doing so, we can have greater understanding and the ability to buffer our reactions to these emotions.

An interesting similarity that spirituality has with psychology (and schema therapy, in particular) is that both delve deep into understanding the relationship between the mind and emotion, their relation to the physical body, and strive to establish harmonious synergy among the three. The major difference is the method in accomplishing this: psychology approaches this by means of a rational, categorical, and methodical perspective, whereas spirituality embarks with a holistic, ethereal, and experiential approach. Interestingly, both have converged on meditation and mindfulness as a means for mental and emotional healing which, in turn, have a positive effect on the body.

As illustrated in the previous chapters, anyone who inflicts emotional, psychological, or physical harm upon themselves is lacking in self-love. This lack of self-love exists because of unresolved fear. The degree to which a person lacks self-love due to unattended fear is what I refer to as "spiritual deficiency." Virtually all of us are spiritually deficient to some extent.

Anyone who emotionally, psychologically, or physically harms another person not only is "spiritually deficient," but since their conscience has been compromised, "spiritually malignant." No soul who is truly themselves - a being of love, loving of self and others - could or would inflict pain of any kind on another person. Most, if not all of us, have been spiritually malignant at one time or another.

Yet if inflicting harm on others reaches a such an extent that the conscience is or has been completely divorced, that person is "spiritually bankrupt." Since the amount of fear that has existed within them has been unresolved and grossly amplified due to repeated acts of causing others harm through offense mechanisms, spiritual bankruptcy is, in essence, amassed fear, or "spiritual debt."

I use the word "spiritual" as opposed to a psychological term since conscience, empathy, compassion, and remorse all require not just the ability to *imagine* the conditions faced by another, but the ability to *feel* the emotions that would emerge under such circumstances. It also conveys our connection to a higher power which, I believe, is unconditionally loving and the notion that our true, highest selves are beings of love. Conscience, compassion, empathy, and remorse all require the ability to experience the emotion of love in order to exist; integrity requires both accurate self-awareness and self-love.

The topics of mindfulness, awareness, and meditation will be discussed later in greater detail, yet I bring these up now to make a distinction with respect to schema reactions. Regardless of whether a schema reaction is a defense or offense mechanism, a person will be *conscious* of the consequence of a schema reaction but not necessarily *aware* of the emotional/psychological foundation for it. For a depressive type, this consequence will take on an amplified emotional state, such as depression, panic, low self-worth, or an anxiety attack since the schema involved sadness, fear, shame, or anxiety respectively. Referring back to the deprivation schema example, such a person will be conscious that they are quiet, withdrawn, and depressed and chose to distance themselves for that reason, yet they will most likely be unaware (or less aware) of the root perception that "no one listens to me" and that the emotions felt are linked to this psychological scar.

For a malignant personality type, the consequence may involve some retaliatory emotion such as anger, contempt, or even a twisted version of bliss that comes with self-gratification, such as the "rush" shop-lifters feel when pilfering an unpaid item from a store or the high experienced by serial killers when murdering their victims. Yet the consequences readily apparent to these types will tend to be ego-based or cerebral in nature, such as the power and control experienced when doling out verbal or sexual abuse, manipulating others, torturing an animal, or exonerating themselves from their flaws or transgressions. As such, the person with a deprivation schema will be conscious that they are domineering and overly assertive in getting their voice heard and may feel powerful, yet they will (unlike the internalizer) be impervious to the depression they feel and even more distant from the deeper perception-identification that "no one listens to me." If sadness, fear, low self-worth, or anxiety is ever felt by these types, it is quickly overridden by the ego which denies their presence by means of mental construct or projection.

For this reason, mindfulness will only be useful to malignant personalities once they allow for the *observation of* the negative emotions associated with schemas. Perhaps greater mindfulness, awareness, retrospection, and introspection will realize this; perhaps not.

Spiritually deficiency, again, is the lack of self-love due to unresolved fear, which pertains to all of us to a certain degree or another. This is true since we all have "issues" or fears which have been unattended. Think of a child who is experiencing emotional pain or trauma. A functional, loving parent would notice their child's pain, ask them what is the matter, listen, and work with the child to resolve his fears. A dysfunctional parent (or one lacking in love) would disregard or admonish the child which, in turn, would validate her fears, causing her to feel insignificant or that her needs are not worthwhile. The loving parent of a child who feels low self-worth will listen to their child's feelings of worthlessness, work with them, and reassure their child that they are lovable just the way they are. The unloving parent may ignore, disregard, or confirm, or even cause the child's sense of low-self worth, causing the child to feel their self-worth is unimportant, feel that their low-self worth is valid, adopt a persona which they believe will be one others will find worthy or lovable, or bully other children. If we do not acknowledge and tend to the fear, sadness, and anxiety experienced by our own selves like a loving parent would their child, it is guaranteed that our issues will continue: the adage "what you resist will persist" certainly applies here. As mentioned before, I do believe that all of our higher selves (or our souls in pure form) are loving beings. Yet when we harbor negative feelings such as fear, anger, and sadness to go unattended, we allow them to contaminate the loving beings we are. Thus, spiritual deficiency is behind any fear-based mechanism whether it be defensive or offensive. For this reason, anyone who is spiritually deficient (read: everyone) is deserving of compassion.

Spiritual malignancy is the violation of the "Golden Rule," or "Do unto others as you would have done unto you." To keep their own negative emotions and fears (and guilty conscience) at bay, a person who engages in spiritual malignant behavior disrupts the well-being of others. Again, spiritually malignant behavior involves offense mechanisms, which will be explored in the next chapter in greater detail. Such transgressions are resolved when the person reacquaints themselves with their conscience by *emotionally* acknowledging the harm they have caused others. The transgression, as we will see later in the second part of this book, can be *absolved* when they acknowledge to the other person the harm they have caused them.

Those who are spiritually bankrupt consciously violate - and oftentimes derive a twisted pleasure in violating - the Golden Rule. Such malignant ego-gratification at the expense of others' well-being may include or be the very act of abuse itself. In doing so, they either ignore or divorce their conscience altogether and directly inflict pain, fear, and suffering on their victims (and to the rest of us in a more indirect or psychic manner.) A spirit with an abundance of love could not and would not inflict mental, emotional, or physical abuse on another.

This intentional (and, at times, sadistic) violation others' well-being is due to the externalization of fears and negative feelings associated with disregarded schemas and, provided the individual is an adult, is cowardly, immature, and selfish in that they choose and allow for someone else to experience the pain they do not yet ought to face. This may sound harsh considering that it may very well be their "inner-child" who is suffering, but as adults these individuals must claim some accountability. Perhaps a bully in grade school who blames someone else for his misdeeds can be seen as too scared, too young, and too depleted in his self-worth to handle being seen as flawed or guilty. Yet for, say, a corrupt politician or supervisor to resort to scapegoatism - out of fear of facing his negative feelings linked to an unlovability and/or perfectionism schema and subsequently placing the blame and thus *his* shame onto another, undeserving person - is selfish, irresponsible, and cowardly. The soul rich in self-love would love himself enough to accept his shortcomings or flaws and hold himself accountable.

In short, with spiritual bankruptcy, the mechanism process is: "You feel and deal with my pain so that I can avoid it and feel pleasure." Having a conscience is all about self-accountability, care for others, and courage. Those who are spiritually bankrupt do not exhibit these qualities and, for this, they conjure contempt.

It should be reiterated that if this chronic offense mechanism practice is routine and not broken, such persons will not only remain spiritually bankrupt (and malignant), their malignancy will likely strengthen as they accrue more spiritual debt (Refer to Figure 1 in Chapter 1.) And the selfishness, immaturity, and cowardice behind this behavior is all rooted in fear - *fear that they are not lovable for who they are*. For this, they inspire pity.

All interpersonal conflict and suffering is due to this: internalized fear in the form of an absence or lack of Unconditional Love. It is my belief that Unconditional Love is the essence of God or, as I refer to, Spirit. Before proceeding, I want to emphasize that it is not my desire or objective to convince others of the existence of God. Although some of the material presented later involves topics which may be related to God or Infinite Intelligence, the existence of a higher power is my own personal belief. Also, I do not believe it is necessary to believe in God to have moral understanding. In fact, most of the atheists I have met have been ethical, conscientious, and morally responsible. If you do not believe in a higher power, most of the information to follow is not based on any doctrine and presented as tangibly as possible. If you are atheist and believe in the *potential* for some sort of "energy" to exist which is not fully understood (and that we humans don't know everything), even better: it's one thing to be skeptical, but it's another thing to be closed-minded.

Whether or not you believe in a higher power, we all have been given (or have) the ability to choose. The free will we possess is, at its most basal level, a choice between love and fear, and there's always a moment before we choose. Think about a time when you lied about something. Wasn't a moment before where you noticed you had an option to either lie or tell the truth? Why did you lie?

The moment we have before making a choice may be fleeting or it may be extensive. If it involves an action or a behavior that has become so routine to the point where it is habitual, it may barely be noticeable or even seem automatic. Yet every choice we make involves a prior moment - for however long - where we weigh out our options and make a decision.

For a spiritually malignant personality to say that a reaction "just happens" without *any* awareness to the emotional stimulus is simply self-excusal and most likely an attempt to manipulate the recipient of their harm. Refer back to the items in the PCL-R checklist and take note that none of them require disconnection from reality and all of them involve the intentional departure from integrity and/or the conscience. No one can lie (whether it be overt or one of omission) without knowing the truth or having a moment to choose to do so beforehand. No one can scam or con without prior strategizing. No one can violate a rule without knowing what the rule is. And no one can attract copious attention to themselves without conscious effort, and so on. As we shall see later, those who are spiritually bankrupt (notably psychopaths and other malignant personalities) often employ a strategy which gradually establishes docile victimhood by incrementally increasing the intensity of victimization. This cannot be accomplished without a good deal of awareness of reality, their actions, their choices, and their victim's psychological state, despite being *emotionally* unaware.

It should be noted that the previous *does not* apply to someone who is *psychotic* or experiences what is known as a *psychotic break,* which occurs when an individual experiences a "disconnect with reality." Here, what I believe occurs is the individual's schema reaction is so strong, it is psychologically, spiritually, and at times physically *impossible* for them to cope with it. This often results in a "blackout" period where all awareness, consciousness, and thus free will are suspended. I knew a person who once attempted suicide after experiencing such a blackout, which was inevitably linked to a potent abandonment schema. After the episode, he claimed to have no recollection whatsoever of attempting to take his life. This dynamic is also behind post-traumatic stress syndrome. The difference between psychotic breaks and spiritual malignancy is that the latter involves some awareness of reality. I do believe there is only so much the human psyche can handle and psychotic episodes occur at the "breaking point," thus the breakdown. Spiritually speaking, there is only so much we as souls can take at one time.

It must also be that acknowledged that spiritual malignancy exists, in part, due to being enabled. As we will see later, by not challenging or confronting the malignant on their behavior, the victim's docility condones the mistreatment which maintains or increases the propensity of repeat occurrences. (Yet, since the methods of victimhood can be quite subversive, the victim may not be fully aware of the harm that is being inflicted.) More importantly, this is not to suggest that malignant behavior exists *due to* this enabling; in fact, *it does not*. Just because it is permissible for a person to violate a certain rule (moral, ethical, legal, etc.) does not absolve them from their choice to do so. The fact that a car is unlocked *is not* the reason for its contents being stolen; the contents were stolen because someone *chose* to steal them. In short, the potential *does not* justify the crime.

Although it was important to initially approach this subject from the solid, analytical foundation of psychology, the realization must be made: *malignant traits exist because - to some degree or another - they are or have been chosen*. Perhaps these choices are infused with deeply ingrained negative emotion, or perhaps they are influenced by our early years or powerful others in our present. Perhaps malignant behavior becomes more automatic with time and repeat offense. Whatever the case may be, in every instance, there is always a moment when the individual, conscious choice is made. Moreover, each of us is equipped with a memory which permits us to recall, revisit, and reassess our behavior at a later time, allowing for retrospection, introspection, and self-analysis, respectively. We can look back at times when we hit or berated our child to gain greater insight into ourselves to avoid repeat offenses. Reasons for not taking such post-episodic measures include irresponsibility, arrogance, laziness, and cowardice. For these reasons, self-accountability - to whatever extent - cannot be denied. Yet fortunately, for these reasons, transmutation of negative energy is possible.

And, as will be explored in this book's second half, *the most valuable possession we can have in this life is a clear conscience*.

Each and every one of us human beings is an individual entity of energy and awareness, yet we are all connected to some degree or another based on the varying levels of emotional and physical proximity and interpersonal contact. In a sense, we all are one. Yet since fear is spread by spiritual malignancy and free will throughout the human network, each of us will encounter fear and its negative emotional byproducts at some point. The key to knowing how to cope with and transmute it is recognizing when it happens. What can we expect upon contact with spiritual malignancy?

†

4

Toxic Tactics: How Fear is Spread

*"If questioned: Lie, Lie, Lie.
If caught: Deny, Deny, Deny.
If punished: Cry, Cry, Cry."*

- Unknown

The previous chapters described how reactions to the various schemas can lead to the outward-oriented mechanisms of overcompensation and projection. These offense mechanisms, again, are spiritually malignant in that they negatively impact others' wellbeing. Before exploring the means by which these mechanisms affect others and thus how negative, fearful energy is spread, it is important to reemphasize that the basis for the malignant person's behavior with respect to others *is their own fear* (be it their schemas or tainted conscience.) I ask that this be kept in mind while proceeding with the contents of this chapter.

As mentioned, the three objectives of spiritual malignant behavior - dominating and/or controlling others in order to create a willing and/or docile victim, reinforcing entitlement, and establishing narcissism or narcissistic supply - are sought by malignant personalities to avoid contact with the negative emotions associated with their schemas and remorse. Moreover, *these goals exist because the spiritually malignant is lacking in unconditional self-love and control over their own deep, inner fears.* Specifically, *these goals are pursued in order to compensate for their own fears and low self-worth by conjuring, exploiting, and capitalizing on fear and low self-worth in others.*

In broadcasting a grandiose sense of self, displaying glib and superficial charm, or whittling away others' self-worth, malignant personalities can demand excessive attention and adulation (which some readily give as narcissistic supply) or narcissistic superiority, robbing others of their own needs for care and attention and a healthy self-concept. When failing to accept accountability for their actions and behaviors, they will often retaliate or shift the blame to others, robbing them of their innocence, reputation, wellbeing, and credibility. By engaging in a parasitic or entitled lifestyle, they coerce others into financing, sustaining, or enabling their self-indulgence, extravagance, lack of productivity, and/or lack of self-accountability. In doing so, they rob others of their energy, funds, psychological and physical wellbeing, or other reserves. By dominating others and quashing their wills, they violate their emotional, psychological, and physical needs.

The offense mechanisms, or "toxic tactics," used to realize the goals of entitlement, narcissism/narcissistic supply, and domination can be passive, aggressive, both, or anywhere in between. However, oftentimes the "boiling frogs" technique is used. According to this metaphor, whether true or not, after being placed in a pot of lukewarm water, frogs get accustomed to the rising temperature of the water if increased gradually. By the time the water reaches a boil, the frogs have already adjusted to the high yet lethal temperature and are not aware that they are about to be killed.

Those who are spiritually malignant or bankrupt tend to work this way: they start by employing passive, insidious, and manipulative offense mechanisms, assess the recipient's psychological/physical state to see if they have adjusted, then gradually increase the aggression in their methods while assessing their recipient's comfortability level. The end result is emotional, financial, psychological, and/or physical catastrophe, contingent on the recipient remaining impervious to what is happening to them.

It must be noted that *the effects of the malignant offense mechanism used are not dependent on the assertion level of the mechanism itself*. Just because a "passive" mechanism is used does not mean the effects will be less than those of a more aggressive nature; the consequences of a passive approach can be just as devastating as one that is more aggressive. Rather, the effects are dependent on the transgression itself. Scapegoatism, for instance, can be used to shift the blame for stealing five dollars, or it can be used to blame someone else for murder.

Also, although it is not uncommon for a spiritually malignant person to "turn up the heat," they may abruptly initiate a toxic tactic at any level of aggression. And, although the mechanisms described below are distinct, it must be noted that a spiritually malignant person can - and usually will - use more than one simultaneously.

Moreover, it is worth mentioning that the harmful effects are directly proportional to the "inner hell" of the person resorting to employing toxic tactics. This inner hell is the spiritually malignant's disregarded fear, including both the magnitude of the fear associated with their ignored issues and the amassed spiritual debt associated with a repeatedly violated conscience as previously described.

Whether the individual is spiritually malignant or bankrupt, for the sake of convenience, the perpetrator in the following examples will referred to as "the malignant." Since passive methods are typically those used first, the following descriptions of toxic tactics will start with the most passive and proceed to others in order of increasing aggression.

I have also grouped the offense mechanisms into six categories and list them in the order in which they are usually implemented to establish domination, narcissistic superiority, and entitlement. These categories reflect the following objectives: *Testing the waters, Establishing Entitlement, Narcissistic Dominance, Avoiding Accountability, Establishing Domination and Control, and Reinforcing Domination and Control.* It should also be mentioned that these mechanisms are categorized based on the objective they tend to realize most, yet most (if not all) will succeed in realizing more than one - if not all - objectives. If applicable, I have included secondary objectives or "by-product" effects in the description.

Lastly, although the word "victim" is used in the following descriptions, this word is used to designate the *recipient* of the misdeed rather than imply that the party should adopt a "victim mentality." That is, it is one thing to be "victimized" yet it is another to take on the identity of being a victim. The former recognizes that they have been wronged, yet will do *something* to address, counteract, or absolve the negative effects of the transgression whereas the latter will absorb the negative affects and/or take it out on someone else. For example, the former could be an employee who has been publicly blamed for something she did not do or was not responsible for. To counteract the "victimhood," she may either allow herself to feel and work through the anger and hurt of the publicized accusation, defend herself at that very moment, make a mental note to speak up if the situation arises again in the future, confront the supervisor at a later time, or quit her job completely. A person who identifies herself as a victim will absorb the humiliation and shame, thus leading her to feel sorry for herself or worse: to take out her frustration on others or publicly humiliate others so that they feel her pain ("I was treated this way, therefore it's okay if I treat others this way.") If the victim's psychological pain is transposed onto others in one manner or another, she has now become toxic to others and is likely to become malignant herself if not "nipped in the bud." Moreover, if she does not set a boundary with the perpetrator (the supervisor), this episode can be expected to take place again.

Now let's have a closer look to see how fear is spread:

Testing the waters:

Preying on trust and rapport:

Although not necessarily a mechanism itself, this is often the first step. It is also the most difficult for the recipient to discern because this step is subversive and innocuous. To begin their quest for domination, entitlement, or narcissistic supply, the malignant needs their victim to be loyal, loving, and trusting; the frog needs to trust the cook enough to go into the pot cooperatively. This is accomplished by manufacturing a pleasant yet phony persona that is gentile, kind, caring, functional, sane, benevolent, conscionable, upbeat, trustworthy, and authentic. (This false persona will be maintained as needed throughout the victimization process yet is likely to dissolve once more aggressive methods are used.) During this initial stage, the malignant covertly assesses the recipient and waits for the moment he senses the recipient likes, loves, or trusts him. When this has been established, the malignant "turns on the stove" and the transposition of fear begins.

Flattery:

Like "preying on trust and rapport," flattery is often the first step. Here, the malignant is overly complimentary and "butters up" the victim. In addition to portraying a false persona, the malignant uses flattery to gauge the emotional or psychological state of the victim. If the victim reacts with excess humility, meekness, or unworthiness, this indicates to the malignant that there is fear to prey upon. The same would apply if the victim's ego soaks up the flattery as narcissistic supply, as this also indicates that there is low self-worth to be exploited. Yet if the victim accepts the "compliment," "praise," or "approval" with some discretion, the malignant will usually back off. However, flattery is essentially the bait which coerces the victim to play along or "go into the pot."

Self-effacement:

This tactic, like flattery, will most likely be used during the rapport building phase. In contrast to flattery, this technique focuses on the malignant depreciating his own toxic capacity, projecting a false impression of being innocuous or innocent. A common example would be for a pathological liar to say, "I'm a horrible liar." A serial killer may claim, "I can't stand the sight of blood." Someone might say, "I'm an empath" yet later proves to be a sociopath. The same applies to "I cry a lot" being said by someone who has shallow emotions. This, of course, is used to inspire trust in the victim which the malignant uses a foundation to manipulate.

Aloofness and ungiving:

This centers on establishing a foundation of gaining attention and control. The malignant will withhold efforts in interacting with the victim in an attempt to condition the victim to consistently be the one to maintain contact. The goal is to passively program the victim to cater to the malignant, and not vice versa, with the mindset, "make them come to me." This is also establishes narcissistic supply.

The lack of reciprocity can involve any resource such as attention, time, energy, money, material goods, etc. A healthy relationship involves a balance of "give and take"; the malignant seeks to always take and never to give.

Underhandedness:

Here, the malignant tests the waters by engaging in sly, secretive, and deceptive spiritually malignant activity against the victim. The purpose of this is to assess the victim's realm of perception, or to "see what they can get away with." Underhandedness is often the first step toward the malignant goal of manifesting entitlement.

Establishing Entitlement:

Conscience bartering:

This mechanism has the motto, "I won't tell on you if you don't tell on me." In this case, the line separating the malignant from the victim is blurred (if there at all) since both may be of the mind: "Are you thinking what I'm thinking?" This scenario can (and oftentimes will) result in a malignant partnership of mutual toxicity and/or repeated conjoined criminality. It is worth noting here that conscience bartering occurs because malignant personalities seem to instinctively know who is like-minded. This tactic and the two following are the seeds which sprout crime-syndicates, whatever the size. Since victimization may not necessarily be a factor between or amongst the parties involved, the malignant's goal here is to have their entitlement enabled. Certainly, a third party (or more) will be victimized somehow.

Mutual enabling:

Similar to conscience bartering, the malignant expects to be enabled since they had previously enabled someone else. The technique "I didn't tell on you so you shouldn't tell on me." This involves an element of extortion, guilt (believe it or not), or threat whereas conscience bartering is more of an agreement, yet both are similar in their mutual toxicity. The goal here is for the malignant to uphold their entitlement while establishing cooperation (if not docility) of the other party, which is most likely also malignant.

Seduction/Bribery:

This is a rewards-based enabling tactic as the victim is created once they have agreed to the terms and conditions and subsequently violate their own conscience. An example of this is a malignant who is unprepared for an exam who offers money to someone else to take it for him. If the victim accepts the offer and violates his own conscience, and depending on the situation, he is now more susceptible to becoming toxic. The end result is similar to the previous two tactics.

Double standards:

Here, the malignant allows himself certain freedoms not enjoyed by others, or self-leeway in violating rules that are respected by or enforced on others. Essentially, others are held to abide or acknowledge a certain standard (whether enforced or through their own volition) which the malignant violates. This mechanism bears the motto: "The rules apply to you, not me." If the malignant is in a position of power or higher status, the motto is, "Do as I say, not as I do."

Narcissistic Dominance:

Undeserved self-praise:

The goal of this mechanism is to establish narcissism (and narcissistic supply), but it also succeeds in dominance and entitlement. Here, the malignant takes credit for results in which they had little to no involvement in creating. For example: A vice-president of a retail chain visits various store locations to assess their performance. When visiting a store she sees as impeccably clean, organized, profitable, and functional, she praises the store manager for their excellent performance. Upon hearing this, the district supervisor, the manager's direct superior - who had no involvement with the operations of the store - chimes in, "Well, I'm the one who hired him!" insinuating that his hiring skills are the reason the store is well maintained. (The same superior will conversely not "take credit" for the poor performance of a substandard manager, rather he will blame her.) While hiring competent employees is certainly an attribute (though perhaps he "got lucky" with hiring this store manager), the district manager had no affect on the store's excellent performance since the management and staff were autonomous. Here, the district manager seeks undeserved adulation, status over the store's hard-working staff, and confirmation of entitlement in that he deserves praise for work he did not perform.

Second guessing:

Here, the malignant questions or criticizes the decisions of the victim repetitively after the outcome of the decisions is known. The purpose of this is to test the victim's self-esteem and assessment abilities by attempting to foster self-doubt in their decision making. This allows the malignant to establish narcissistic supply and/or domination, since the victim may start to believe that the malignant "knows better" than they do. By dismantling the victim's decision making ability, the malignant disrupts their ability to assess other situations as well, which permits the malignant to "get away with more" and thus strengthens his entitlement. By manipulating the victim into cognitive dependence and disrupting their critical thinking abilities, the malignant fortifies the goal of domination by creating a willing, docile victim.

Schadenfreude:

"Schadenfreude" is a loanword from the German language referring to the pleasure derived in observing another's misfortune; "Shaden," meaning "damage" and "freude" meaning "joy." The malignant will outwardly express their "joy" for the victim to hear, attempting to induce humiliation or shame in the victim. The goal is to establish narcissistic superiority and supply.

Invasiveness:

This is usually coupled with second guessing in that the malignant proactively seeks opportunities to test boundaries by questioning the victims performance or activity. Here, the malignant is constantly observing and assessing the victim's actions, performance, behaviors, or demeanors, imparting on the victim the feeling of someone "breathing down my neck" or "up in my business." This can also involve frequent snooping into the victim's privacy or personal life. A more covert form of invasiveness is spying by means of aliases, hidden cameras, or any other means in which the victim will not know they are being assessed. Therefore, it is not necessary for invasiveness to be partnered with second guessing, yet the purpose is to disrupt the victim's personal peace, autonomy, and privacy. The goal is to establish domination/control, superiority, and (potential) victimhood.

Invisible insults:

With this technique, the malignant makes what appears to be an observation or a "blank statement" yet it contains a hidden meaning left for the recipient to decipher, and the meaning is neither "neutral" nor complimentary. For example, a malignant walks into the living room of the victim's home for the first time and says, "Oh. There are a lot of mirrors on your wall." The victim is left disoriented as they try to "read into" the reason for this comment being made. The victim may also feel like they are being overly sensitive for reading too much into the "comment." Chances are, this was simply a shallow attempt to belittle the victim by ushering a passive insult masked as an observation. The invisible insult may also come in the form of an "opinion" or an "assessment." Say the same malignant then walks into the victim's kitchen and, after opening and examining the refrigerator, remarks "This refrigerator would be too small for me." This passive remark insinuating inadequacy is another attempt to belittle the victim. The goal is domination by creating a disoriented, un-confrontational victim and the establishment of narcissistic superiority.

Backhanded compliments:

Similar to the invisible insult, this tactic is manipulative and insidious. Instead of making an "observation," the malignant masquerades an insult to appear as a compliment. Here, the victim receives a "sugarcoated slap in the face." Backhanded compliments are a bit more overt than invisible insults in that the insult appears as subtext. An example of this is "You're smarter than you look!" The goal is the same: domination by creating a disoriented, un-confrontational victim and the establishment of narcissistic gratification.

Potshots/Put-downs:

Potshots are like backhanded compliments but without the sugar-coated spin. The malignant makes a comment or asks a question with the insult contained as subtext. An example of this would be, "Are you going bald or is that just how you style your hair?" The malignant will also seize opportunities to "piggy-back" the insult on something the victim has said. For instance, the victim might express after consuming a large meal, "Wow! I feel stuffed!" to which the malignant responds, "I can see that!" The goal is the same as the previous two mechanisms.

Guilt trips:

A way of playing the victim, guilt trips are used by malignants to induce behaviors by adopting a "poor me" role. The false or exaggerated sense of being in some sort of pain or turmoil allows the malignant to emotionally manipulate the victim into catering to their will, providing excessive attention, or some other objective. The guilt inspired can be related to someone or something other than the malignant. "Think of all those starving children…" may be said to a child to guilt them into finishing food even after they are full. The goal, of course, is to manipulate the victim into acquiescing to the malignant's will.

Shame:

A more overt form of a guilt trip, shame involves the malignant directly condemning the victim. A wife confronting her cheating husband may be shamed, "How dare you ask me that!?", "How could you even think I would do such a thing!?," or "What the hell is wrong with you!?" The accuser is made to feel bad about herself for confronting, a feeling the malignant will hope she keeps. The goal is the inverse of guilt trips: first, to establish dominance and control; second, to force the accuser into docility via guilt.

Shame can also take place when the victim has done something which they feel bad, ashamed, or embarrassed about and the malignant seizes the opportunity to make them feel worse. This is known as "kicking them while they're down." Someone who was at fault in an accident, feeling bad about damaging the vehicle, will be sarcastically told bythe malignant, "Good job!" or "Well, that just goes to show what a shitty driver you are." The guilty feeling has now been enhanced by the shame.

Derision:

Here, the malignant mocks, belittles, berates, ridicules, or deprecates their victim due to an action, behavior, perspective, or result the malignant finds undesirable or inadequate, whether intentional or unintentional. The husband who misplaces a checkbook will be inculcated with verbal abuse about how "stupid, dumb, and irresponsible" he is by his abusive wife. The goal here, like interrogation, is to establish narcissistic superiority and dominance/control.

Insatiability:

In short, this tactic establishes the notion that nothing is ever good enough. This may take the form of rewarding capitulated demands with more demands. The thought process is, "You did so well, here's more for you to do well!" This is not only domineering and entitled, but narcissistic in that the malignant feels the reward for someone who pleased him is to please him more, not to be grateful. In addition to narcissism, this tactic not only fosters parasitic entitlement, but also strengthens the tyrant/victim dynamic as well.

Favoritism:

This tactic must involve a third party - present, absent, or conceptual - in order to be utilized. It is used, via compare and contrast, to elicit a certain behavior or action from the victim that is displayed in a third party or to denigrate the victim's sense of self-worth. It usually involves the insinuation that the victim is substandard in a certain capacity. "Why can't you be more like Jennifer?" a supervisor may ask his employee. "Most three-year-olds are more well-behaved than you!" a mother might admonish her five-year-old.

In both cases, it attempts to create and exploit low self-worth in the recipient.

This tactic can take a more subversive approach in that the third, more desirable party will receive more "perks" - such as attention, freedom, praise, leniency, etc. A director may give one subordinate more direction, attention, and praise than another (even though both have equal responsibility) in an attempt to convey that one is approved of and the other is not.

Since this tactic coerces the victim into believing they should strive to "please" the malignant - or the malignant's approval is to be catered to - the primary goal here is to establish narcissistic dominance.

Avoiding Accountability:

Denial:

This toxic tactic is simple: The malignant commits a transgression, the victim confronts them, and the malignant denies accountability. If the victim does not press on, the transaction is over and the malignant avoids accountability while victimhood is confirmed. If the victim continues to confront the malignant, he will do one of the following: 1) repeat the denial until one of the parties relents, wait for the the victim to find him in good favor again, mistreat the victim, and attempt to use this tactic again; 2) fall in line or out of sight if the victim is unrelenting; most likely it will be the latter since the victim won the battle of wills; 3) resort to a more assertive offense mechanism.

Avoidance:

This technique, although seemingly the most passive, usually occurs after the malignant knows the victim has the capacity to confront. It may also be the first mechanism employed if the malignant senses that he will be confronted by the victim. The dynamic is simple: the malignant distances himself after the transgression until he feels the victim has forgotten or no longer cares about confrontation.

Deflection/distraction:

This is another mechanism used to avoid accountability that involves changing the subject or shifting the focus when the malignant is being confronted. After being confronted, the malignant will conjure an unrelated topic in an attempt to distract or confuse the victim. This technique is also used in establishing narcissistic supply when the malignant personality consistently shifts the focus away from other people and topics and refocuses it on himself. In short, the subject is changed to them.

Lies of omission:

A lie of omission occurs when some factual details are given yet others are left out in order to distort reality. For example, a malignant tells his girlfriend: "I'm sorry I couldn't call you last week; I was camping and didn't have cell-phone reception." While it is true that he was camping and was unable to call, he leaves out the detail that he was spending this time with another woman. The goal is, of course, to avoid accountability and maintain entitlement.

Half-truths:

Similar to lies of omission, half-truths leave out the entire truth. The statement of a half-truth may be completely true, but does not represent the entire truth. An example of this would be: "You shouldn't trust Michael; I've seen him take money from people." While it is true that the malignant has seen Michael take money from people, it is because he works as a bank teller. Both half-truths and lies of omission are used to avoid accountability and manipulate the victim. Half-truths also involve statements which are misleading but are perceive a certain way due to their context. An example of this would be the employee who calls out of work because they are "not feeling well." The employer may take this to mean the employee is physically ill but, in actuality, the employee is cranky.

Exoneration:

Here, the malignant avoids or lessens accountability by means of an excuse or reinventing history. The excuse, whether partially valid or invalid, is pawned off by the malignant as a "reason" which prevented him from behaving a certain way. Or, it can be an invented "circumstance" used to absolve him from meeting a certain obligation. The exoneration, "Well, I couldn't be respectful toward you because I'm having a bad day" may have some validity since it is more difficult to be pleasant when having a bad day, but it certainly does not make it impossible. A more extreme version would come from a physically abusive spouse whose claims, "I just lost control." Or, the excuse behind the exoneration may have no validity whatsoever. An employee who comes to work an hour late without calling the establishment to report their tardiness may say, "I couldn't call because registering for classes took too long" when it is known that the employee owns a cell phone and her school has a telephone. Clearly, the employee could have used either her phone or the school's to notify her manager at some point when she knew she would be late. Exonerations are often used to buffer accountability with "apologizes": "Well, I'm sorry, *but...*" with the remainder of the sentence involving an excuse rather than a reason.

The malignant can also shift blame to the circumstances themselves, such as someone justifying his collection of thousands of dollars in a tax-return scam, claiming "I wouldn't have done it if I couldn't get have gotten away with it." The twisted logic is, "If I'm able to get away with it, it's not my fault."

Whether it is the excusal of a character flaw, a lack of performance, or abuse, the goal for the malignant is the same: to protect their narcissism, domination, and/or entitlement.

Playing the victim:

This is similar to exoneration yet the excuse given portrays the malignant as a victim or a person facing poor circumstances. The excuse may be based on something external, such as "I had to take money from the safe or else I wouldn't have been able to pay rent." Or the excuse may lay with the victim, in the case of the cheating spouse who alleges, "Well, if you were around more I wouldn't have slept with him!" when her husband had been physically available. Not only is entitlement and the creation of a docile victim reinforced with this tactic, but it seeks to employ a role reversal as well. This can cause psychological harm if the victim begins to second-guess himself. Playing the victim may also involve the invention or amplification of trying circumstances faced by the malignant in an attempt to inspire compassion or lenience. This is commonly known as the "drama queen." An example would be an employee exonerating her lack of accomplishment by claiming, "I couldn't get anything done today; it's been so busy!" when, in reality, it wasn't.

Minimization:

This is a form of exoneration where the malignant reduces or eliminates his accountability by depreciating the effects of his misdeed. For instance, a malignant whose dog rips up and destroys someone else's rug may state, "Well, it was only twenty bucks" without compensating the owner. By minimizing the cost of the rug, the malignant frees himself from being responsible for his dog's behavior, leaving the financial brunt with the owner. The motto here is the solipsistic assessment: "No big deal." This tactic both establishes/reinforces entitlement and avoids accountability.

Spin:

This is similar to minimization but, instead of accountability being reduced or eliminated, the malignant proffers his transgression as a benefit. A toxic manager who is informed that one of his employees broke down in tears during a shift he knew to be very busy and short-staffed would say, "Good, that will toughen her skin." The goal is the same as minimization, yet it builds the malignant's narcissism as well.

Scapegoatism:

This is also similar to deflection/distraction and exoneration yet, instead of shifting the focus by changing the subject or providing a manufactured excuse, the blame is shifted to someone else who is either present or absent. The more passive version of this tactic involves an absent third party who is not able to defend themselves.

Scapegoatism can also involve shifting the blame onto *something* else, usually about the victim and simultaneously involves exoneration. Take for example the cheating lover who is confronted on their infidelity. They may say, "I can't talk to you until you calm down." The blame is placed on the victim in suggesting that their emotional state of (understandable) hurt and anger makes it impossible for the malignant to speak with them. The replacement of blame is scapegoatism; the claim that it is impossible to engage is exoneration. The goal of scapegoatism is identical to exoneration.

False consent:

Here, the malignant exonerates himself in engaging in devious, unauthorized activity by falsely claiming the victim or someone else had authorized or consented to it. A teenager who arrives home after curfew may tell her mother, "Dad said it was okay" when her father made no such concession. Forgery also falls under this category. Whether a signature is forged on a permission slip or an employee signs her supervisors name on her work to avoid checks and balances, the goal is the same: entitlement. And, as a result, due to the fact that the victim's boundaries are abolished and harm can ensue as a result, victimhood is created.

Dialectics:

This technique must require two or more parties outside of the malignant. The goal is to coerce the two (or more) parties into blaming each other for the actions of the malignant. The two (or more) other parties can be persons or groups of people. The creation of "us versus them and not me" allows for the malignant's acquittal since the other parties lose focus of the misdeed's source as they inaccurately find the accountability to lay with the other (or another) party. To establish this, the malignant must convince both (or all) parties involved that the other (or another) party is at fault and not him. Once it is established that the other parties find each other to be the adversary, the malignant now has free reign to engage in additional, uncontested, and corrupt activity provided he can manipulate the parties into believing the other (or another) is responsible.

Dialectics are easily established if the malignant is in a position of power and the other parties are experiencing an environment of stress or high "fear-factor." The reason for this is two-fold: first, the parties are psychologically burdened and susceptible to externalizing their frustrations; second, since the parties find the malignant to be more powerful, they will prefer to use each other as a scapegoat, since the playing field is more level and therefore more convenient.

Not only are all of the malignant's goals of entitlement, parasitic lifestyle, and despotic control achieved, but others are conditioned to be malignant as well.

Establishing Domination and Control:

Deaf ears:

This occurs when the victim confronts the malignant and, despite acknowledging accountability at the time, the malignant repeats the same transgression or maintains the toxic condition. This is a passive way of avoiding accountability in that it "goes in on ear and out the other" although it appears otherwise. It underhandedly establishes victimhood in that it passively sends the message, "Complain all you want; it's not going to change anything." It also manipulates the victim into thinking the malignant cares when, in actuality, they don't.

Carrot-dangling:

Here, the malignant underhandedly elicits a continuous desired behavior or performance from the victim with the false promise that cooperation and/or follow-through will present the victim with a reward for their efforts. Regardless to the extent the victim capitulates - whether with respect to time or performance - the reward is "always within reach" but never obtained. This inevitably leads to the victim indefinitely chasing the "carrot" while the malignant continuously reaps the benefits of the victim's ongoing labor.

Setting up failure:

This tactic tends to be used when the malignant has some sort of status over the victim. Here, the malignant places unreasonable demands on the victim within circumstances that guarantee or lead to failure. The circumstances which ensure failure may involve a lack of resources (time, material, manpower, information, energy) or conditions which would not allow for the demand(s) to be realized. The purpose of this tactic is to whittle away at the victim's self-worth when they do not meet the demands placed upon them. If this tactic is successful, the malignant derives a sense of narcissistic superiority and domination over the victim.

Interruption:

This tends to occur in everyday conversation to some extent, yet the malignant will use interruption to disrupt being confronted or losing control. The malignant will thus interrupt the other person if his viewpoint/agenda is being challenged (thus reinforcing both domination and narcissism.) This also allows the malignant control and dominance by not allowing the victim to get a word in edgewise. Interruption is also used to maintain or establish narcissistic supply by interrupting the topic if the topic is not the malignant. It is similar to deflection/distraction in that it changes the topic, thwarts confrontation, and establishes narcissistic supply, yet different in that it is more abrupt and overt.

Transposition:

This tactic is identical to scapegoatism yet the scapegoat is the person confronting the malignant and the allegation is the same as the transgression. Here, instead of shifting the focus of blame onto someone else not present, it is shifted directly to the victim. An example of this would be for a malignant who is miserable to brandish their victim as miserable even though, in reality, this is not or hardly true.

This is not only more brazen, but can cause the victim to second guess themselves. The victim may consider whether the malignant's allegation has any validity especially if the victim does not perceive the malignant as manipulative. Such a tactic can take a psychological toll on the victim since their sense of self has been disrupted; in this case, the victim may start to believe they are in fact miserable. Projection often takes on the situation where the victim and the malignant go back and forth as they hurl the same accusation toward the other. In reality, it is applicable to one but not the other, but it is "their word against yours." An example many of us can relate to is a crazy person calling a sane person "crazy."

Inappropriate accountability:

This occurs when the malignant holds the victim accountable for a lack of performance outside of the victim's realm of responsibility. In essence, the malignant blames the victim for something that under someone else's realm of responsibility. For instance, a malignant supervisor employing inappropriate accountability will blame one employee for the poor performance of another, insinuating that this employee should be responsible for another's lack of performance. The goal here is to establish domination by means of docile victimhood.

Interrogation:

This is sort of like second guessing but more overt in that it causes the victim to repeatedly defend their actions, behavior, or lack thereof. It imposes unreasonable or impossible demands on the victim, or incessantly requires the victim to justify or defend their behavior. In other words, the malignant attempts to put the victim "on the defensive." An example of this is an abusive store owner who unrelentingly demands, "Why did this happen!?" to an employee who made an error with a particular transaction. The answer, "I made a mistake," while valid, is not good enough and is incessantly challenged by, "I want answers!" The owner will continue to demand answers long after the employee provided the most honest, self-accountable answer.

Interrogation can also take the form of control in that the malignant will demand the "who, what where, when, and why" over every aspect of the victim's life. Since the answers to these questions is sought, spying can also be enhanced here, such as with private investigators, shills, or toadies. Not providing (or obtaining) answers to these questions will most likely result in the victim facing a more aggressive tactic, if not abuse. The purpose of both is to establish domination and control and thus a docile victim.

False accusations:

This is akin to inappropriate accountability, yet the malignant accuses or insinuates the victim has *committed a transgression* he or she is not guilty of. An example of this is a girlfriend being blamed for flirting when she was simply talking another man. A more overt example would be the malignant who falsely claimed to have been raped. The goal here is clear: to establish dominance and control over the behavior and activity of the victim.

Blackmail/Extortion:

Instead of providing an incentive to the victim as a means of capitulation, blackmail uses the threat of an exposé based on either valid or false information about the victim to obtain something - money, a service, a certain behavior, etc. The goal here is domination by means of forced capitulation. It plays on the victim's fears of being embarrassed and humiliated, whether in be in front of a third party or in public. An example of this is a malignant demanding money from the victim with the threat of informing his wife (or the public) about an extra-marital affair, whether or not the affair is real or invented. This tactic can take a more passive approach in the form of "emotional blackmail" in which, instead of a threat, uncomfortable emotions such as guilt or sympathy are used to coerce the victim into capitulation. This is similar to "playing the victim," yet it involves a threat and the "victimhood" is contingent on the decision of the victim. An example of this is, "If you don't let me go to Paris, I'll never forgive you."

Slander:

Slander is similar to blackmail, but the step of threatening to expose the victim is bypassed and the information broadcasted is false. This can be used to smear someone socially or defame someone publicly, and the damage may be irreparable. This can involve character assassination ("Stay away from her; she's crazy!) or reputation damage ("Did you know he's a drug addict?") The goal here is obvious: to create a humiliated, docile victim.

Abandonment:

Abandonment is a passive-aggressive means of subjugating a victim. When the victim does not comply with the malignant's demands or desires, he vanishes emotionally, physically, or both. This differs from aloofness and ungiving in that the separation is intended as a punishment as well as method of control, often leaving the victim in a state of vulnerability and need or "on their own." A malignant who feels he is not getting enough attention from his girlfriend at party suddenly takes off without notice, leaving his girlfriend embarrassed and stranded since she can't account his whereabouts.

Ostracizing:

Similar to abandonment, this tactic involves the intentional exclusion of a person from a group. The victim may be shunned due to dissension, un-cooperation, being envied, or challenging the purpose of the group's leader or the group itself; here, "the squeaky wheel gets removed."

Reinforcing Domination and Control:

Brainwashing:

This tactic is used to impose false beliefs on the victim and/or distort their perception of reality, often by means of manipulation such as propaganda. Its purpose is to coerce the victim into a certain action or behavior or divert their awareness.

Subjugation:

This mechanism ensures that the will of the malignant always take precedence over the victim's. This can be accomplished by being overly demanding or through verbal abuse, repercussion, or manipulation. The goal is to reinforce control and willing, docile victimhood.

Retaliation:

In order to reinforce the toxic goals of entitlement, narcissism, and domination, the malignant will retaliate against the victim after being confronted on such behavior. This measure is taken to punish, if not debilitate, the victim for not condoning or enabling the malignant's falsehoods, narcissism, entitlement, superimposed fear, or excessive control. The vengeful harm can be psychological, emotional, financial, or physical, yet it often centers on an area the malignant knows the victim to be vulnerable.

Capitalizing on Crisis:

This tactic involves exploiting an incident or trend that leads to dire circumstances that conjure a fear-based feeling - panic, anxiety, anger, or some other distressing emotion - which the malignant capitalizes on to pursue their own self-serving, devious agenda. This may be part of a scheme if the crisis is planned or anticipated, as the malignant will have preconceived plans on how to exploit and benefit from it. Or, this tactic may involve the malignant capitalizing on a genuine crisis. This too can be used to swindle money, usurp freedoms, divert awareness, and violate trust. An example would be a cheating husband who takes advantage of his wife's need to be out of town with her ailing mother to engage in his affair.

The crisis, if both real and planned, will most likely be one involving shock. The goal is clear: entitlement and the establishing of a willing, docile victim.

Fear Creation:

Like Capitalizing on Crisis, this tactic takes advantage of distressing situations, whether they are circumstantial or schemed. Fear Creation takes this a step further by playing on the panic, anxiety, anger, or some other distressing emotion situation creates in order to further a devious agenda. .The "problem-reaction-solution" paradigm falls under this category. For example, a wife may deliberately damage her car and, while she is "panicked and stranded on the side of the road," ask her husband for one-thousand dollars to fix it when it only cost four-hundred - and pocket the remaining six-hundred.

On a larger scale, Fear Creation is the tactic behind events known as "false flags."

Shock:

Shock is used to disrupt the psychological health and balance of the victim by employing an aggressive and (usually) unprecedented toxic tactic "out of the blue." In short, the victim becomes shellshocked in a brief instant as their relative peace is disrupted by some form of abuse or trauma. Although the moment may be short, the lasting affects are prolonged if not indelible. Shock can and most likely will leave the victim psychologically and/or physically debilitated, enabling the malignant to exploit them even more. Due to this, the victim, unfortunately, can expect more escalated, abusive measures to be taken against them as the abuser realizes their goal of physical and/or psychological tyranny. Shock is used when the malignant feels it is time to pursue (more) despotic control. When shock is used, it is safe to say that the malignant is a psychopath.

Constant-surveillance:

This method is more despotic than invasiveness and interrogation in that, instead of disrupting or demanding information about the victim's personal privacy, it is taken away completely. The victim bears the feeling of "always being watched" because, in truth, they are. This tactic involves monitoring as much of, if not all, the victim's life activity: location, activity, relationships, communication, demeanor, finances, habits, hobbies, diet, etc. The victim has no ability to shield their privacy from the malignant, leading to an extreme sense of vulnerability, hyper-tension, fear, and anxiety. "Big Brother" is a term used to describe this. The goal is clear: to employ despotic control over every aspect of the victim's life and to build not just narcissism, but a persona of supreme, invincible omnipotence.

Intimidation:

This tactic involves the use of verbal or physical threats to coerce the victim into cooperation. "Do this or else!" is the motto here. The goal of course is to frighten the victim into submission and establish control. Intimidation can involve either a direct threat or creating a standard by which the victim fears for her physical or emotional safety if she does not cooperate.

Enslavement:

This is subjugation to the extreme. Here, all of the victim's actions are monitored *and* controlled. What the victim does, how long the do it for, who they do it with, etc. is all determined by and subject to the malignant. The victim has no say in what they do, how they do it, or for how long they do it: this is all up to the jurisdiction of the malignant. This helps to complete the establishment of ultimate domination and tyrannical control.

Confinement:

This is physical subjugation to the extreme. Here, the location of the victim, usually constricted, is entirely up to the discretion of the malignant. The victim cannot go anywhere the malignant does not want him to be. Tyrannical control is reinforced with confinement, as is the creation of a willing and docile victim. The victim may become so willing and docile, they may develop what is known as "Stockholm Syndrome" in which they develop positive feelings for their captor. Oddly, the captor may develop reciprocal positive feelings for the captive.

Physical duress and abuse:

This is the psychopath's use of physical force or abuse to manage the victim. Physical duress involves managing their victim through physical restraint or coercion while physical abuse involves inflicting any sort or physical harm as punishment or coercion. The malignant may carry out the physical onslaught himself, with an accomplice, or through someone else. "The beatings will continue until morale improves" is a phrase often used to describe the use of physical abuse to force a certain response or behavior.

Torture:

Here, the psychopath inflicts continuous, unrelenting pain - whether mental, emotional, physical, or psychological - to ruthlessly punish, admonish, incapacitate, torment, and agonize the victim beyond submission. Its goal is despotic control, elevated narcissism, and unabashed entitlement.

Despotism:

The psychopath has realized his goal of complete despotic control over every aspect of his victim's life - physical, geographical, psychological, personal, financial, emotional - and the victim is nothing more than a shell. The psychopath feels omnipotent and powerful while the victim is psychologically and at times physically catatonic.

Murder:

The psychopath exercises the ultimate control over his victim's life as he attempts to destroy his own issues (and guilty conscience) by killing the scapegoat onto whom he has projected (and now personified as) his inner hell. To relive this feeling of unparalleled power, he will need to repeat the process since the recipient of victimization is no longer alive. The goal is the epitome of domination, entitlement, and narcissism.

This is clearly an extensive list of outward-oriented tactics yet it is likely to be incomplete. Moreover, just because a person is noticed using a toxic tactic does not necessarily mean that they are "toxic." Most of us have demonstrated some of the lesser offense mechanisms at some point or another. Some may do it occasionally, some more often. Others who engage in these tactics routinely are spiritually malignant (or bankrupt) and most likely have a personality disorder.

So when it is appropriate to refer to someone as "toxic?" My definition of a toxic personality is someone who, more often than not, does not adhere to the Golden Rule yet believes the Golden Rule should be applied *to* them. A toxic person will consistently expect to have others' undivided attention while they give little attention to what others have to say. Or, they may demand respect for their privacy while they routinely violate others'. Or, they expect to be sympathized with despite being devoid of sympathy for others. Or, they will have access to rights and privileges which they deny others.

The degree to which one is toxic would depend not only on the frequency of these tactics used, but also the severity of the effects experienced by others as a result. A good litmus-test is whether or not we feel "sapped" after interacting with another person, yet this could be due to being in the presence of someone who is wallowing in self-pity or filled with "piss and vinegar." The "drain" we feel from these persons, although palpable, is substantially more passive than that from toxic individuals.

To self-assess our own degree of toxicity requires a good deal of self-awareness. It is helpful to be mindful of the times we've displayed any of the above behavior and the effects it had on others. It is also important to understand the *intent* behind the tactic. For instance, sometimes backhanded compliments or pot-shots can be used to playfully tease someone. (Yet, in this case, they usually do not contain an element of truth which might offend or hurt the recipient.) Was your intention to make them laugh or put them down (to feel better about yourself)? Were you trying to humiliate the person or potshots themselves? If you can't tell, the recipient most likely will (provided they are not overly sensitive) and the answer can be found with them. If they don't respond favorably, it may be time to self-assess or acknowledge a boundary. Also, what may appear as a "second guess" may simply be a differing in viewpoint. Were you dissenting to due honoring your own perspective or were you attempting to coerce the other party to doubt theirs?

To understand and acknowledge our own level of toxicity, we must be both honest and observant with ourselves. Any manufactured or disregarded emotional or mental state will prove counterproductive. Understanding ourselves is not an easy process; it is very hard work, in fact. But it is our duty - to ourselves and others - to transmute our own inner-negativity to make ourselves and our world better. Mindfulness, meditation, and other techniques that aid in this will be discussed in the second half of this book. Yet, in understanding ourselves more, we come to understand the "victim" process as well.

However, if a person is highly spiritually malignant (or bankrupt), perhaps the worst thing to say is, "I love you." Ironically, it is love that they need yet, if it comes from someone other than themselves, it is regarded as narcissistic supply and/or enabling. Worse, this statement is liable to send the signal, "I'm yours; do want you want. I'll love you no matter what." This is detrimental *especially* after toxic tactics have transpired. The malignant will see this as the slate being wiped clean. It is akin to hitting the hitting the "reset button" since the malignant, now knowing that good rapport exists, will either begin to prey and start the whole process again or proceed more aggressively. At best, it's back to square one. At worst, they will up the ante. Whatever the case, it is regarded as carte blanche to victimize however they please. The unconditional love they feel should come from themselves, not you, *and it should be used to address their own internal fears.* To say "I love you" to a person who is malignant conveys, "I love you and I'm okay with how you've harmed me.'

A common question is, "Who gets victimized?" or "How do toxic personalities or psychopaths choose their victims?" From what I have noticed, there is no clear answer except that it depends on the malignant's own internal turmoil and who is available. The common conception is that the malignant chooses someone who is more vulnerable in some capacity: physically, psychologically, emotionally, financially, intellectually, etc. While this is likely, it is not always the case; sometimes it is hardly the case. The victim may be someone whom the malignant senses will not capitulate to his goals of domination and despotic control, narcissistic supply, and/or entitlement. Such is the case with the despotic, narcissistic supervisor whose docile staff provides him with excessive leniency and narcissistic supply. The employee who does not will be seen as a liability and is likely to be expunged. The victim may be also someone the malignant fears, such as the worker who notices her colleague is more talented, gifted, and competent. The colleague will be seen as a threat to the worker's quest for advancement (of not just career, but narcissism and power as well) and will bear the brunt of a host of toxic tactics aimed at diminishing her good standing or sabotaging her performance. It could also be someone the malignant envies: since the victim reminds him of what he is not, it abrades his own narcissistic sense of self (read: low self-esteem.) Such a scenario would start the toxic process at diminishing the victim's self-worth and judgement making, with the goal of creating a docile, downgraded victim. The victim could also be someone the malignant wants to "possess" in some manner, as in the case of the "trophy wife" or the "model employee." Just the presence of their "prize victim" boosts his narcissism, yet they had better be at his beck and call: they are his "prized possession" after all. This particular victim, though rewarded at first, will be discarded once they have lost their novelty or ability to generate narcissistic supply for the malignant.

Unfortunately, it seems that no one is spared outside of other like-minded malignant personalities. In this case, just the opposite can occur. Conglomerates headed by a malignant personality can expect to see "birds of a feather" flocking to the top as their "malignancy in common" forges a bond and results in promotion. They advance within the chain of command because it allows the malignant the power to broaden his realm of despotic control, since they act as extensions of his ego. This propensity for malignant personalities to "join forces" is also the causality behind crime syndicates, mafia rackets, and co-conspiring.

Subordinates unwilling to adopt a reciprocal toxic (or victim) mentality, as we will see later, have one of three options: avoid, confront, or appeal to a higher power. If unsuccessful, they will be expunged. Those who acquiesce to the toxic relationship run the risk of becoming "secondary psychopaths."

The silver lining, however, is this: learning about and coming into contact with these these toxic tactics can shed light on our own ways of mismanaging unresolved fears. As will be explored later, using this knowledge productively can strengthen our self-love.

Otherwise, we will be susceptible to be caught up in an interpersonal network of defense and offense mechanisms that leads to an epidemic of fear.

But, as illustrated in the next chapter, groups infested with malignant personalities - whether a dysfunctional family, a toxic work environment, or a country dominated by a tyrannical regime - are bound to display negative traits indicative of a toxic environment. Such symptoms include an escalated fear factor, a general sense of caution or "walking on eggshells," robotic/drone-like behaviors and demeanors, a lack of fun or enjoyment, operational dysfunction, distinct double standards and hypocrisy, overall discord and disunity, widespread stress and burnout, outbursts of anger and resentment, rebellion, and a reluctance or fear of being authentic. Consider one of my own personal experiences...

5

The "Zombie Effect": A Toxic Epidemic

"Shit rolls downhill."

- Unknown

It was a mid-autumn morning when I left my apartment to start my new job as a temporary call center representative with a high-end retailer. Having been unemployed for many months, I was looking forward to working again, especially with a company owned by a prestigious parent company with an excellent reputation.* A friend of mine whom I had worked with previously had started with this company a few months before. Although relatively new himself, he had favorable things to say about his job, especially in comparison to the last company where we had both worked.

Like any new position, the first week was reserved for training. On the first day, I had become acquainted with the other temps as we waited in a small conference room for our orientation to begin. The seven of us were soon joined by the Senior Customer Service Manager, an attractive, well-dressed young woman with a pleasant and cordial demeanor. She was one of two people I had met with during the interview process and would be one of our trainers. The other trainer, a young woman with whom I had met for a second interview, was a "team lead" who directly reported to the Senior Manager. Due to the various needs of the department, the two would alternate training our group as we learned the various protocols and policies of our new positions.

During this time, the temps enjoyed each others' company as we learned about our duties in a light yet productive atmosphere. Toward the end of the week, we were briefly introduced to the Customer Service Director, who oversaw all operations and productivity within the department. He reported directly to the company president and had been with the company for over a decade, starting out in our exact position: a customer service representative in training.

After a week of orientation and training, we were brought into the department to join the other twenty-five representatives. The format of the second week would be divided:

during the first half, we would "shadow" some of the other representatives as they performed their duties; during the second, they would "shadow" us. Overall, the dispositions of the representatives we were paired with were either moderately friendly or dutifully obliging. During this week and the weeks which followed, the other representatives - whose cubicle walls were often wallpapered with photos of pop-stars and fashion models - didn't seem to be too engaging, welcoming, or interested in getting to know the new-hires, though I felt there "were eyes on us." I figured this was due to our temporary status.

The holiday season, although busy and stressful at times, went by quickly. I became more acquainted with some of the permanent employees, but mostly interacted with my friend and the other temps. We all knew that decisions would be made during the first month of the new year regarding which temps would be made an offer of permanent employment and which ones would be released. Yet, before the season's end, the Director had publicly reprimanded some representatives for poor performance which, inevitably, was not their fault. The Senior Manager, despite knowing this was the case, said nothing to correct him. Regardless, after being unemployed for so long, I was hoping to be made permanent. Considering my performance as a consistent top seller within the department throughout the season, I was optimistic. I was also hopeful for another temp who was a top seller as well; she was also very efficient and had an excellent rapport with her customers.

I was a bit surprised when the decisions were made and neither of us were offered a permanent position. Although I was disappointed, I wrote it off as kismet. I gave it my best shot, I figured, and at least I would be taking away favorable sources as future references. I continued to perform as best as I could for the remainder of my employment.

However, after another week and a half, luck turned my way: one of the permanent employees was let go and a vacant position was now available. To my relief, I was offered the position. This was a load of my back since my previous bout of unemployment had revealed the lack of opportunity available, and I was not looking forward to hitting the pavement again. But now I could rest easy, finally feeling a sense of security I had missed for so long. My temp friend was not so lucky, and I sincerely wished her the best.

During the following months, I gradually began to know the other representatives more. And, oddly and unlike other retail operations I had worked for, the stress load did not decrease after the holidays; it increased. Accompanying the growing familiarity with my coworkers was an increased exposure to gossip and "venting," which I respectively disregarded and detached from. I also noticed that various customer service issues which I was not authorized to handle were being deflected by the team leads responsible for managing. I was either asked to direct the issue to another team lead or the issue would go unresolved, typically leading to situations where I had to find a way to placate irate customers. However, the monthly performance reviews (assessed by a team lead or the Senior Manager) I received were positive overall, yet these were based on surveillance monitoring which I disliked. I was also given more responsibility in responding to customer e-mails since someone above me (I don't know who) liked my writing skills. This additional duty, however, created even more stress. Like the others in the department, I found myself multi-tasking to the point of feeling burnt out by the end of the day. By this time, it was clear that virtually everyone "clock-watched" and left the second their shift ended.

As the stress escalated, I began to look forward to going to work less and less. The workload was increasing and finding a team lead to resolve escalated customer service issues was becoming more difficult. One team lead seemed to be extremely overwhelmed by the amount of work placed on his shoulders; on occasion, the poor guy would snap. As for the other leads, their whereabouts were unknown, and it was becoming more and more apparent that they were simply not around. Other times, I noticed some were socializing with each other while the reps were going mental with multi-tasking. The Senior Manager appeared not to be addressing urgent matters as well, preferring the customer to call back or leave a message on her voicemail. She too would be missing in action at various times for reasons unknown. (My friend eventually made the observation that she never wore the same outfit twice, which time proved to be accurate.) Fortunately for me, I was eventually blessed to work the same shift as one team lead who was a nothing short of a godsend. This young woman was exceptional in her ability to diffuse any sort of issue and was always available for support.

The Customer Service Director, whose office with a view was more distant than the others, was even more of a mystery. His start times, if noticeable, varied with each day. No one, including the Senior Manager, knew when he was "expected to be in." The duration of his lunch breaks was arbitrary as well. Also, the time of his departure would vary, but it was usually within a few hours after he came in and no one would be notified. What aroused the most curiosity was the actual work he performed, since did not speak or interact with any customers and allocations, merchandising, and vendor relations were all handled by other departments. One customer service rep postulated that he took care of the shipping accounts, but this later proved to be untrue: one of the team leads was assigned this duty. During the times he *was* in his office, he would be seen chatting with employees from the parent company or on his computer. But his actual contribution to the department was unknown to me and, as I would soon learn, everyone else within the department.

By now, I felt regret over their decision to keep me as a permanent employee and, more troubling, concern over the viability of the company itself. The toxic, dysfunctional signs of this work environment uncomfortably paralleled the symptoms of decline I noticed at the two previous companies where I had worked - and both had gone under. In both cases I was able to jump ship after seeing the writing on the wall that the companies were going to fail. Would I be as fortunate this time?

During the beginning of the following summer, the company announced its poor performance to the employees during the first quarter. Just after this announcement, I took a brief period off to go out of town to attend a friend's wedding. While away, I received a panicked phone call from one of my co-workers. Shocked and in tears, she told me she had been let go for being five minutes late one too many times. Not only was I amazed that she was let go for being five minutes late (the state law regarded tardiness as anything over seven minutes), but she was one of the best representatives (if not, the best) we had on staff. Moreover, I could not get over the fact that the Customer Service Director had made this decision, since he was clearly working part-time hours for a handsome full-time salary.

Upon returning to work, the increase in the fear-factor was palpable as was the representatives' depleted morale. Everyone was walking on eggshells and fearful of being let go. People who took public transportation were particularly nervous since it wasn't always reliable. With one of our "heavy hitters" gone along with others who had left (and weren't replaced), the work load increased even more. Representatives were now making more mistakes, leading to more work in correcting them, leading to more fear and negativity, leading to more mistakes - in short, a cyclic negative feedback mechanism.

Due to this, there was a marked increase in the toxicity within the department. Those who were already aloof, robotic, and antisocial became even more so. Their rare moments of free time would be devoted to watching videos of Beyoncé or pictures of cats. Some people began to monitor each other and, in turn, admonish their peer's mistakes and lack of follow through, even though they were guilty of the same thing due to the workload being more than any of us could humanly handle. Others, in an attempt to rebel against the extreme conditions they were facing, were intentionally performing poorly. Some of the "old-timers" lamented the days when the department functioned smoothly and morale was high. In general, there was a widespread lack of empathy, compassion, and cohesion within the department, despite the fact that we were all in the same boat.

Cliques began to form and solidify, and the "conversations" within them - when they could occur - were strange to observe. It was like watching two monologues take place as each person took turns talking about themselves while the other pretended to listen. People seemed more self-absorbed in general - that is, when they weren't reprimanding each other. One employee, though, was perennially chipper. I tried to diffuse the tension with some humor, but that only went so far. After so many attempts to "lighten up" the atmosphere were met with disdain, not only did I give up, but I started to feel resentment toward my coworkers as well. I noticed that more and more people, including myself, were frequently (and truly) sick. To top if off, we were told during a training session that one of the incentives of our job was being able to work for a well-known, high-end brand.

Yet everyone began to feel the fear factor as opportunities to "write up" associates were being sought. People were becoming paranoid that the next mistake or episode of tardiness in returning from their lunch break would lead to their dismissal. Plus, our whereabouts were tightly monitored: a bathroom break exceeding more than five minutes was guaranteed to be reprimanded. We were also constantly monitored to make sure we were at our own desk and not someone else's. By now, the work environment felt like a cross between "Survivor" and "One Flew Over the Cuckoo's Nest." It was getting to be way too much: my friend and I made the mutual confession that we uncorked a wine bottle as soon as we returned home.

The one thing that did not change was the Senior Manager's saccharin demeanor. It was a strange yet fabricated veneer of pleasantness, despite the fact that her staff was stressed out, over-worked, and miserable. She seemed to be as emotionally dissociated from her employees' morale almost as much as the Customer Service Director was physically. On the "tough days", though, she would buy the department doughnuts - which she would never eat. Otherwise, the only praise to be given went to sycophants and "yes-men;" or, they were favored in one way or another. Those who brought up deficiencies and/or opportunities to make the department's operations more efficient were told, "Thanks for the feedback!" or "Great idea!" yet nothing came from it.

I began to job hunt during whatever free time I had.

Then, after a glaring episode of employee favoritism, I blew a whistle. In short, this resulted in a closed door meeting with the Senior Manager, which I hoped to make as diplomatic yet productive as possible. In addition to the matter at hand, I attempted to discuss the various counterproductive protocols and operations that, if changed, would benefit management, the department, productivity, and the company as a whole.

Since the talk appeared to be going well, I decided to "go there": I brought up the Customer Service Director. After a respectful prologue, I asked her, "What does he do?" After nearly a year, I still had no idea and was sincerely hoping for some sort of answer. If there were none, hopefully she would see the light and realize that we were all being required to perform excess work outside of our responsibilities, beyond our capabilities, and within dysfunctional operations. Instead, she stared at me with a shocked look on her face - as if I were flippant or committed a blaspheme. I asked again, since no one else seemed to know either. I never received an answer.

Soon after this meeting, I was invited by the Customer Service Director to "sit-in" on an interdepartmental meeting less than a half-hour before it was to start. Present at the meeting would be the president and the directors from other departments. Apparently, one customer service representative is selected to sit in on this meeting each quarter. When I met the Customer Service Director and another manager outside the conference room a couple minutes beforehand, the director asked me, "Okay, Matt. Are you ready to give a presentational assessment of the Customer Service department?" Believing him to be joking, I jested, "Yep, I brought my diorama." But, when it came time for the director to give his presentation at this meeting, he turned to me and posed the same question. Dumbfounded, I struggled for words yet somehow whipped up an assessment, yet I could sense that the others in the room empathized with my predicament. Being a representative, I was not in a position to give a complete, objective overview of the status of the department, only recommendations based on observations germane to my position.

Shortly after both the meeting and the shock, it occurred to me: *the reason he asked me this question is he did not have an answer*. It wouldn't have made sense that the Senior Manager had relayed the content of our conversation to him; it would have been too confrontational for her. Yet I was livid (though not surprised) at the degree to which the director would pawn off his responsibility: that question was for someone in his position to answer, not mine. Prior to this, I was frazzled in keeping myself afloat with performing my own job and more with little resources and dysfunctional operations, and now he expected me to do his. Not only was he testing my willingness to be a victim, but enforcing it with shock and failure set-up as well. Needless to say, I didn't take this kindly. Moreover, my job hunt was proving to be futile.

Our department was sitting beneath two-thousand pounds of expensive dead weight and was about to be crushed if it didn't move. In an attempt to mobilize the other reps, I began to discuss the director's apparent absence of work, trying to convince them that our stress was due to his responsibilities being pushed away or downward. Appealing to the Senior Manager proved useless and I wasn't about to address this to the director himself. I hoped that others in my department would cooperate in an effort to do something about it. If we could displace him, we could hire more reps to handle the workload. Some listened and agreed, but seemed reluctant. One apathetic rep bemoaned, "Well, there's really not much I can do" and caved. The cheerful one was still inexplicably cheerful. Only two others in our department of now eighteen people were willing to take action.

Unfortunately, and before we could approach her, the president was let go by the parent company due to poor performance. I genuinely liked and respected her but wished she had seen the red flag waving about at the last interdepartmental meeting; perhaps that would have saved her. She was savvy and bright, yet the trust and faith she placed in her Customer Service Director was undeserved and detrimental.

After a new president was brought in, the two others and I waited to approach him until he was more immersed. To our benefit, however, he chose to meet with each employee one-on-one to discuss ways in which to make the company more profitable and efficient. Not only did the three of us seize this opportunity to blow the whistle on our director but, unbeknownst to us at the time, our voices were joined by others from outside our department. Mercifully, it wasn't long before the director was asked to leave.

As he walked out for the last time, the Customer Service Director seemed genuinely shocked by his termination. The Senior Manager expressed in an e-mail how much she and the department would miss him. I returned home with a cold bottle of champagne.

Sadly, and for reasons I will not get into, our company could not be turned around. After the following holiday season, the parent company announced its plans to shut down its dysfunctional child, which was to take place at a later date in the summer. With this announcement, the department tried to hold onto as many reps as possible, but wasn't too successful. This led to an even thinner skeleton crew as we tried to cope with the incessant demands of the operation, which led to more blame, accusations, breakdowns, and negativity amongst the reps. One wished she had a soundproof room to scream in, to which I agreed. Another coworker, I had noticed, always waited for me to say "hi" to her first, yet never seemed to reciprocate. Noticing this, I stopped to see if she would ever take the initiative to say "hello"; unfortunately, we never spoke again. Regardless of the inner-negativity, the environment was still bared a political yet odd "Stepford Wives" feeling about it. The shut-down date could not come soon enough.

The "after party" in the break room had a bittersweet air as the members of the customer service department were in each others' company for the last time. There was a subliminal ruefulness to the atmosphere, yet it didn't seem to be about sadness over the company's demise. Looking around the room, I couldn't tell if everyone wanted to say "good-bye" or "I'm sorry." Were they remorseful in how they treated each other? Would they miss each other? Did they regret not taking any action to make their workplace better? And sooner? Were they experiencing any hindsight?

Whatever the case, I left right after I lost the raffle. Now that I had some severance pay, I could enjoy some downtime to detox from this place. As I rode down the elevator to the street-level exit, my eyes swelled with tears of gratitude. "Never again," I promised myself. "No fucking way."

As portrayed in many horror movies, getting bitten by a zombie was infectious: the victim would join the ranks of the living dead assailants and seek out prey as well. Only those who knew how to effectively protect and defend themselves were safe.

It is evident from this previous story that the passing of responsibilities from the top of the pyramid downward increased the stress and fear factor of the department, causing a sort of "zombie effect" where fear and negativity became an epidemic. People who ordinarily were pleasant, responsible, engaging, understanding, and kind to others - in short, "people" - became caustic, short-tempered, irrational, and aloof. Moreover, many became predatory, retaliatory, malignant, and toxic toward each other. When another person came into contact with their toxicity, they too would feel their negative energy and, if not addressed in a healthy manner, were likely to convert into a "zombie."

If enough people succumb to offense (and defense) mechanisms as a means of coping with fear-based stress, the likelihood of this mentality permeating the entire group is sharply enhanced. This is similar to the "hundredth monkey syndrome," a phenomenon which describes the trend behind a group instantaneously exhibiting certain behaviors after they are adopted by a certain threshold percentage within it.

This phenomenon suggests that our energies are transferrable and that the resulting collective energy - or "synergy" - of a group or an organization, regardless of its size, is not just the sum of its parts, but originates within a certain portion of the group. When this threshold percentage is toxic, the "zombie effect" emerges. It can arise in any sort of collective, such as a family, a work environment, a religious congregation, a company, or a country. The energy behind the toxic tactics described in the previous chapter catalyzes the infection of this portion of the group, followed by the subsequent and spontaneous conversion of the group to reflect this toxicity as a whole. And, within this network of chain-reaction, more toxic tactics are born out of reactions to fear.

What makes the victim/criminal conversion within this network of chain reaction possible is how the person responds to being "victimized." This conversion - the tendency to behave against the conscience due to the fear conjured from the malignant's behavior - comes easily in those known as "toadies." These sycophantic types seem almost or just as self-gratifying as the malignants they cater to. Their servile, appeasing behavior signifies a remarkably low threshold in coping with the negative emotions involved with schemas reactions: that is, they essentially join "evil" to feel protected and avoid facing fear. But the fact that their own "self-worth" is based on placating perceived yet malignant authority figures, a deeper level suggests underlying low self-esteem. Having narcissistic personality disorders themselves, their need for recognition and dependance on approval make them prime candidates for promotion, since it is known that they will do anything to appease. Regardless, these types are prime candidates for becoming secondary psychopaths.

For the rest of us, when we to fail to defend ourselves against malignant behavior, we can avoid becoming "zombies" ourselves by making the conscious choice not to be overly reactive and/or take out our frustrations on others. This is important since it keeps our own vibration up and consciences intact. However, this is only possible when we have not reached our own threshold; if we have allowed our selves to absorb too much toxicity, this will be much more difficult to do. When we amass and harbor toxicity, we are liable to engage in the self-oriented defense mechanisms described previously, which can lead to self-destructive behavior (such as my turning to the "happy sauce.") Not only are we more susceptible to self-destructive behavior but, as we will see later, these negative emotions are stored in the body and can cause dis-ease. What is worse is that we may begin to take out our negative energy on others in the form of offense mechanisms. Fortunately, there are ways to "detox" from this negative energy which will be outlined in the second half of this book.

Outside of remaining impervious or impenetrable to negative energy, in dealing with malignant personalities one can either avoid them, confront them directly with or without the recruitment of others, or appeal to a higher power. In the previous story, avoidance wasn't an option and confrontation would have likely proved useless, but recruiting others and appealing to a higher power inevitably worked, but it proved to be too late.

In hindsight, it is clear that there were no "winners" in the previously described work environment. Everyone had succumbed to their fears in some way or form and some had become malignant themselves. The toxic tactics were flying about like oxygen molecules in air: scapegoatism, exoneration, entitlement, denial, spin, avoidance, inappropriate accountability, fear creation, false accusations, deaf ears, slander, constant-surveillance, and confinement were just some of the tactics frequently seen.

There were no winners since everyone reacted to their fear instead of honoring their self-love. Some were concerned about not being perfect. Others capitulated to the insatiable demands, but felt deep resentment or low self-worth underneath. Many acted out on their negative feelings of anger and resentment from being subjugated by deliberately performing poorly. Others projected the negative emotions stemming from deprivation, subjugation, vulnerability, abandonment and more onto their coworkers. And virtually all buckled in their fear of confronting malignant authority.

The reason for the differences in response to toxic authority was based on the difference in the various *perceptions of toxic authority itself and how to cope with the fears associated with it*. Those who were unduly loyal acted as "toadies" and did so out of being conditioned that their self-worth was based on obedience. Their allegiance was based on a fear that, if they did not acquiesce to the demands - no matter how toxic and abusive - they would be seen as "bad" or not get what they needed. In short, their fear-based yet false sense of self-worth was based on the approval they received. These types perceived the toxic authority figure as "good" since their capitulation at least bought them some praise, regardless of the degree to which they abdicated their true sense of well-being as well as others'.

Those who gave into the excessive demands and felt deep resentment as a result did not challenge authority because they were afraid of it. Their aversion to vocalizing their needs was rooted in a subjugation-based fear, dreading retaliation or some sort of repercussion. Thus, their very well-being took a back seat to their fears and they suffered in silence as a result. These people saw the authority figure as malignant yet omnipotent and had grown accustomed to harboring their negative feelings as much as they could.

Those who intentionally sabotaged performance - their own as well as the department's - honored their feelings of resentment, but in a non-productive manner. Their "rebellion" did nothing to address the source of toxicity, probably because they too feared confrontation since they saw authority as malignant yet omnipotent. They evidently had grown used to "acting out" on their frustrations in order to alleviate them. Although they regarded the malignant authority with fear, they did not perceive it to be powerful enough to prevent them from "getting away with" some defiance.

Those who took out their anger on innocent others also perceived the toxic authority as omnipotent, and likewise avoided confrontation out of fear. Instead, their negative feelings were more easily honored by directing them to their less imposing coworkers, which was probably a practice cultivated over time. They also saw authority as too powerful, yet they were callous in their treatment of others.

In all cases, these people had allowed their own self-worth and innate needs to be overridden by fear - fear of confronting authority - and the ways they reacted to this fear shaped their character.

I wonder if my fears had shaped my reaction, too. Had prior episodes of dealing with toxic authority conditioned me to strive to expel it in some way? Should I have spoken directly to the Director about his lack of involvement with the very department he was supposed to oversee? If I had approached it out of concern for him, would he have responded well? Or would he have just "smiled and nodded" like the Senior Manager or would he have had an adverse reaction? Was I just being realistic, knowing that broaching the topic with him would lead to becoming a target and being dismissed since I was not willing to enable his apparent absence of work? I seemed to be one of few willing to stand up for his own worth and that of the department, but was my reaction fear-based?

It seems as though there were as many "directors" as they were perceptions of him. A minority (including himself, apparently) saw nothing wrong with him; in fact, they were loyal to him. Others saw him as toxic, yet challenging authority and dissension were not an option. A few regarded him as malignant and powerful, yet felt they had they ability to do something about it.

Although the various perceptions were as many as the representatives in the department itself, some were closer to reality than others. However, in retrospect, all of them were skewed.

Recounting the dynamics at play within this work environment is beneficial in that it acts as a microcosmic (and, perhaps, less toxic) model for what is now occurring at a national - even global - level. As will be explored, the many means of dispensing fear by a powerful minority causes much strife within the whole. Moreover, many of our coping mechanisms in facing these imposed fears have mimicked those of the representatives in the previous story: many of us have internalized, diverted or anesthetized, denied and/or overcompensated for, and projected our fears onto each other rather than address and transmute them.

For a while after the company's closing, I held a good deal of resentment toward the leadership of our department - the Director in particular. This man seemed to have a very charmed life for doing very little. His entitlement was like nothing I had ever seen: the fact that he was physically present for less than half the time he was getting paid was appalling. The enabling of his behavior was unparalleled: the fact that no one seemed to know - or care about - what work he performed during his halved workday was astonishing. His despotism was lofty: the fact that others were being fired for being five minutes late after performing tasks relevant to his position was mind-blowing. His utter disregard for others' wellbeing could not have been worse: the fact that he was absolutely impervious as to what it was like to be one of his employees was ire-inducing. He could not have been more feckless: the fact that he was completely oblivious to the functioning of his own department was mind-boggling.

But, I had an epiphany when considering what sort of person would behave this way; it was eye-opening: *This man was miserable. It wasn't just that shit was rolling downhill; this man's inner life was shit: this man was fear-full.*

In this moment of revelation, I could not help but feel very, very sorry for him. But, as bad as I felt for him, the absence of any authentic love this man had in his heart pales in comparison to the power players on the global stage.

Out of an agreement with and respect for the parent company, I've withheld both its name as well as the name of its former child company. From what I had seen, the parent company was both dignified and ethical in its business practices, which were reflected in the treatment of their employees.)

6

"The Elite": Lonely at the Top, Pitiful at the Core

"We don't pay taxes. Only the little people pay taxes..."

- Leona Helmsley

They have many labels: "The Globalists," "The Military-Industrial Complex," "The Corporate Multinationals," "The Establishment." Most commonly, they're known as "the Elite." This highly dominant, powerful, executive, and exclusive class is comprised of various cross-pollinating groups and figures influencing financial, political, economic, and military policy at national and global levels. Their realm of influence spans the culture, media, and social conditioning of many populations around the world, including that of the United States.

Its members include the heads of international economic organizations and central banks such as the Bank for International Settlements, the International Monetary Fund (IMF) and the Federal Reserve, executives and officers of large commercial and investment financial institutions, high-ranking foreign and domestic political figures, former and current heads of state, directors of and high-ranking officials within sensitive intelligence and government agencies, media and casino moguls, energy and natural resource tycoons, chief officers of various corporations, including those specializing in the manufacturing of arms and military equipment.

Some of the organizations believed to be linked to this privileged minority include conglomerates of political and economic think tanks, such as the Trilateral Commission, the Bilderberg Group, the National Security Council, and the Council on Foreign Relations; secret societies such as Skull and Bones, the Bohemian Grove, the Zionists, and the Illuminati; and ruling class families and political dynasties.

Their power can be attributed by the amount of wealth they have amassed, and so is their opulent yet insular lifestyle. The multiple mansions they own, though extravagant and massive, are highly secluded, protected, and clandestine. In some cases, the locations of their residences are effectively withheld from public knowledge. Their personal travel and whereabouts are even more protected, since most - if not all - own private jets that allow for unhindered mobility and protection from public scrutiny. Their very wealth and assets are protected in the form of off-shore accounts, shielding them from any investigation into how it was "earned."

To masquerade their own influence and amoral activity, many use decoys, "puppets", figureheads and façades such as foundations, political action committees, and front companies. Most of their unethical conduct is performed via proxy in general. They have the ability to create or destroy careers in politics, military, finance, economics, media, journalism, entertainment, advertising, and governance.

Those whose careers are maintained and promoted benefit the elite in some way. Moreover, they possess jurisdiction over policy, legislature, and elections themselves, regardless of the general public's opinion, will, or belief in the existence of a democratic, self-determining process. Their manipulation of various political administrations essentially renders them controlled regimes. Most notably, they manipulate and exploit financial markets for profit. Such abilities are routinely used and it is to their own advantage.

By their direct or indirect control of intelligence agencies, law, military, and law enforcement, these objectives are secured.

Through their control of media, journalism, academia, entertainment, and advertising, they influence, manipulate, indoctrinate and oftentimes brainwash members of the general populace to adopt and even endorse ideologies and political belief sets which counter their best interests. Through media, this is accomplished with such toxic tactics as spin, half-truths, lies of omission, as well as blackout, falsehoods, and punditry. This often conditions the population to inappropriately hold other groups within the population accountable for social and economic ills. Within academia, corporatist, economic, and political doctrines are promulgated while the respective institutions are kept prosperous by means of financial donations and contributions. In the entertainment and advertising industries, this is accomplished by means of embedded ideological conditioning, celebrity endorsement, and attempts to spin or even reinvent history in films which supposedly portray it; in short, propaganda.

Not only is the general population influenced by the elite, they are closely monitored as well. New technology and practices are now employed to track purchases, communications, and whereabouts of any member of the populace.

Dissenters, whistleblowers, or anyone who sufficiently disquiets them can expect retaliatory measures to be silenced in some way or form.

They plan well in advance, have excellent cognitive ability in realizing relationships of cause and effect, and implement sufficient understanding of human nature and behavior and the manipulation thereof. They would not be so "successful" if they did not.

They are the top of the pyramid and accountable to no one. The rules exist for their benefit; the rules exist of others to obey.

The elite sit atop this hierarchal pyramid of power which is largely based on extracting wealth from the tiers below it. The tier directly beneath consists of international economic organizations and national and international central banks. This tier is responsible for establishing, monitoring, and profiting from interest based currency systems and their relationship to each other internationally. This tier creates the supply of money as well as large financial institutions such as "big banks," which determine credit interest rates and loan creation, and investment banks. Special low-interest loan rates and other financial support are given to corporations, which comprise the next tier. National governments, the next tier, are highly influenced by the tiers above it. "Symbiotic" transactions among them are smoothly accomplished through lobbying groups and political action committees; they ensure the viability of both the governments and the higher tiers above them. Due to the immense cross-pollination of central-banking, financial, corporate, and government personnel, the divisions among these tiers are blurred, as is their direct connection to (or inclusion within) the elite. Subsequent tiers include those associated with state and local government, judicial processes, law enforcement, academia, media and journalism, advertisement, and entertainment. Their ties to the elite may be strong, weak, or non-existent.

Lastly, at the bottom, is the general public whose wealth is tapped and concentrated at the top by means of taxation and interest, which the elite effectively circumvent. This hierarchal structure, which will be referred to in the chapters that follow, not only orchestrates the flow of money to its top, but the flow of fear toward its base. To condense, the flowchart of fear is:

Figure 2:

The Elite → Central Banks → Investment Banks → Retail Banks → Corporations → Government → Law→ Law Enforcement → Academia → Media → Public

Currency manipulation is not the sole method of generating wealth. Because of the elite's close (and blurred) ties to government, other means are at their disposal. Expanding on the quote by nineteenth century military theorist Carl von Clausewitz, "War is a continuation of policy [or politics] by other means," it must be noted that *politics is a continuation economics by other means.* This is well understood by those comprising the elite, since their prosperity is also derived from the direct manipulation of natural resources, economic and financial policy, politics, and in some instances, war. Such endeavors have inevitably resulted in strife experienced by others, be it a diminished quality of life, loss of political freedom, or physical harm.

The first point of contact is the usurpation of territory or property known to contain an abundance of natural energy resources (such as oil or natural gas) or precious commodity (such as diamonds, gold, or other minerals.) The proceeds derived from extracting such natural commodities remain in the hands of a few by means of minimizing or bypassing taxation, regulation, and any labor protection (such as minimum wage, maximum hours worked per day or week, and benefits) if such laws exist.

The second tactic involves the systematic subjugation of foreign and domestic policy for concentrated profit. As illustrated in her highly-acclaimed book *The Shock Doctrine,* Naomi Klein demonstrates with numerous examples the ways in which unregulated capitalism has resulted in the transfer of public wealth into the hands of a few, namely the elite's. This is accomplished through subversive economic policy, covert intelligence agencies, and can involve the exploitation of crises (real, imagined, or made) known as "disaster capitalism," or the use of shock in the form of coups or juntas, often brutal. By means of collectivization, privatization, and deregulation of nationally based industry and public services, the elite is able to extract public wealth by monopoly, discarded price protection, and, again, taxation. The result is high-unemployment, high-inflation, poor working conditions, depreciated public services, a disappearance of the middle class, and soaring costs of living.

The third approach - and perhaps last resort - to realizing excessive gain is war. Combat measures are taken when a government or percentage of the population resists capitulating to the objectives of policy, resource ownership, and deregulation. War will generate even more profit for certain members of the elite if it is privatized: the companies contracted to manufacture weapons and/or military equipment or provide mercenary services will realize profits for its executives and investors. Since tax dollars are used to subsidize wars, this will increase the amount of public wealth to be transferred into private hands.

Since they have the ability to manipulate both foreign and domestic legislation, not only do laws benefit them, they are above "the law" and have the power to avoid accountability. This allows for them to add more to their millions and billions of assets by ways and means that would be (and are) criminal for the general public to engage in. In addition to insider trading, it has been alleged that this may include the transnational trafficking and selling of illegal drugs, weapons trading, money laundering, prostitution rings, and child and human trafficking. Other means more devastating have been also been asserted.

Lastly, it seems to be a common conception that "the elite" is a group unified in its objectives and moral standards (or lack thereof.) Although its members may objectives in common, I feel this is an inaccurate assumption. This is not an excusal, yet a recognition that some members of its rank have more scruples than others which most likely leads to some dissension within the stratum.

It is not an imperative of this book to specifically designate who benefitted from currency control, unregulated "free-market" capitalism, foreign/domestic policy manipulation, and other means for two reasons. First, it involves some speculation due to, in part, withheld evidence, records, and information. Moreover, determining who comprises the elite would be based not only on the toxic ways and means of the garnering wealth, but the amount of profit as well; both of which are subjective.

Second, and more importantly, *it is not the intent of this book to incriminate or judge individuals.* As we will see later, these actions are truly and ultimately the individual's own responsibility, regardless of how morally corrupt others may find them and the ill-effects of their actions impacted others. Rather, it is to *understand* and gain insight into the spiritual nature behind their behavior. By doing so, we can proceed with the most morally and logistically effective means of resolution while honoring our highest selves.

I have tried to keep the previous description of the elite as relevant, neutral, and bias-free as possible. (Hopefully, your perspective is similar at this time.) The purpose of providing this description is not to inspire passion, but to provide a foundation from which to gain deeper insight into the nature of those who comprise the elite.

To understand what is occurring on a psycho-spiritual level with persons as spiritually bankrupt these, it must first be acknowledged that their malignant behavior is rooted in offense mechanisms. To delve further, it is necessary to make the correlation between these outward-oriented mechanisms and the schemas they react to. By doing this, we can understand the foundation of their spiritual deficiency (absence of self-love replace by fear) which inevitably gave rise to spiritual bankruptcy.

Based on the previous description, the following toxic tactics are evident: Mutual enabling, Seduction/bribery, Double Standards, Invasiveness, Favoritism, Denial, Avoidance, Lies of Omission, Half-truths, Exoneration, Spin, Scapegoatism, Dialectics, Deaf Ears, Projection, False Accusations, Blackmail/extortion, Slander, Abandonment, Ostracizing, Brainwashing, Subjugation, Fear Creation, Capitalizing on Crisis, Shock, Constant Surveillance, Intimidation, Enslavement, Confinement, Physical duress and abuse, Torture, Despotism, and Murder. Most likely, all of the toxic tactics described earlier have been apparent to some degree or another. (If any of these are not readily noticeable, they will be as various other trends within the lower tiers are explored.)

The end result is a realization of the goals of spiritually malignancy discussed previously: domination (or creating a willing and/or docile victim), reinforcing entitlement, and establishing narcissism and/or narcissistic supply. Not only are these goals realized, they all are achieved on a vast, macroscopic scale and often catastrophic.

Although all of the toxic tactics are most likely applicable, it is sufficient to use those listed above to correlate to their associated schemas. If relevant, a toxic tactic is assigned more than one schema. The following correlations are based on the malignant personality profile detailed in Chapter 2, Table 3:

1) **Abandonment:** Avoidance, Ostracizing, Abandonment, Subjugation, Enslavement, Confinement, Despotism.
2) **Deprivation:** Mutual enabling, Seduction/bribery, Double Standards, Invasiveness, Projection, Slander, Abandonment, Ostracizing, Brainwashing, Subjugation, Fear Creation, Capitalizing on Crisis, Shock, Intimidation.
3) **Subjugation:** Seduction/bribery, Double Standards, Favoritism, Lies of Omission, Half-truths, Spin, Scapegoatism, Dialectics, Deaf Ears, Blackmail/extortion, Slander, Brainwashing, Subjugation, Intimidation,
Enslavement, Confinement, Physical duress and abuse, Torture, Despotism, Murder.
4) **Mistrust:** Invasiveness, Denial, Lies of Omission, Half-truths, Spin, Scapegoatism, False Accusations, Blackmail/extortion, Slander, Brainwashing, Fear Creation, Capitalizing on Crisis, Shock, Constant Surveillance.
5) **Unlovability:** Scapegoatism, Double Standards, Favoritism, Exoneration, Scapegoatism, Projection, False Accusations, Blackmail/extortion, Slander.
6) **Exclusion:** Abandonment, Ostracizing, Enslavement, Confinement, Physical duress and abuse, Torture, Despotism, Murder.
7) **Vulnerability:** Invasiveness, Denial, Scapegoatism, Projection, False Accusations, Blackmail extortion, Slander, Brainwashing, Fear Creation, Capitalizing on Crisis, Shock, Constant Surveillance, Intimidation, Enslavement, Confinement, Physical duress and abuse, Torture, Despotism, Murder.
8) **Failure:** Seduction/bribery, Double Standards, Denial, Lies of Omission, Half-truths, Exoneration, Spin, Scapegoatism, Dialectics, Deaf Ears, Projection, False Accusations, Blackmail/extortion, Slander, Brainwashing.
9) **Perfectionism:** Double Standards, Denial, Avoidance, Lies of Omission, Half-truths, Exoneration, Spin, Scapegoatism, Dialectics, Deaf Ears, Projection, False Accusations, Blackmail/extortion, Slander, Brainwashing.
10) **Entitlement:** Mutual enabling, Seduction/bribery, Double Standards, Denial, Avoidance, Lies of Omission, Half truths, Exoneration, Spin, Scapegoatism, Deaf Ears, Projection, False Accusations, Blackmail/extortion, Slander, Constant Surveillance, Intimidation, Enslavement, Confinement, Physical duress and abuse, Torture, Despotism, and Murder.

Your assignments may differ, but one thing is clear: *the toxic tactics behind the collective spiritually malignant behavior of the elite can be reduced to most if not all of the schemas.*

By assigning the elite's overcompensating and projecting toxic tactics to their underlying schemas, the extent of their inner, unresolved hell becomes apparent. These people, as a whole, are tremendously scared of abandonment. Deep down, they are perhaps deathly afraid of not having enough or being cared about. They are deeply afraid of not having any control. They're scared for their own wellbeing. They are extremely frightened that no one would love them for the human beings they truly are. They're afraid of not being included or involved. They are terrified of ever appearing not good enough as they are with being seen as anything less than perfect. And, of course, they would experience extreme anxiety if they ever were denied what they wanted, how they wanted it, when they wanted it or realized they weren't special; it would prevent them from being able to avoid such fears.

Most of all, any attempts to address or expose their criminal behavior would stimulate their repressed paranoia.

Yet, the extent to which they have avoided their fears in denying their existence by overcompensating for and projecting them onto others is unprecedented. This has truly led to a downward spiral into deep spiritual debt to the point of being incredibly bankrupt. Countless others - if not the entire world - have felt the effects of their mechanisms.

Their shortcomings and misdeeds have catalyzed an insatiable need for more money, power, and control to make themselves feel better, safer, and stronger. The expensive homes, the luxury cars, the pomp and circumstance, and the lavish lifestyle exist to make themselves feel admired and adulated to avoid feeling inadequate and unlovable. The power over global policy, national affairs, and other people and populations make themselves feel they have control, cushioning them from any emotional strife resembling deprivation, subjugation, mistrust, and vulnerability. The mass spying, surveillance, and exposing of skeletons in others' closets compensate for their own personal demons and shame. Their insular, reclusive, and highly-protected lifestyle shield them from scrutiny, vulnerability, and accountability. Their criminal practices require more and more protection and control to keep themselves feeling safe and secure. Their lies need more power and control to keep them from being found out.

It is quite a bit to avoid facing one's inner fears and guilty conscience.

As a result, billions have lost their jobs, their homes, their health, their credit, their savings, even their lives to starvation, malnourishment, and committing suicide or being assassinated, disappeared, and murdered.

It is unlikely that any of their interpersonal contacts love them for who they are. They associate with them out of kindredness since they share the same malignant offense mechanisms and the fears behind them. Or, they associate with them figuring proximity and "good graces" equals protection. Or, similarly, they associate with them because of the false sense of self-worth they can derive. Whatever the case, it is unlikely that any of their associations love themselves either.

Whereas I felt very sorry for the Customer Service Director described earlier, *these people break my heart*. The irony is that they believe they're enviable, but there's nothing about them to envy. Their wealth was earned illegitimately, as was their power. The "love" that surrounds them is bogus: it is, at best, mutual enabling, cronyism, and narcissistic supply. Their own "self-esteem" is based on anything and everything - a grandiose sense of self; positions of power and prestige; manufactured awards, coronations, and commemorations; a false persona portrayed by the media; false accomplishments; false friends; false wealth, etc. - *anything except for authentic, intrinsic value*. In short, nothing about them or their lives is genuine. So, how can they be envied if their entire lifestyle is based on something false? *How can anyone be lovable if nothing about them is true?*

Their rule over the world serves as a diversion for confronting their own inner-hell which, ironically, only grows as a result. They have earned millions and billions, but the one thing their money will never buy and that they are likely to never possess is true: unconditional self-love. *To understand this about them is excruciatingly heart-wrenching*. And it's ironic that, if anyone would know what they don't have, it would be the elite. But the grandest irony is that, with the help of courage, responsibility, and a genuine care for self and others, this unconditional self-love is free of charge. Actually, I'll correct myself: the cost would be confronting their fears and guilty consciences and replacing them with love and self-accountability. Sadly, their money can't pay for that either.

But it can certainly pay for spreading their fear.

✦

7

Pyramid Power

*"The powers of financial capitalism had a far-reaching aim,
nothing less than to create a world system of financial control in private hands
able to dominate the political system of each country and the economy of the world as a whole."*

- Carroll Quigley

In this and the next few chapters, we will examine how these toxic tactics (or offense mechanisms) are used in pyramidal or hierarchal organizations to engage a "fear for power" trade. Here, those who are at the top superimpose and subject others within tiers below to fear in order to gain despotic control, avoid rules, and plump up their egos. The type of organization varies: it could be anything from a corporation, to a religious institution, to a dysfunctional family, to an institution for higher education, to a big bank, to a country, to a political regime, to a mafia ring, to a pyramid scheme, etc.

Whatever the pyramid, *those at "the top" extract power* - which could be in the form of financial wealth, excessive "liberty" such as having to never or barely work, exoneration from standards (moral, ethical, logistical, legal, etc.) required of the majority, and despotic control - *by dispensing fear and stress downward the pyramid onto the successive tiers below.* Thus, in the hierarchy, members of a "higher" yet smaller tier will dispense toxic tactics onto the larger tier beneath. As "those below" increasingly feel the downpour of stress that comes with fears of being subjugated, excluded, abandoned, mistrusting, violated, unlovable, failing, deprived, and needing to be perfect, "those above" increasingly amass control, entitlement, and narcissism. As time goes on, and if this dynamic isn't challenged, the final result digresses into a situation where a narcissistic, controlling, entitled, conscienceless, remorseless, seemingly stress-free yet tyrannical "elite" - that is, *a group of psychopaths* - at the top of the pyramid dominate a system compromised of an overly-burdened, fearful, and stressed-out majority of decent human beings who can no longer self-determine and desperately try to survive, most prominent at the pyramid's base:

Fear   Power

Inevitably, and at some point, the whole pyramid collapses. And the pyramid that is the United States of America is beginning to wobble.

The Federal Reserve

"It is well enough that people of the nation do not understand our banking and monetary system, for if they did, I believe there would be a revolution before tomorrow morning."

- Henry Ford

As mentioned in the preceding chapter, much of the elite's wealth and power is derived via currency control. And, as previously described, wealth and power is sought solely to provide protection from facing their fears.

The hierarchal pyramid structure behind the principle of currency control used to realize this, as we will see in the following chapters, serves as the elite's template for amassing additional profit while spreading more of its fears.

Central banks, such as the European Central Bank, People's Bank of China, and the Federal Reserve System in the United States, were created to manage a nation's money supply and interest rates. In the United States, the Federal Reserve was established in 1913, reportedly in response to a series of financial panics. Yet, unlike other central banks established as public institutions, the legislation behind the creation of the Federal Reserve - drafted in 1910 by Senator Nelson Aldrich and leaders of top finance and industrial groups - attempted to create a *privately* owned central bank. This would have provided a centralized, independent, private group with monopolistic control over the production of currency, which was to be elastically based (in that the supply could be expanded and contracted) on a gold and commercial paper standard. Since the money printed by the Federal Reserve on behalf of the US Treasury created interest, it would create a debt based system since the federal government would need to compensate for the interest accrued on the money it borrowed - a debt the general population would inevitably be responsible for. The revenue from this interest, of course, would be reaped by those in control of the Federal Reserve.

Aldrich's bill was met with much opposition in Congress primarily due to his close ties to established finance and industrial leaders. Some members of Congress favored public ownership via a system owned and operated by the government. Others favored a private yet decentralized system which would circumvent monopolistic control. This opposition effectively prevented the Aldrich bill from passing. However, a revision of this bill, the Federal Reserve Act, was passed in 1913. The essential difference between the two bills was the transfer of control from the Board of Directors to the government, known today as the Board of Governors.

Today, currency management by the Federal Reserve bypasses much regulation or accountability. The Federal Banking Agency Audit Act of 1978 granted the Government Accountability Office (GAO) the ability to audit check-processing, currency storage and shipments, and some regulatory and bank examination functions. However, the GAO is not permitted to audit transactions for or with a foreign central bank or government, non-private international financing organizations, deliberations, decisions, or actions on monetary policy matters. It also cannot audit transactions made under the direction of the Federal Open Market Committee, and communication among or between members of the Board of Governors and the Federal Reserve's officers and employees.

Since the money supply can be increased and managed with little regulation or oversight, this not only allows those controlling its production to create as much as they want, yet doing so depreciates its overall value. This leads to inflation, ultimately affecting those who have less. To compensate for inflation, taxation, and decreasing monetary value, people turn to loans or credit, both of which involve more accrual of interest, which is determined by rates set by big banks. Part of the revenue generated from this interest will be paid to the central bank that created the money to begin with. Yet, since the central bank operates today in privacy, secrecy, and with little oversight or accountability, it appears to be neither "federal" nor "reserved."

Because this hybrid of private and (supposedly) public control of money supply created in 1913 still maintained a debt based system, the government still required a means to subsidize the interest accrued on the money it borrowed. This was accomplished by the establishment of the Internal Revenue Service in the same year. The sixteenth amendment was ratified and allowed congress "the power to collect and lay taxes on incomes." Thus, the American citizen was now required to pay for their government's spending as well as the interest owed to the Federal Reserve which, considering the amount the government can spend, led to a handsome profit for those in control of the money supply.

Failure to file a tax return or remitting payment for the amount of taxes owed results in a marked interest rate increase; the penalty serves as a financial injury to the citizen from which the Federal Reserve benefits. A person who does not file and is audited can expect to be inundated with numerous notices. If accrued penalties are not collected over a period of time, this can lead to criminal charges, repossession of assets such as homes or cars, and even imprisonment.

The end result is a debt-based monetary system which creates serfdom among the general population and a very rich and powerful few. The mechanisms used to manifest and enforce the Federal Reserve system have distressing parallels to the boiling frogs effect described earlier. The stages are the same: Testing the Waters, Establishing Entitlement, Narcissistic Dominance, Avoiding Accountability, Establishing Victimhood/ Control, and Reinforcing Control. Readers who are familiarized with respective congressional hearings and inquiries will notice specific toxic tactics used to avoid accountability, establish entitlement, and create docile victims. (It is likely that all of the toxic tactics have been used behind closed doors.) Those who are not familiarized can understand that this scheme is reinforced by government-backed subjugation, fear-creation, enslavement, and captivity, all of which the citizen subsidizes with tax dollars.

We can see how the pyramid model realizes this: The elite use the central banks to control the money supply and designate interest rates; the big banks set additional loan and credit interest rates while providing the central bank interest; the corporations and business file tax forms for each employee (as they receive tax breaks and special interest rates); the government enacts and enforces tax-evasion laws and regulations; attorneys and law enforcement assist in enforcing of laws, media broadcasts tax deadlines and often exposes those guilty of tax evasion; the public capitulates by filing and paying taxes because no one wants to lose their homes, cars, valuables, or be imprisoned. *This is a big bully taking a lot of milk money.*

To understand what is occurring from a spiritual perspective, consider the dynamics of fear involved: The elite fear not being in control, not being lovable, not being protected, not being perfect, not being successful, not being without, not being alone or included, and/or not being special. They turn to money as a source of power to buffer their fears by means of central banking.

They recruit others who willingly capitulate to their demands out of similar fears (of powerlessness, unlovability, vulnerability, abandonment, exclusion, deprivation, and not being special) to work directly with or for them in government, corporations, and finance (all of which the elite establishes, influences, or has some involvement in) to maintain the central bank's profit and viability. In return, they are given power, money, and status to appease their fears.

Now, for these individuals to further compensate for these subconscious fears as well as remorse, they recruit proxies within law, law enforcement, military, and media who also seek money and power to counter similar fears of their own. Being sycophants, they find salvation in those more powerful and thus do their bidding.

The end result is the enforcement of laws, regulations, and mores that cause poverty in the general public, leaving them feeling like subjugated, deprived, ordinary, unlovable and imperfect failures (since they now cannot self-determine and appear poor) because they have inherited the fears which were originally the elite's. Thus, as the money of the public has floated upward the pyramid, the elite's fears have trickled all the way down to the general public. Actually, the elite's fear still exists at the top; money just covers it up along with a stockpile of remorse.

It is often said that "money is the root of all evil," yet when noticing how money is siphoned as fear is dispensed, something deeper is revealed regarding the nature of money: *Money is desired to calm people's fears.* Anyone who has faced foreclosure or had an automobile repossessed knows this all too well. We earn money out of fear of not having food, clothing, shelter, or transportation; no one wants to be homeless, naked, stranded, or starving. We seek money to calm our basic fears of survival and to have some semblance of freedom.

But, like a drug, any surplus money sought by malignant personalities via malignant means is to anesthetize their excessive fears (and, in turn, guilty conscience.) For instance, consider those people who strive for excess money because they want higher status, or vice versa. People who want higher status or excess money want to be envied and adulated. People who want to be envied and adulation are deficient in self-love because anyone who possessed true self-love would be happy with themselves and not give much of a care about what anyone else thought of them. Thus, the money is sought to numb their fears of not being lovable or special.

The amount of extraneous wealth one has can be considered to be directly proportional to the amount of unattended fear she or he has, provided it was "earned" through malignant means. Conversely, the amount of wealth one has usurped by malignant means is inversely proportional to the amount of self-love they have, since the fear which blocks this self-love is numbed with money. In the case of the elite, this self-love devastatingly little. Also, the excess money that they have affords them greater ability to employ toxic tactics, which generates more money to cover up the negative feelings associated with their schemas (and guilty conscience.) Therefore, *it is not money that is the root of all "evil," rather it is fear.*

Is this to suggest that everyone with excessive wealth is "evil" or has a stockpile of unresolved fear and remorse? Absolutely not. Many wealthy individuals have earned their money through an honest living or "labors of love" and subsequently enjoyed appreciable - and usually unexpected - profit. These artists, novelists, entrepreneurs, and others have realized wealth on the basis of their own creation. I would imagine that their happiness is *not* based on the amount of power and wealth they have; rather, it is based on vocational freedom, creative expression, and the ability to affect others in a positive manner. Moreover, their wealth was not derived from toxic tactics or establishing despotic control, narcissism, or entitlement. Specifically, they did not follow a pyramid model which involved projecting their fears onto those less fortunate as wealth was siphoned by exploiting this imposed fear. Sadly, these morally-intact individuals are few, and the pyramid model exists outside of currency control to make money by projecting fear.

Corporations

"What's wrong with taking care of No.1?"

- Ned Gerrity, former Vice President of ITT (International Telephone and Telegraph Company)

Corporations and financial institutions are companies recognized by law as single bodies with their own powers and liabilities separate from the those of its individual members. Their hierarchal structures are similar to that of the elite. Policy, decision making, execution, and communication are all directed by a managing officer or the Chief Executive Officer (CEO.) Their leadership is assisted by an executive council or board of directors, often including presidents, vice-presidents, and other executives and officers whose roles involve overseeing operations, communication, legal issues, and human resources. Depending on the institution, subsequent tiers include department heads, zone or area managers, regional managers, district managers, branch or store managers, assistant managers, and associates. Both corporations and financial institutions exist to realize large, reliable, and legal returns for their owners, investors, and shareholders.

Corporations emerged during the Industrial Age to increase productivity and minimize man-power, both of which would ultimately result in greater profitability for investors and shareholders. A business can become incorporated by obtaining a charter from the government and, after doing so, is recognized by law as a legal personality with its own powers and liabilities. Its powers are now the same as an individual citizen: it can purchase property, apply for loans, and seek legal recourse. Yet, since the corporation is its own entity, its shareholders can avoid certain liabilities associated with proprietorships. In particular, shareholders of a corporation have "limited liability" for the corporation's debts and obligations. As a result, their losses cannot exceed the amount which they contributed for the purchase of their shares, and thus reduces the amount that a shareholder can lose in a company. Another advantage is the "perpetual lifetime" status of the shares themselves. Since the corporation - as an individual - is likely to outlive its shareholders, the assets and accumulation of capital can be bestowed upon beneficiaries.

However, since the corporation is endowed with its own powers and liability, personal accountabilities for the decisions made within the company are dispersed. Moreover, not only is decision making spread throughout its leadership, it is also based on its shareholders, unlike sole proprietorship. This affects not only the decision making process, but the judgement process as well.

The executive council, as previously mentioned, is primarily concerned with maximizing profits for itself and other shareholders. Since the decision making is in the hands of a group with the basis of its decisions relating to the whole, a merging of many minds take place. In this sense, the corporation *is* a personality, yet it is a large personality composed of multiple consciousnesses with its mind comprised of those of its board. Like the 1980's anime series *Voltron*, a cartoon featuring the adventures of five heroes who connect their vehicles to form a giant super robot, the minds of the executive board converge to form that of the corporation.

Yet with the converging of group's minds also converges their unresolved schemas, defense and/or offense mechanisms, and varying degrees of conscience. The personality of the corporation will not only be a fusion of these yet, since accountability is decentralized, the liability for the effects of the collected offense mechanisms can be attributed to the corporation itself. This not only increases the likelihood of malignant repercussions, it exponentially increases the magnitude as well.

Those who comprise the executive branch may not be fully aware of any toxic contribution they (or others) are personally making due to the group dynamic at play. Like a Ouija board, one set of hands will most likely not cause the window to move, but adding other hands decreases the awareness of personal influence while subconscious anonymity moves the window. In both cases, a personality takes over. To whom it belongs to is anyone's guess.

However, this nebulous accountability can result in a host of malignant behavior affecting the corporation internally as well as outside of it. Since the goal of the corporation is to maximize as much profit as possible, its feedback can be devastating considering the wealth it creates serves to counter fear.

Within the corporate structure itself, this can lead to "shit rolling downhill." If the collective consciousness of the corporation has enough unresolved "issues," it will be insatiable in garnering mass profit to anesthetize its fears. Amassing surplus profit would involve increasing productivity, reducing manpower, and minimizing wages as much as possible. This has given rise to the trend met with much chagrin known as "Corporate

America" where employees are viewed, not as people, but as a component of the profit-making process. It is by no coincidence that the term "personnel" (sounding like "personal") has been replaced by the label "human resources." This semantically convenient - and Orwellian - term enables the corporation to establish a culture in which employees are perceived as a source of energy rather than human beings. The objectives of the "corporate mind's" fear-based mentality to realize maximum profit are delegated to personnel in subsequent tiers to enforce. These individuals - zone or area managers, regional managers, district managers, etc. - are often compelled to motivate by fear in order to safeguard their own positions during which they scapegoat their own issues in the process. They capitulate to the demands of maintaining lower wages, tighter surveillance, excessive delegation of responsibility, and more since their job security, promotability, and "self-worth" depend on appeasing these demands. They do so out of fear of not being able to put food on the table or their children through school, appearing "less than" to their peers, having savings for retirement, retaliation, not being seen as "good" employees, not being able to challenge authority, etc. - in essence, out of fears of vulnerability, unlovability, mistrust, subjugation, and more. Any fear-based stress they encounter can be easily projected onto their subordinates through a variety of offense mechanisms, thus bestowing upon them feelings of vulnerability, deprivation, perfectionism, etc.

Those working within the bottom tiers will surely feel this the most. They will be controlled and subjugated into working harder, faster, and stronger for as long and affordably as permitted by law. The amount of time they are permitted to rest or tend to illness is highly regulated as is their pay raises, which often do not meet the rising cost of living. Although they will receive paychecks, they will be fortunate if their wages subsidize their own living necessities (let alone anything outside of them.) Their labor-burdened lifestyle of "working to live and living to work" renders them serfs, while their low morale (or disdain for the job itself) will surely affect the functioning of the corporation as a whole. If their needs and feedback are not vocalized, met, or heard, internal resentment will lead to vexation and sabotage against the company, oftentimes manifesting in a pronounced fear factor, poor performance and theft. If anything, they are likely to feel deprived, subjugated, excluded, failing, less than perfect, etc on a daily basis.

The result is a large negative feedback mechanism: the executive branch imparts more control to ensure profitability through labor productivity, more control creates more internal resentment and an escalated fear factor, more resentment and fear negatively impacts the company's productivity and profitability, and more control is needed to counter this deficit in productivity and profitability to the point where the environment resembles a fascist regime. The very fact that more control is enforced affects the corporation's profitability since energy and funds are required to reinforce it.

However, the conditions faced by those within the bottom tiers are likely to be tolerated due to the lack of career mobility and job opportunity, since many corporations have outsourced internal positions to foreign markets with less regulation and labor protection. This increases the corporations' profitability, yet affects job creation domestically.

If the laborers are not domestic and live in a country with little to no labor protection, their fate will likely be much worse. Some workers in foreign sweatshops have been known to earn less than one percent on the retail value of the product they've made. They can barely feed or clothe themselves let alone self-determine on such a pittance.

Whether the "human resource" is foreign or domestic, the effect is the same: they inherit the fears of vulnerability, subjugation, mistrust, deprivation, unlovability, abandonment, exclusion, failure, perfectionism, and entitlement which the corporate personality originally sought to avert through profit. Like the pyramidal central banking model, the end result is identical: by means of offense mechanisms, the top projects its fear toward the bottom while the wealth concentrating at the top anesthetizes its fears. In 2011, the national ratio for CEO-to-worker pay ratio grew twenty percent from the previous year to 325 dollars to one. [8]

Also unfortunate is that the effects of externalizing fear are often not localized within the corporation itself. The primary imperative of maximizing profit can persuade an executive branch to disregard ethical and legal safety standards which can affect the health of the environment and the general population. This is especially evident with respect to corporations which manufacture a product or produce energy. To reduce costs associated with waste management or raw material expenditures, a corporation may bypass regulations on toxic dumping and/or health and safety standards. In the latter case, the consumer base itself is affected and oftentimes may not be readily aware. With the help of a talented legal team, lobbying, and bribing government officials, such corporations can circumvent both regulation and accountability. Worse, a corporation may resort to using more malignant offense mechanisms such as extortion, blackmail, slander, retaliation, intimidation, and even murder to exonerate itself from its toxic behavior.

Like the toxic work environment described earlier, there are no winners in this paradigm. Although jobs are created by the corporation, its base is founded on serfdom (or something closely resembling it.) Its workers - subjugated, dominated, and controlled - are miserable, poor, resentful, and, most of all, fearful. Their direct supervisors are almost as subjugated, dominated, and controlled, yet their money and power came at a cost of violating their conscience, which has done nothing to alleviate their own inner-fears; rather, their money and power has only served as a diversion. Consumers, although benefiting from cheaper products and services which ease their own financial burdens, now fear for the safety of their environment as well as themselves. Shareholders, owners, and corporate executives reap financial benefits to afford an exceptionally comfortable lifestyle, yet the inner-fears that compelled them to do so in the first place not only have grown, they are accompanied by a growing amount of remorse born out of the unethical treatment of others, all of which requires more wealth to be anesthetized.

As such, the only product truly produced by such a malignant mega-personality is fear.

Investment and Retail Banks

"Their problem is that they play a lot of golf, which is right up there
with heroin abuse as a killer of our nation's productivity.
The only difference is that golf is more expensive."
- Dave Barry, humorist

Corporations are established with the assistance of special rate loans provided by large financial conglomerates such as big banks. These, along with investment banks, operate by similar corporate structures as mentioned earlier. The executive branch is headed by a CEO and comprised of its board of directors and executive officers. Subsequent tiers include department heads, zone managers, regional branch managers, district branch managers, branch managers, assistant managers, and associates.

Similar to corporations, commercial (or retail) banks need to maximize profits for shareholders. This is accomplished primarily through interest based loans (mortgages, student loans, credit cards), application fees, account fees, ATM fees, and overdraft and penalty charges.

The ability to provide loans to customers is enhanced by a fractional reserve system in which a portion of a customer's deposit in kept in house while the remaining is used for loans to other customers. The amount of money or funds a bank must physically have on hand in comparison to the amount it can lend is called a reserve or liquidity ratio. The reserve ratio is determined by the Federal Reserve's Board of Governors and is follows: institutions holding less than $11.5 million have no minimum reserve requirement; between $11.5 million and $71.0 million must have a reserve ratio of 3%; exceeding $71.0 million must have a ratio of 10%.[9] Thus, any "big bank" savings or checking account only has 10% of its value retained by the bank. The remaining 90% is loaned out, deposited in another bank with the same reserve ratio or less, and loaned out again with interest. The net result is creating even more "money" and more interest to that which had been created by the Federal Reserve. Now, in addition to currency interest and taxation, those with loans or credit card debt - out of necessity, irresponsibility, or both - bear even greater financial burden.

While the profit building of retail banks is (or, was) relatively conservative and safe, investment banks reap greater profit in an more high-risk and speculative manner. The profit margins are substantially higher in investment banks as are the stakes. Some of the revenue is derived from fees charged for managing market capital transactions, yet other means require more savvy.

One such method is proprietary trading, in which an investment bank will trade currencies, commodities (goods and services), and securities (stocks, bonds, treasury bills, commercial paper) and derivatives it had purchased with its own funds to garner profit. A derivative is essentially any financial instrument which has value derived from the inherent value of something else.

An investment bank may also act as a market maker in which the company quotes both a buy and a sell price of a financial instrument (stocks, bonds, loans, deposits, certificate of deposits, derivatives) or commodity in the hopes of making a profit off its bid-offer spread. Though similar to proprietary trading, market making is less profitable due to regulations on spread size.

Investment banks also gain profit by advising companies with mergers and acquisitions. By assisting the companies (or acquiring company) with the legal and strategical means of buying, selling, dividing, reconstructing, and combining enterprises, the bank receives a commission or fee contingent on the size of the deal. To facilitate mergers and acquisitions, a bank may assist an acquiring company in generating funds to take over another through corporate action. Here, the bank will solicit potential investors or other institutions to financially back the company's endeavors either by investment or purchasing shares. Or, the bank itself may subsidize the acquiring company by purchasing unwanted shares (for an additional fee) which it could sell at a later time for profit, similar to proprietary trading. This, known as underwriting, increases both risk and profit potential.

An investment bank may also derive profit from selling structured products, which are pre-packaged investment strategies based on securities, commodities, currencies, debt issuances, options, and swaps. The Banking Act of 1933 established the Federal Deposit Insurance Corporation (FDIC), an agency which oversaw banking reforms intended as speculation control and asset protection. Four of the provisions of this act are commonly known as the Glass-Steagall Act, which limited commercial banking security activity and affiliations to investment banks. These measures ensured the protection of deposits made into a commercial bank by preventing the bank from using those funds to engage the in high-risk, speculative ventures associated with investment banks.

Although the separation of commercial and investment banks began to erode during the early 1960s, the restrictions of the Glass-Steagall Act were repealed in 1999 through the Gramm-Leach-Bliley Act. Furthermore, deregulation of financial markets had been en vogue since the early 1980s when less government had become preferable, giving rise to a laissez-faire, free market, and unregulated economy. The belief was that unregulated markets would regulate themselves; those who worked hard reaped profit whereas those who did not work hard did not.

This "separation of state and economics" philosophy was shared by those in charge of the Federal Reserve and the US Treasury, with their pro-business perspective being one of "the less regulation, the better." Initially, the results were quite favorable: the economy in the mid-to-late 1990s surged, aided by a potent boom in the technology sector.

Yet the market for over-the-counter (OTC) derivatives was shrouded in secrecy and completely opaque. Contracts involving these complex, complicated products were entered into privately with no requirements for in-house record keeping. Members of Congress as well as government regulatory agencies had little to no understanding about the nature of derivatives, their activity, how large the derivative market was, or who was involved. The absence of any oversight of these "narcissistic assets" - with their grandiose and inflated value being based on outside substance - left the door wide open for fraud. Moreover, the absence of regulation was a gateway for unabashed entitlement.

The Commodity Future Trading Commission (CFTC), an independent government agency regulating futures and options, became aware of such fraudulent activity when Proctor and Gamble filed suit against Banker's Trust. The company claimed that the institution not only sold them an in-comprehensive product, but one they knew to be toxic. This bank and others were found to have repeatedly provided their customers with incorrect valuations of the derivative products they had sold and were fully aware of the scam.

Brooksley Born, chairperson of the CFTC at the time, feared that the high-stakes derivative market - now involving of trillions of dollars and the largest banks of the country - had the potential to decimate the entire financial system. She thus found it imperative to enforce some regulation on this market. This was met with considerable opposition by those affiliated with the Federal Reserve and the US Treasury who not only attempted to impose on her the belief that such regulation would cause the worst financial crisis in history, but erroneously condescended that she did not have such power to do so. The Secretary of the Treasury, under additional pressure from players on Wall Street, issued a statement denouncing regulation, and that "Congress should act with all deliberate speed" to block it. The media was also tapped to broadcast the sentiment that Born's views were not to be trusted.

The financial sector, outnumbering each congressman with a posse of lobbyists, rallied hard to stave off Born's attempts at regulation. The expediency of the subsequent Congressional hearings served as swift and strong action to weaken Born's position. Since many members of Congress were unfamiliar with the derivative market, they relied on the word of reputable sources which denounced regulation, using the current economic success as defense. As a result, the derivative market continued unregulated and without oversight.

A couple of months later, Long Term Capital Management (LTCM), a hedge fund company whose clients included fifteen of Wall Streets largest banks, began to collapse. Like other investment banks, its derivative activity operated outside of any oversight and regulation and had realized huge profit margins, leveraging five billion into more than one trillion in derivatives. Now, their computed models were tanking by millions each day.

Its clients were unaware of the extent of LTCM's exposure in the market or that many other OTC derivative dealers had been lending to them as well. Yet, this became apparent when LTCM's clients attempted to collect their collateral. LTCM seemed destined for collapse and the American (and global) economy was hanging by a thread. To avoid disaster, the Federal Reserve pressured fourteen of the banks to bail out LTCM with $3.5 billion of their own capital.

This second brush with catastrophe rekindled the call for derivative regulation. Yet this was also bypassed by Congress, being told by financial leaders that this was an anomaly. Instead of placing accountability on the investment banks which provided toxic products, it was attributed to the irresponsibility and unwise investment decisions of its commercial bank clients. The derivative market continued with no transparency or oversight and thus no prohibition of fraud or manipulation. Moreover, and most ironic, Born's ability to enforce regulation was then stripped by Congress.

Wall Street continued to "regulate itself" which inevitably led to the detonation of the economic time bomb ten years later in 2008. OTC derivatives were the prime culprit, and the toxic assets of the biggest banks led to a devastating financial crisis. This time, the American taxpayer was tapped for financial rescue, as the government had committed $12.2 trillion dollars to support the collapsing financial system.

Like the structure of the corporation, the financial sector is a pronounced example of the fear-for-power pyramidal model, as negative feelings are projected from the top to its base, while money is siphoned from the base and concentrated at the top. The decision of investment bank executives to knowingly sell toxic products to their customers was clearly out of fear-based addiction. The surplus profit brought them more wealth which, in turn, made them feel more powerful, included, enviable and adulated, secure, exclusive, successful, and perfect. This counteracted their fears of subjugation, vulnerability, abandonment, unlovability, deprivation, exclusion, failure, and perfectionism, respectively. Their issues of mistrust were superimposed onto their respective customers by selling them bad assets and violating their financial health. Their insistence on barring any regulation despite the many financial failures emphasizes the degree of their entitlement and spiritual malignancy.

They realized their wealth-generating objectives through a variety of toxic tactics, including testing the waters (preying on trust and rapport, underhandedness), establishing entitlement (conscience bartering, mutual enabling, seduction/bribery, double standards), narcissistic dominance (undeserved self-praise, insatiability), avoiding accountability (denial, avoidance, deflection/distraction, lies of omission, half-truths, exoneration, playing the victim, minimization, spin, scapegoatism, false consent), establishing victimhood (setting up failure, projection, inappropriate accountability), and reinforcing control (brainwashing, subjugation, fear creation, capitalizing on crisis, shock.)

The subordinates within the financial structure capitulated to similar behavior out of the same fears. Wanting to anesthetize their own issues of unlovability, failure, deprivation, etc., they also sought surplus money to appear enviable, successful, wealthy, etc.

These fears were felt by large banks and other clients once they had realized they had been manipulated and subjected to fraud, as they now experienced the fears of vulnerability, mistrust, failure, deprivation, abandonment, et al originally present in the investment bank sector's leadership. Although some took the hit at first, the fears born out of the devastating 2008 collapse were passed onto the general public as their money was taken away from them. Considering the US population in 2008 was close to 3.1 million, the $700 billion tax-funded TARP (Troubled Asset Relief Program) bailout alone amounted to $2,258 per citizen (*not* taxpayer.) Considering the amount of bailout reserves spent by 2011 was $2.5 trillion, this amounted to over $8,000 *per citizen* (again, *not* taxpayer.)

In a brazen act of reinforcing entitlement, many leaders of Wall Street investment banks anticipated on using this bailout money for their bonuses. None of them have been prosecuted for what amounted to trillions in fraud and thievery, nor have any restitutions been made. And, despite the additional financial burden on the US taxpayer after enduring such a cataclysmic economic crisis, the derivative market to continues to operate unregulated, despite presidential campaign promises to the contrary.

Due to the economic collapse in conjunction with being required to pay trillions to repair it, many Americans lost their savings, homes, and jobs. Collectively, they have spent trillions, yet only have fears of vulnerability, abandonment, mistrust, unlovability, deprivation, subjugation, exclusion, failure, imperfection, and mistrust to show for it. Money flowed to the top; fear flowed to the bottom.

Government

"They who can give up essential liberty to purchase a little temporary safety, deserve neither liberty nor safety."

- Richard Jackson, as quoted in Benjamin Franklin's An Historical Review of the Constitution and Government of Pennsylvania

"Our only political party has two right wings, one called Republican, the other Democratic."

- Gore Vidal

On September 17th, 1787, the Constitution of the United States was adopted by the Constitutional Convention in Philadelphia, Pennsylvania and went into effect on March 4th, 1789. This document laid the foundation for supreme law and structure of the United States federal government. The structure provided for the separation of powers of supreme law by establishing three branches of government: an executive branch led by the US President, a legislative branch involving two houses of Congress, and a federal judiciary branch led by the Supreme Court.

For the new republic to "prevent misconstruction or abuse of its powers" reminiscent of the despotic control it experienced as British colonies, ten constitutional amendments known as the Bill of Rights were ratified and came into effect on December 15th, 1791. These are:

Amendment I

Congress shall make no law respecting an establishment of religion, or prohibiting the free exercise thereof; or abridging the freedom of speech, or of the press; or the right of the people peaceably to assemble, and to petition the Government for a redress of grievances.

Amendment II

A well regulated Militia, being necessary to the security of a free State, the right of the people to keep and bear Arms, shall not be infringed.

Amendment III

No Soldier shall, in time of peace be quartered in any house, without the consent of the Owner, nor in time of war, but in a manner to be prescribed by law.

Amendment IV

The right of the people to be secure in their persons, houses, papers, and effects, against unreasonable searches and seizures, shall not be violated, and no Warrants shall issue, but upon probable cause, supported by Oath or affirmation, and particularly describing the place to be searched, and the persons or things to be seized.

Amendment V

No person shall be held to answer for a capital, or otherwise infamous crime, unless on a presentment or indictment of a Grand Jury, except in cases arising in the land or naval forces, or in the Militia, when in actual service in time of War or public danger; nor shall any person be subject for the same offence to be twice put in jeopardy of life or limb; nor shall be compelled in any criminal case to be a witness against himself, nor be deprived of life, liberty, or property, without due process of law; nor shall private property be taken for public use, without just compensation.

Amendment VI

In all criminal prosecutions, the accused shall enjoy the right to a speedy and public trial, by an impartial jury of the State and district wherein the crime shall have been committed, which district shall have been previously ascertained by law, and to be informed of the nature and cause of the accusation; to be confronted with the witnesses against him; to have compulsory process for obtaining witnesses in his favor, and to have the Assistance of Counsel for his defence.

Amendment VII

In Suits at common law, where the value in controversy shall exceed twenty dollars, the right of trial by jury shall be preserved, and no fact tried by a jury, shall be otherwise re-examined in any Court of the United States, than according to the rules of the common law.

Amendment VIII

Excessive bail shall not be required, nor excessive fines imposed, nor cruel and unusual punishments inflicted.

Amendment IX

The enumeration in the Constitution, of certain rights, shall not be construed to deny or disparage others retained by the people.

Amendment X

The powers not delegated to the United States by the Constitution, nor prohibited by it to the States, are reserved to the States respectively, or to the people.

The first amendment protects freedom of religion (by prohibiting Congress from making a law "respecting an establishment" of religion and protecting the right to free exercise of religion), speech, press, assembly, and petition. The second protects the rights of citizens to possess weapons and bear arms. The fourth guards against unwarranted searches, arrests, and property seizures or without a "probable cause" for the alleged crime; privacy rights are also protected by this amendment. The fifth is regarded as the "rights of the accused" amendment, otherwise known as the Miranda Rights. It forbids punishment without due process of law and protects against one testifying against himself, or "pleading the Fifth." The sixth guarantees the right to a fair trial, including trial by a jury of peers and legal counsel. The seventh assures trial by jury in civil cases. The eighth protects against cruel and unusual punishment and excessive bails or fines. The ninth ensures that the rights of the people detailed in the Constitution are not exclusive to those it designates; rather, the people themselves define their own rights. The tenth defers any powers to the states (and people) the Constitution did not delegate to the United States.

These rights can be reasonably perceived as direct protection against spiritually malignant offense mechanisms. The freedoms of speech, press, assembly, and petition allow for calling out, broadcasting, and holding others accountable for criminal and unethical conduct. They counter denial, avoidance, deflection/distraction, lies of omission, half-truths, exonerations, spin, scapegoatism, false consent, projection - in essence, any toxic tactic mentioned previously. The right to bear arms, due process, and legal search, arrest, and seizure defend against any tactic used to establish and reinforce victimhood and domination, such as inappropriate accountability, false accusations, blackmail/extortion, slander, constant surveillance, intimidation, retaliation, physical duress and abuse, enslavement, confinement, torture, despotism, and murder. Protection against cruel and unusual punishment safeguards against similar mechanisms. The ninth and tenth amendments ensure that the public has more power than its government and is therefore in control.

In summary, these rights empower the public to defend itself against the spiritually bankrupt goals of domination (or creating a willing, docile victim), establishing entitlement, and narcissism; in short, protection from: "The rules apply to you and not me because I'm special and you're not." They allow us the ability to address fears being imposed on us by those in positions of power who are spiritually malignant. Because of these rights, we can counter malignant offense mechanisms which attempt to superimpose fears of abandonment, deprivation, subjugation, mistrust, unlovability, exclusion, vulnerability, failure, perfectionism, and entitlement. In doing so, we are able to honor our own self-love and self-worth and defend our liberty. And, in doing so, we remind others that projecting and overcompensating for their fears (as opposed to dealing with them directly) is unwise behavior.

Today, the structure of the US government has evolved into a pyramidal structure more intricate and vast than the corporate and financial models described previously. Each branch of government - executive, legislative, and judiciary - operates in its own pyramid structure.

The executive branch, headed by a democratically elected president and vice president, is assisted by the Cabinet of the United States. Cabinet members are nominated by the president, confirmed by the Senate, and head various federal executive departments. These include the departments of State, Treasury, Defense, Homeland Security, the Interior, Justice, Commerce, Agriculture, Transportation, Labor, Health and Human Services, Energy, Housing and Urban Development, Education, and Veterans Affairs. Each department, overseen by a Secretary (or Attorney General in the case of the Department of Justice), is assisted by assistant secretaries, undersecretaries, and deputies who oversee various divisions, commissions, departments/departmental offices, and bureaus, each having their own hierarchal structure.

The judiciary branch consists of three successive subbranches of courts: original jurisdiction, appellate courts, and the Supreme Court. Courts of original jurisdiction consist of ninety-four district courts (one in each federal judicial district) and courts of specific subject matter (such as bankruptcy courts, Court of Federal Claims, Court of International Trade, Tax Court, Foreign Intelligence Surveillance Court, Court of Private Land Claims, Alien Terrorist Removal Court.) Appellate courts include eleven US court of appeals, the US Court of Appeals for the District of Colombia, and courts for specific subject matter (US Court of Appeals for Veterans Claims, Court of Appeals for Armed Forces, Court of Appeals for the Federal Circuit, and Foreign Intelligence Surveillance Court of Review.) The Supreme Court of the United States, the highest court, consists of a chief justice and eight associates justices who, like cabinet members, are nominated by the president and confirmed by the Senate.

The bicameral congressional legislative branch consists of the Senate and House of Representatives, both of which are comprised of democratically elected officials. Within these houses, committees are formed and headed by senators or representatives elected by their peers to be officers. Congress is also aided by the GAO (which, mentioned previously with respect to the Federal Reserve, is responsible for auditing and evaluation), the Library of Congress (its research library), the Congressional Research Service, and the Congressional Budget Office (providing economic data.) Members of both houses have their own staff and offices as well. Moreover, policy making is also influenced by lobbyists, who represent outside interests and sway congressional decisions to meet their clients' interests.

The outside interests represented by lobbyists can represent any entity or enterprise: include various industries (gaming, oil, tobacco, etc.), foreign interests, corporations, associations, unions, non-profit organizations, or any other group or organization. Lobbyists are hired guns who seek to promote the agendas for whichever organization is paying their fees. They do their bidding, and their success is largely based on the results they achieve. Through fundraisers, political action committees (PACs), and donations, lobbyists raise campaign funds for politicians who pledge support for their causes.

Previously, it was mentioned how lobbyists influenced Congress' decision to override the regulation of financial markets which led to the economic collapse of 2008. These lobbyists represented the large investment banking conglomerates that sought to maintain a structure from which they would reap great profits. Their influence, evidently, had not proved beneficial to the general public by any means.

Currently, Wall Street procures the most lobbyists and is consequently the largest campaign donor to Congressmen, Senators, and presidential candidates. Oftentimes, the politicians sought out by lobbyists are not party-specific. In fact, an institution may seek to influence members on both sides of the aisle to ensure their agenda is carried out: one can't lose if they bet on both black *and* red.

Lobbying has become so lucrative and in demand, by 2011, over $30 billion dollars had been spent nationally on lobbying. In 2011, $3.33 billion was spent on congressional lobbying, with 12,654 *registered* lobbyists employed by various firms.[10] Taking into account that there are 435 Congressional representatives, 100 Senators, one President and one Vice President, the ratio of registered lobbyists to elected officials in Washington is about 24:1.

Since these officials - Senators, Congressmen, and Presidents - are elected by the people to represent the people yet carry out the wishes of those who paid their campaign finances and bribes, the democratic process is compromised if not dismantled. For example, a politician who promises regulation, transparency, policy change, accountability etc. on their presidential campaign trail will thus endorse contrary legislature to appease their campaign benefactors after taking office. The government supposedly "for the people, by the people" morphs into one that is "for the wealth, by the wealth." Money talks, and the voice of the elite gets heard while the population's is drowned out.

Also controversial is the trend of lobbying by foreign-owned corporations and foreign interests. By having the ability to affect Congressional activity through lobbying, non-citizens of the US have the ability to influence, manipulate, or create policies of the United States, often more so than the voting ability of the US citizen base. The government "for the people, by the people" now serves "others, by others."

Candidates, to date, are not required to disclose information regarding the sources of their campaign's financing.

Unfortunately, the toxic tactics of seduction/bribery and mutual enabling behind lobbying are not the only ones used to coerce elected officials into endorsing an outside agenda. Such groups can (and do) resort to tactics of blackmail, extortion, slander, false accusations, constant-surveillance, and intimidation to enforce capitulation. These aggressive tactics are, at times, coupled with seduction/bribery to achieve an objective. Thus, a politician may be given the choice to accept a few hundred thousand dollars or face an exposé about a recurring affair he has been engaged in.

Not only is the democratic process tampered with, but the very electoral process itself. Ballot stuffing, voter fraud, issuance of false delegate slates during caucuses, voting by non-citizens, rigged electronic voting systems, and rule bending have all been reported in recent years.

The very constitutional rights have also been challenged and eroded by the very government elected to protect them. On October 26, 2001, in response to the September 11th attacks, the USA Patriot Act was signed into law. This act permitted search and seizure of businesses and homes without warrant, consent, or knowledge of the owner. It also permitted the Federal Bureau of Investigation (FBI) the ability to search e-mail, telephone, and financial records without a court order. The government was also allowed to order files from communications providers, such IP addresses, login times, and sites visited. Also under this law, business, library, and financial records became accessible to law enforcement. This act clearly countered the provisions specified in the fourth amendment, which protected against unwarranted searches, arrests, and seizures and a right to privacy.

Also in 2001, the Transportation Security Administration (TSA) was created as part of the Aviation and Transportation Security Act. This agency was given power to exercise security measures with regard to transportation within the United States. Primarily involved with airport passenger screening, the TSA oversees security for other means of public transportation, such as highways, railroads, and mass transit systems. However, similar to the Patriot Act, the authority given to the TSA allows for warrantless search without probable cause.

Perhaps the most flagrant - and troubling - violation of Constitutional rights came with the signing of the National Defense Authorization Act (NDAA) on the eve of the 2011 New Year. This act allows the military to *indefinitely* detain anyone "who was a part of or substantially supported al-Qaeda, the Taliban, or 'associated forces' that are engaged in hostilities against the United States or its coalition partners, including any person who has committed a belligerent act or has directly supported such hostilities in aid of such enemy forces." This act, however, does not define the terms "substantially supported" or "associated forces." Because of this ambiguity, such military detention can be applied anywhere worldwide (including domestically) and without trial or any oversight. This act is applicable to Americans, obliterating the rights protected under the fourth, fifth, and sixth amendments.

Curiously, these freedom-stripping, unconstitutional measures - along with financial bailouts and war funding siphoning the wealth of the American population by the trillions - were passed with little to no debate within a bipartisan Congress. Could it be their objectives, despite contrary rhetoric, are essentially the same?

If catering to corporate and foreign interests, excessive taxation, and and whittling away Constitutional rights were not enough, the financial health of the American population is further debilitated by being required to subsidize "inverted pyramids." Here, instead of money flowing from the bottom to the top, it is siphoned downward to an opportunistic minority which the government requires the general population to enable. One such inverted pyramid involves those taking advantage of tax-funded welfare and disability programs. Intended for citizens who have faced economic hardships and physical disabilities, some able-bodied members of society without any reason to be non-productive (aside from a poor economy) expect others to finance their leisurely lifestyle.

Another such inverted pyramid involves disenfranchised illegal immigrants. After the economies of their countries of origin had been decimated by the collectivization and privatization of corporate multinationals, a substantial influx of non-citizen migrants ensued. Instead of the corporate multinationals providing any restitutions, the general population - uninvolved in any sort of economic pirating abroad - is tapped again to accommodate the burden imposed on tax-funded programs, such as welfare and education. This financial burden is increased by the *billions* considering many of these illegal immigrants have engaged in tax fraud. Using an ITIN (Individual Taxpayer Identification Number) as opposed to a social security number to file taxes, many of these non-citizens have taken advantage of the Additional Child Tax credit, which provides a fully refundable credit of $1000 per child. Intended to assist working families with children at home, this program is exploited by those engaging in fraud who claim dependents, *in some cases over ten children*, even though the children are living outside of the country - and collect refunds worth thousands of dollars as a result.[11] Despite the IRS being repeatedly notified for years, nothing has been done about this. In fact, the IRS has instructed its employees to ignore such fraudulent activity.[12]

These areas and many more could be explored in greater depth, yet it is not the purpose of this book to delve into such topics in detail. However, it is apparent from this alone that the system of government which had allowed for its citizens to preserve the ability to honor both self-worth and self-determination is not only eroding, but it has been replaced with a "bipartisan" regime which seemingly intends to deactivate the general population of its financial health, political influence, and Constitutional rights.

Like the central banking, corporate, and financial models, the pyramidal structure of the federal government has evolved into one where wealth and power coagulates at the top as fear is dispensed toward the bottom. While it was originally created to ensure that power and wealth were maintained at its base and with "the people," it is evident that this is no longer the case. Moreover, "the top" has been superseded by a semi-ambiguous governing body which has, in part, gained power through coercion, manipulation, bribery, and intimidation.

The mechanics of the "fear-for-power" transfer are the same as the other models. Those comprising "the top," consisting of those representing outside interests, seek money and power to counter their own fears of failure, perfectionism, exclusion, deprivation, entitlement, vulnerability, unlovability, etc. To accomplish this, they employ offense mechanisms of seduction/bribery, intimidation, blackmail, extortion, slander, etc to coerce elected government officials into capitulating to their agenda, despite its harmful effect on the general population. These officials, in turn and acting out of their own fears, acquiesce to these toxic demands and pass equally toxic legislation. To ensure these policies are carried out, similar offense mechanisms are used on subsequent tiers within the pyramid (law, law enforcement, federal and state government), and their capitulation is also based on fear. This exchange of fear for security, like the other models, spreads toward the bottom which now inherits the same fears of failure, perfectionism, exclusion, deprivation, entitlement, vulnerability, unlovability, etc. which had existed at the top. Again, the same schema-based fears still exist at the top; however, they are anesthetized by siphoned wealth and power. Since the fear has reached its base, the general public, it has nowhere to be displaced except within itself.

With the case of the government, not only does the pyramid model effectively pass down its fear to its base, wealth is collected and condensed through taxation, as previously mentioned. Apparently, sufficient wealth has amassed at the top to afford employees attending a September 2011 Department of Justice conference cookies and muffins costing, respectively, $10 and $16 apiece.[13] I find it difficult to believe the high cost of baked goods can be attributable to inflation. Such transfers of wealth and power to the top through taxation and policy is accompanied by the transfer of fear to the bottom through subjugation. Money, power, and $16 muffins float to the top as fear, vulnerability, and food stamps sink to the bottom.

In closing of this chapter, it must be understood: whether it is a federal agency, a religious institution, a secret society, a news outlet, a military branch, an educational facility, or a retail store chain - *any organization which has a pyramidal hierarchal structure is, in essence, a CULT.*

The United States of America has morphed into an interlocking network of cults.

The cult leaders dictate downward through successive tiers what the cult followers are to do, what they need to give, how they are to behave, what they are to believe, what rules they follow, and more. The cult member eventually loses any semblance of autonomy, self-identity, and self-reference. The ability to think independently, question "authority," and formulate beliefs, decisions, and conclusions on their own is eradicated. Instead, the individual is coerced into adopting the cult's identity as his own. *This is accomplished by creating and exploiting fear.*

Yet, not only does the fusion of corporations, the finance sector, government, and so much more project its collective fear toward the bottom yet, as we will see, *it conditions the general public to "manage" this inherited fear with the same spiritually malignant offense mechanisms used to dispense it.*

8

Weapons of Mass Dysfunction:

The Media

*"The Central Intelligence Agency owns anyone
of any significance in the major media."*

- Former CIA Director William Colby

"The first casualty of war is truth."

- Aeschylus

Historically considered the "fourth arm of the government," the media has acted to inform the general public of both political and domestic matters regarding local, national, foreign, and international affairs. With this, and aided by freedom of the press, many media sources had acted as investigative journalism by whistle-blowing. However, due to the consolidation of power within the media structure, such truth-telling and transparency is now endangered.

The independence of the mainstream media was permissible due to its power being dispersed amongst many hands. In 1983, roughly fifty corporations controlled the vast majority of media outlets, including television, radio, daily newspapers, magazines, books, and motion pictures. By 2004, the control of the nation's mass media industry was narrowed to five corporations, yet is dominated worldwide by the following dozen: Disney/Capital Cities/ABC, Time Warner/Turner, Murdoch's News Corporation, Bertelsmann, Tele-Communications (TCI) /AT&T, General Electric/NBC, CBS Inc., Newshouse/Advance Publications, Viacom, Microsoft, Matra, Hachette-Filipacchi, Gannet. The term "corporate media" is thus often applied to the small, corporate monopoly over the industry.

The corporate media, of course, has a pyramidal structure like that of any corporation.

And, like many corporations, these for-profit media mega-firms are managed by a core group of profit-seeking elite. The corporate media thus conjoins with the pre-entwined banking/corporate/government conglomerate to promote its collective elitist interests; they would not have the necessary funding to operate such large broadcast systems otherwise. Because of this, they are subject to the demands of shareholders and, like corporations, cater to special interests, namely those of the elite.

Because of the elite's widespread control over media and objective to protect their own interests, corporate media outlets will avoid any topics or disclosures which could jeopardize the elite's agenda of profitability, entitlement, and control. Rather, many media outlets will use offense mechanisms of spin, half-truths, lies of omission, debasement, slander, minimization, scapegoatism, and blackouts (or avoidance) in reporting "news" to coerce (read: manipulate) its viewers to perceive elitist objectives as favorable, even though they are often contradictory to their own best interests. This allows expansive propagandizing ability for these corporations to influence news, political opinion, popular culture, popular ideology, popular opinion, information, and social interests.

As mentioned, corporate media structure is based on a pyramid model. Sitting atop is the board of directors and executives which, most likely, are comprised of controlling shareholders of the corporation. Also influencing are other major stockholders who invariably have ties to other corporations, the finance sector, or the government. The executive peak serves as the encompassing content filter for information, whether it is skewed, absent, or promoted. Like the other pyramid models, the apex of corporate media is also fear based which is the force behind censorship. To safeguard wealth and power and thus shield the banking/corporate/government/media conglomerate from facing its own fears of vulnerability, failure, entitlement, subjugation, mistrust, et al, the corporate media is used by the elite both as a megaphone and a tool for manipulation.

This is accentuated by appointing those who adopt or are willing to comply with their objectives. With others, it involves subjugation - often covert - as control over the activity and performance of subordinates is finessed by sensitive intelligence agencies. Consider, for instance, the CIA's infamous Operation Mockingbird of the 1940s, which sought put reporters on the CIA payroll, thus purchasing behind-the-scenes influence (with tax dollars, no less.) Those who are unwilling to comply to censorship are expelled - in some fashion - from their respective industry (news, journalism, motion pictures, etc.)

Thus, many program and production managers, editors, producers, directors, newscasters, reporters, directors, actors, and any professional within the lower tiers of the chain of command capitulate to their superiors' demands out of cronyism or fear - just like the other pyramid models described. To ensure their advancement and/or job security, they amend, censor, promote, withhold, endorse, and broadcast as dictated or bribed. The fears of unlovability, subjugation, vulnerability, etc. originating with their elite superiors (who, again, sought such power to override) have been superimposed onto them through a cacophony of offense mechanisms, from those more passive such as mutual enabling and seduction/bribery to those more aggressive such as blackmail and constant surveillance. Many of those within these lower tiers then, like infected zombies, use spin, manipulation, half-truths, projection, scapegoatism, or any offense mechanism to carry out the toxic agenda, with the general public bearing the brunt. The net result is the imposition of a massive schema cluster onto the national (if not, world) population.

The first - and most direct - point of contact is news broadcasting. Headlines, breaking stories, and current events are not only filtered, but the frequency of their broadcasts is managed. Most notable are stories which involve some fear-inducing component, such as a claimed terrorist attack or mass shooting. Air waves, television stations, and corporate owned internet sites will bombard the viewer with incessant details to seemingly keep the topic afloat to stoke a certain public response, usually panic or ire. This is inevitably at the behest of the media executives (and their affiliates) to create a problem-reaction-solution scenario. Here, a problem (authentic, amplified, or created) is exploited through mass and incessant broadcast to illicit a response from the general public. The public, reacting out of fear, is then coerced into accepting new, constraining conditions which are sold as responsive solutions. Examples of this would be the signing of the Patriot Act and the creation of the TSA after the September 11th attacks. These solutions, however, are usually pre-planned and contrary to the general public's interest.

Such coercion does not need to be based on shock or catastrophe. For more than a decade, punditry has become more commonplace and prevalent in virtually every media source. Like politicians who are lobbied (and most dogs, for that matter), some news personalities and commentators succumb to rewards-based behavior. Readily abdicating their personal moral codes and conscience, they defend the malevolent policies, decisions, and character of their benefactors, regardless of the amount of spin, lies of omission, half-truths, scapegoatism, and blatant inaccuracy of their "position." By capitalizing on their pre-existing fears and frustrations, they attempt to sway the opinion of their viewing audience. Often, their "views" take on much audacity. One pundit, when commentating on the nuclear disaster in Fukushima, Japan, made the claim that radiation is "good for you."

Unfortunately, punditry has only been one of many tools of media sway. It is becoming more rare that a story will be composed solely of "who, what, where, when" as reporting is almost always infused with a commentary of some bent. Either embedded or supplemented, commentaries and opinions (and, sometimes, fervor) from passers-by, an "expert", or the reporter himself (all of which are either pre-selected, pre-planned, or post-edited by the media's manufacturer) will frequently accompany the "facts" of the story. The general public is not only provided tinkered information, they are proscribed the way they should feel about it. Unless viewers are capable of critical thinking, they will often not distinguish between fact, opinionated fact, and opinions.

This, of course, is predicated on the notion that the public will be provided with the truth, the whole truth, and nothing but the truth. Yet, if this were the case, the media corporations would be out of business - so half-truths, spin, lies of omission, and blackouts are relied upon. The signing of the National Defense Authorization Act, for example, went widely unreported by corporate media outlets. Only a couple major television news outlets covered the story, albeit partially: except for one, it was left out that *Americans* (not just foreign nationals) could be detained without trial or oversight. The sole newscaster with the media outlet providing the thorough commentary no longer has a job with his respective employer.

Since ownership of the corporate media is still (somewhat) plural, some competition still exists. Whatever remaining differences (real or concocted) residing within elite ownership are expressed - not only through punditry - but often in the culture of the outlet itself. This gives rise to dialectical dichotomies within the corporate media and, most conveniently, conditions its respective viewer base. Thus, the members of the population at large who subscribe to a particular media outlet (read: ideology set) will find themselves allied to one "team" and opposed to another (or, more appropriately, "the other.")

Whether it is "Republican vs. Democrat," "Liberal vs. Conservative," or "Left vs. Right," many individuals will be prone to accept a label and choose a team. The inherent danger in conforming to this "us versus them" mentality is that ideological positions regarding a variety of issues - foreign affairs, economic policy, taxation, politics, cultural mores, wars, illegal immigration, etc. - are lumped as a corporate package rather than through individual logic and critical, independent thinking. The belief that "might makes right" exempts the viewer from using their own mental faculties, conditioning them to adopt political, ideological, and cultural perspectives they may not have accepted otherwise were they not grouped with others. The fusion of selected facts with opinions only enhances this. What much of the public has seemed to bypass is the notion that news solely based on "who, what, where, when" facts would not lead to such mud-slinging division; the viewer could formulate his own opinions without influence and avoid treating politics and ideology like a team sport. Sadly, both "teams" are coached by the elite and it is the spectator who consistently loses. And neither team seems to wholly reflect the public's best interest - at all.

A resulting issue many other members of the viewing public face is not knowing what to believe. One commentary will espouse a certain set of facts and opinions while another expresses something completely contrary, leaving many viewers baffled, confused, frustrated, and not knowing where to place themselves.

Yet the overall dualistic polarization serves the elite well. The dichotomy of ideological and political endorsement shifts the focus from the elite to the "us" and "them" of the general populace, as one side finds fault and accountability with the other. If members of such "fan bases" truly seek fault and accountability, the most efficient way to accomplish this would be to look into the closest mirror, for there they will find an accomplice. By abdicating their own inherent ability to employ logic, independent, and critical thinking, they have allowed a powerful few to lie, manipulate, steal, violate, injure, and murder on a mass level. By employing such offense mechanisms as exoneration, debasement, lies of omission, half-truths, and scapegoatism toward each other in handling the fears passed onto them, they can claim ownership.

Of course, the more wedge issues the elite have at their disposal, the better, even if they are baseless and inane. One such topic is gay marriage. As someone who is gay (and although I do not condone discrimination, inequality, or double standards in any capacity), I find it strange that a country which supposedly embraces the freedom of religion and promotes the separation of church and state would even indulge this topic - or the "legality" of any marriage for that matter. The irony is that this country is founded on freedom, yet both sides seem bound and determined to enforce their own ideology, often taking prioritization over trillions of dollars in debt, a collapsing economy, and multiple, endless wars. Defying logic and common sense, some believe such calamities are a byproduct of gay marriage.

The corporate news media further affects mass culture by those it chooses to publicize. Air time is frequently given to pundits who bully, railroad, and condescend to "guests" whose opinions differ from theirs or their employer. Much of the viewing public is conditioned to find such rude behavior "normal" and, in turn, find it acceptable to interrupt, belittle, and verbally barrage anyone whose views do not compliment their own. Waning are the days where a rational discussion of opposing vantage points can take place.

If the personality is not cantankerous, manipulative, and/or belligerent, they are physically good-looking, as it seems to be an apparent prerequisite that a broadcaster or news anchor appear as a former catalogue model or pageant contestant. Such parades of beauty on local and national news broadcasts not only foster a cultural code of narcissism and perfectionism, it reminds the average viewer of who they are not: constantly made prim. Since the message that success and smarts is contingent on (enhanced) good looks is broadcasted alongside enhanced news, the person watching will not only be conditioned to feel "less than" and unlovable, but a failure as well, unless they can attain the same status of beauty. Besides: "sex sells." Complimentary, commercial "breaks" between beautiful broadcasts will feature diet and weight loss ads (often featuring former overweight, sullen-looking people), fashion ads, and beauty products. The viewer who has subconsciously received and absorbed the message that she is unattractive will be most susceptible to these. Also unsurprising is that female broadcasters in particular will be fortunate to have their careers outlast their relatively youthful beauty. Like models and trophy wives, they too have a short shelf-life.

Yet the emphasis on beauty expands much farther than news programs. Television programs and motion pictures consistently promote beauty and narcissism which are readily absorbed by the viewer. Such messages are often subconsciously adopted since the audience watching such media will do so in a semi-conscious, alpha brain-wave state, unaware that such messages are being promoted. Often, "good" equals "pretty" or "hot" while "bad" equals "ugly" or "fat." Similarly, narcissism is promoted. Many sit-coms, for instance, will feature an older, slovenly husband figure who has a younger, attractive, doting wife. Or, the storyline is one of "guy gets girl" where the guy is average but the girl is a prize; there is always "happy ending" but it is never realistic. Also en vogue is the portrayal of middle-aged plus women who refuse to accept their years and dress and behave like a sorority. The viewing public is subsequently conditioned to accept such trends as cultural norms.

The advent of "Reality TV" has done much to promote both narcissism and entitlement. A person - any person - can be a "star" simply by being a bratty, quasi-attractive, entitled, self-important, solipsistic, difficult, toxic, materialistic, obnoxious, intoxicated, dizzy, and/or narcissistic spectacle-diva without any discernible gifts or talents. Since these traits are delivered as merit-worthy, cute "attributes," many viewers will behave in like fashion: if they themselves cannot be a star, at least they can feel like one through mimicry, attracting "friends" who, like much of the audiences of these shows, act as narcissistic supply.

Incidentally, one no longer needs singing talent to become a pop-star. All that is needed is marketability, new-found pubescence, narcissism, and/or willingness to publicly endorse any ideology as dictated by an elite-affiliated sponsor. Any vocal ineptitudes can be modified with post-studio, pitch-correcting software or lip-syncing during a live performance. The lowered-bar of competence makes the "carrot" all the more tangible to the public; adulating fans grow to believe that they, too, require only attitude for success and fame. Unfortunately, the overwhelming majority will go hungry (since vast narcissistic supply is required for sales) and continue down a career path which resembles serfdom.

Narcissism and entitlement are not the only traits promoted within reality television, or television in general for that matter. Process-of-elimination "reality" shows such as "Survivor," "The Apprentice," and "The Bachelor" (or "The Bachelorette") all depict contestants engaging in a variety of offense mechanisms as they attempt to surpass their competition, such as debasement, schadenfreude, invisible insults, backhanded compliments, potshots, setting up failure - overall, any behavior that is underhanded, manipulative, entitled, esteem-crushing, and/or narcissistic. While engaging in this malignant "ends justify the means" behavior, the contestants strive to please whomever is holding the carrot (whether it is a cash prize, a position of employment, a rose, a ring - anything to make them feel lovable, adulated, included, special, perfect, etc.) by capitulating to their wants, desires, or stroking their egos thus providing narcissistic supply. Even if they face extreme humiliation or ridicule from the discerning carrot-wielder, they "keep their eyes on the prize." The message to the audience is simple: for one to get what they want, one must be both dominating and cutthroat with their peers (no GoldenRule here) and appease and capitulate to whomever is holding the prize no matter how toxic or sociopathic they may be. Since there is only one prize, they must do what it takes: even if it means they abandon their own conscience and self-esteem.

Much if the viewing public, watching these programs in a relaxed, semi-conscious, alpha-brain wave state, will absorb such messages at a subconscious level. Like the subconscious nature of fears associated with schemas, their effects will manifest at a conscious level to a certain degree. And the messages are many. Some shows, like "Big Brother," even promote constant-surveillance. Not only is watching people voyeuristically as they perform their sensitive daily functions okay, it makes for great entertainment. Professional sports are promoted in a similar vein and, if a team sport, bears the potential to foster the "us versus them" mentality within in the viewer base.

But, as far as narcissism and entitlement are concerned, there are only so many ego-carrots to go around. The vast majority will have to settle for accommodating its own issues of unlovability, exclusion, entitlement, deprivation, subjugation, et al by living vicariously through celebrity worship. If they cannot have the status of being adulated, adored, admired, catered to, and imitated that comes with fame and fortune, they can at least experience it secondhand. Thus, narcissistic supply is given in exchange for remote identification, which gives rise to celebrity culture. And, since the compensation for low self-worth is vicariously derived from such famous persons, products or ideologies endorsed by celebrities will be adopted by those who adulate them. The vicarious (and fictitious) bond they have with a specific celebrity will, in turn, cause them to embrace their specific cause or product. The net result is a fantastic industry of television programming, motion pictures, internet sites, books, magazines, and advertisement and marketing campaigns based on celebrity.

The profitability of celebrity culture need not only play on the internalizing and avoiding defense mechanisms rooted in the general public's self-oriented fears in order to thrive: tabloid marketing takes advantage of the public's offense mechanisms as well, and accomplishes this by inspiring schadenfreude. By exposing a famous personality as unattractive, overweight, scandalous, divorced, gay, etc., the viewer can shift and project her negative feelings of unlovability, vulnerability, mistrust, abandonment, etc. onto a celebrity. The viewer now not only feels (superficially and shallowly) better about herself, she can elevate her own narcissism by comparing herself to a celebrity standing on a shorter pedestal with a bruised ego. Unfortunately for the viewer, her own poor, fear-based self-concept still intact, just less palpable through compare and contrast. This sort of gossip is often branded as "news."

If not used to bend public opinion and behavior to compliment its objectives, the elite use media to deflect attention from them. This is not only accomplished by narcissistic programming, but frivolous and diversionary reporting as well. Despite ongoing worldwide conflict, political corruption, and widespread economic turmoil, fluff pieces will appear bearing such headlines as,"Toy Stuck in Kid's Nose for Years," "Clever Chimp Signs Crafty Message," and "What Your Cat is Really Up To." (These articles were all found on the same day, same webpage.)

Since corporations maintain a monopoly over mainstream media production, the bulk of the viewing public will be subjected to news that is heavily filtered, edited, biased, or drivel (save for broadcasts from a brave, conscientious journalistic minority who stick out their necks), along with television programming that conditions both themselves and their culture. To obtain news that is remotely accurate and unobscured, the discriminating viewer (who possesses some semblance of critical thinking which yields that the truth, the whole truth, and nothing but the truth has been withheld, and that the pot of water they're sitting in is getting quite hot) will gravitate to independent, alternative sources on the internet. Unfortunately, their discerning skills will still be needed as many of these sources themselves become increasingly filtered, skewed, and compromised through infiltration and subjugation.

Moreover, such extensions to promote any freedom of the press are threatened by broad, ambiguous legislature. Such bills include the Cyber Intelligence Sharing and Protection Act (CISPA), which would quash privacy laws and mandate Internet providers and websites to hand over personal data to any federal government agency, and the Stop Online Piracy Act (SOPA), which would give the government the power to shut down any website simply because the "allegation" of copyright violation was made. Such legislation is billed in the name of cyber-security and homeland defense. This is most ironic since it is anathema to both freedom of press and privacy, protected by the first and fourth amendments. I would be remiss if I did not include the "internet kill switch," which grants the president the freedom to shut down the entire internet at will.

Thus, the elite owned and operated corporate media and their control over independent sources serve a variety of purposes. The first is to protect the image, activity, and agenda of the correlated corporate/finance/government conglomerate itself, resulting in an offense mechanism cluster used to counter its own issues of unlovability, deprivation, abandonment, subjugation, mistrust, vulnerability, entitlement, etc. Since the elite acts as the primary filter for its own media broadcasts, this is easily accomplished through managing what is broadcasted, how it is broadcasted, and how often. In doing so, the elite maintain and reinforce their success along with realizing the spiritually malignant goals of establishing narcissism and entitlement.

The second purpose is to serve as a fear-dispensing vehicle to achieve the other spiritually malignant goal of dominating a willing and docile victim (that is to be the general public.) This is accomplished by delegating to fear-motivated subordinates in progressively lower tiers the use of fear-trumpeting as well as blackouts, spin, half-truths, lies of omission, debasement, intimidation, fear-creation, and a plethora of other offense mechanisms. Such sycophants capitulate out of similar fears and abrade their own consciences in the process. Inevitably, the general public receives manipulated broadcasts and messages which cause them to inherit the same fears of vulnerability, mistrust, unlovability, deprivation, subjugation, et al. The negative, fear-based energy originating from the spiritually bankrupt top has spread throughout the pyramid and amassed at the base. Since the public now experiences a myriad of fears, the elite can now exploit such fears to further their preferred agendas, which involve the extraction of rights, money, and narcissistic supply, often in concert.

Yet, the pyramid structure of the corporate media is not only used to protect the elite's own malignant lifestyle and further its agenda by projecting its own fears onto others. Since fear has travelled from the epicenter at the top onto the general population, the means by which the public handles this imposed fear must also be managed: if not managed "properly," the whole dysfunctional system would collapse. By broadcasting and promoting programs, articles, shows, etc. which display various personalities in engaging in a variety of toxic tactics geared at establishing narcissism, reinforcing entitlement, and dominating others, society is conditioned to followed suit. Believing such behavior to be culturally normal, much of the viewing public will either acquiesce to providing narcissistic supply, enabling entitlement, and/or abdicate their own self-worth in relinquishing their God-given rights or they will embody the opposite: the will fall into the belief that success and happiness (and thus self-worth) is predicated on narcissism, entitlement, and dominating others.

Whether this messaging causes the public to adopt a negative self image (and self-oriented defense mechanisms of internalization and avoidance in the process) or one that is spiritually malignant (based on offense mechanisms of overcompensation and projection), the goal is uniform: to ensure that the general public is spiritually deficient in lacking authentic self-love and mishandles its "issues." Marketing would not work otherwise, and the funds and leeway used to maintain the elite's power and wealth would be cut off. As will be explored, a person who has fears of unlovability based on their physical appearance could overcompensate for this fear by gravitating to narcissism, coercing them to spend money on clothes, make-up, diet products, beauty products, enhancements, etc. A person projecting their fears will be prone to support the tabloid industry by purchasing related periodicals or watching relevant television programming.

A person diverting their unlovability issue could turn to a variety of products - such as food, alcohol, drugs, etc. - or activities like "retail therapy" (which could also pooh-pooh a narcissistic tendency) The person internalizing this issue would remain disempowered and docile, readily embracing the notion that they are defective, act as narcissistic supply (since others are "better" than they), and turn to a variety of self-destructive behavior, all of which requires money to carry out. A person at peace with their physical appearance would have no need to partake in any of the previous activity and would thus not feed a system which thrives on fear.

However, the types of fears imposed by media and advertising are many, and its conditioning of the general public to respond to its fears in unhealthy manners has enhanced the vast network of toxicity and scarcity. This fear emanates from broadcasts to the masses and inevitably permeates the culture we know today.

Consumerism

"This is an age of mass production.
In the mass production of materials a broad technique
has been developed and applied to their distribution.
In this age, too, there must be
a technique for the mass distribution of ideas."

- Edward Bernays

The various forms of corporate media and celebrity endorsement are not the only means by which the elite play on fear and condition cultural behavior to garner profit. The industries of advertisement and marketing have also made use of exploiting the public's emotional subconscious to promote a cause, product, behavior, or ideology - commonly known as "propaganda."

The concept and widespread use of propaganda was enhanced during the early twentieth century by Edward Bernays, nephew of psychology pioneer Sigmund Freud. By combining pre-conceived concepts behind crowd psychology and the ideas of his uncle, Bernays developed methods of persuading, even controlling, social conduct, opinion, norms, mores, behaviors, and habits. He referred to this method as the "engineering of consent." Most notably, the implementation of his methods by various corporations proved highly profitable.

With propaganda (which Bernays later rebranded as "public relations" due to negative feedback; "propaganda" apparently needed propaganda), products, concepts, ideologies, and selected facts are communicated alongside an emotion-inspiring component. The objective is to subconsciously coerce the viewer to correlate the inspired emotion(s) with the message, thus swaying opinion and clouding judgement. The goal nowadays is the same as it was then: to control mass behavior and opinion. Such control enables corporations to catalyze consumer activity.

Moreover, the success of propaganda plays on swaying opinion and behavior en masse and capitalizing on the social nature of most human beings to gravitate and/or succumb to the trends of a larger group. This affecting of a significant percentage of the population takes advantage of the "herd" or "sheep" mentality.

Oftentimes the insinuated emotion behind such coercion is fear. In the 2002 documentary *Bowling For Columbine*, a portion of the film focused on certain faction of society protesting Marilyn Manson, whom they considered to be responsible for the high-school gunmen's behavior due to their listening to Manson's music, asserting that its lyrical content "fueled their desperation and anger." Subsequent footage showed the filmmaker interviewing Manson who, after responding to those sentiments, offered his perspective as to the way media operates: "keep everyone afraid, and they'll consume."

This campaign of fear and consumption can be seen in many commercials and advertisements, which often make use of a "before and after" scenario. Before using the product, the actor (or model) will be seen as achy, sleep deprived, sick, overweight, irritable, in danger, and so on. This segment is usually accompanied with a somber, depressing, or ominous musical underscore and equally dismal atmosphere. The scene after the product is used features the actor as healthy, energetic, rested, agreeable, chipper, safe and so forth as pleasant music plays and the ambiance literally appears brighter. Or, the condition supposedly alleviated by the product will itself become a third character within the thirty-second psychodrama. The "villain" could be anything from gingivitis, to mucous, to pet hair, to body fat, any of which the heroic product or service being proffered will protect the consumer from. The message - playing on the emotional subconscious of the viewer - is that the product alleviates misery, distress, illness, low self-worth, etc. - in short, the negative emotional manifestations of fear.

Clearly, fear is not the only emotion used in advertisement. Any emotion - happiness, excitement, empowerment, carefreeness, confidence - can be used to coerce the viewer to perceive the product in a certain light. Any connected positive emotion indirectly plays on fears in that it exploits what the viewer subconsciously feels he or she lacks.

For instance, a product which is featured in a joyous, high-spirited, celebratory, or party-like group atmosphere will exploit the viewer's issue of abandonment or exclusion. He or she will unknowingly associate the product with feeling accepted, involved, and included. Similarly, the product or service can be depicted in multiple scenes, each with a new and different user, bearing the connotation that many people take part. A specific and common usage of this tactic is a print or photo ad featuring numerous faces of a variety of ages and ethnicities. The subliminal message communicated is that "everyone" is using the product or service.

Or (in addition), the product can be depicted to be used by people who appear hip, sexy, smart, popular, successful, beautiful, in shape, etc. This will directly plug into the viewers subconscious fears that he or she is uncool, ugly, stupid, an outcast, failing, unattractive, fat - in short, their unlovability, failure, and perfectionism schemas: all of which have been ingrained or reinforced by other means of media. The message the viewer receives is that they can depend on the product to feel better about themselves: "If I buy those jeans, I can look as sexy as her."

The product can play on mistrust issues as well. By promoting feelings of security and safety alongside a product, a person harboring mistrust issues will buy right in. Similarly, a product which depicts the user as being in charge, in control, powerful, or privileged will target those who have issues of subjugation or entitlement. And, if introduced with a backdrop of abundance, material ease, luxury, or comfort, a person with an unresolved deprivation schema will be particularly susceptible.

Whatever the case, the broadcasting, exploiting, and capitalizing off of a positive trait or lifestyle lacking in much of the viewing public is probably the most widespread and underhanded use of an invisible insult: "We've got what we think you think you're not."

As mentioned before, much of this positive spin is accomplished through celebrity endorsement. As opposed to linking the product to emotion, it is linked to a persona who represents positive attributes. The consumer subconsciously correlates the wealth, beauty, status, confidence, and/or personality, etc. of the celebrity to the product and, if they bear an unresolved schema the celebrity persona counteracts, they will gravitate to it. There is a reason a starlet or sports hero is recruited to be "the face" of a company: the corporation uses their image as their own. It need not be a specific celebrity endorsement either: product placements in television and motion pictures accomplish the same objective.

In essence, virtually all advertisement capitalizes on fear and unresolved schemas. The fear can either be blatantly featured as part of the campaign or, conversely, it can be absent: the fear will appear instead as subtext, being underhandedly presented as an alternate reality or personality subconsciously reminding the viewer of what they lack - freedom from inner-fears; more specifically, self-love.

The objective of product advertisement is universal: it is to condition the general public to manage their inner-fears by purchasing products. The problem is, the reliance on material goods to alleviate inner-turmoil - or "retail therapy" - is both superficial and ineffective. Once the new dress no longer makes its owner feel sexy, or the make-up is taken off, or the pill is swallowed and its effects have worn off, or the alarm system is installed, or the electronic gadget that everyone else owns is purchased and loses its novelty, the owner returns to feeling ugly, vulnerable, unsafe, and excluded. The issues of unlovability, abandonment, deprivation, subjugation, mistrust, exclusion, vulnerability, perfectionism, and failure which were exploited to coerce the purchase of the product in the first place still exist and will resurface.

Regardless, the elite have effectively conditioned the general public to their own image, as the public has been taught to follow their lead: one doesn't need to tend to their inner-hell, as there is always something out there they can get or control that will make the pain go away. Yet because of the inability (or unwillingness) of many to divorce themselves from the belief that salvation from inner-fears comes with status or a receipt, they keep purchasing. And, since their fears keep reappearing, they keep purchasing. They continue purchasing until they find themselves in debt, owing more money to elite institutions, generating more fear, leading to more purchasing to quash their fears, more tapped credit, more debt, more enslavement, and so on. This downward spiral is only catalyzed when the person, succumbing to their social nature, purchases even more to "keep up with the Joneses."

Yet it doesn't stop there. The consumer culture of anesthetization through materialism has taken on more spiritually malignant characteristics of narcissism and entitlement, as customer service and marketing caters to both. The concept that the customer is "in charge" or can have "what they want, when they want it, how they want it" is becoming a more prevalent practice and selling point. Terms like "on demand" and slogans such as "You're way, right away" reinforce the narcissistic and entitled consumeristic culture. A personality on a day-time talk show team once declared, "If you don't get what you want, complain to a manager." If one doesn't get last month's sale price, throw a fit. If one is required to pay a late fee, cop a nutty to get out of it. Having worked in customer service for years, not only have I witnessed countless occurrences of this, but belittling, manipulative, and verbally even physically abusive behavior - temper tantrums as well. Just like the elite, the public has means to bypass self-accountability. Although the establishment will bear the financial brunt of enabling such narcissism and entitlement, it most likely will not be felt by the company's executives or shareholders; rather, it will be compensated for in lowered employee wages, pay raises, and benefits.

Products themselves increasingly reflect the promotion of narcissism, whether it be sweatpants with the word "juicy" imprinted across the seat or underwear with "papi" embroidered in the waistband. The general public now has not only been conditioned to anesthetize its issues with material goods, but to employ the same toxic tactics to maintain its consumer dominance, narcissism, and entitlement. The spiritual malignancy of those pulling the strings reflect even more in the puppets attached. And, like other fear-for-power pyramid models, the net result is the same: money and power float to the top; fear settles at the bottom.

However, it is not just products and services which propaganda is used to sell. As previously described, political opinions and ideologies are also imposed onto the general public through various forms of news which, as owned by members of the elite, compliment their own interests. Even advertising can be used by various political entities and other organizations. Most notable is the same fear-based consumption marketing often used by adversarial candidates, with the gloomy, ominous, or depressing music accompanying the selected information about the opponent or opposing view, whereas the contender is heralded with bright, cheery colors and equally optimistic music. And, unsurprisingly, celebrity endorsement is also used to promote a political candidate or ideology.

If adults lack the savvy to understand when they are being manipulated, children surely will, too. Being young, vulnerable, and impressionable, they are particularly susceptible to various marketing schemes (based on extensive research) which take advantage of ways to manipulate child behavior, psychology, and development. Corporations spend an estimated fifteen billion dollars each year on sophisticated, slick marketing to children, which amounts to $200 per child. (They would not do this if they did not realize an appreciable return.)

Since these corporations have tight bonds to media (or, in some cases, eggs in both baskets), programming can be created to condition children to engage in behavior to get what they want. For instance, the 2003 documentary *The Corporation* featured a segment on a 1998 marketing study on nagging. "This study was not to help parents' cope with nagging," according to Susan Linn, Professor of Psychiatry, Baker's Children Center, Harvard, "It was to help corporations help children nag for their products more effectively." The researchers, incidentally, found a strong correlation between the purchase of such items as theme park tickets, fast food, and movie tickets and parents' being nagged for them. No doubt such techniques have been embedded in childrens' programming. Such conditioning fosters a foundation for younger generations to disregard boundaries. By proceeding to incessantly nag, whine, or throw a tantrum to get what they want after being told "no," children will grow up conditioned to believe "no" has no value. As adults, they will cultivate the same sense of entitlement: by being persistent, incessant, and disrespectful of others' boundaries, they can get what they want - and that is all that matters.

Marketing and production not only capitalizes on the entitled culture children have been conditioned to, but the narcissistic component as well. Consider the "Bratz" dolls, for instance (or the name alone): small, sexualized, fashionista figurines with attitude and skimpy, tight outfits - including miniskirts, fishnet stockings, and feather boas.

Now, not only has propaganda manipulated the general public to trade their wealth, power, and critical thinking ability for fear, it has conditioned them to continuously numb their fears - however temporarily - with material goods and egotistical means. Furthermore, the corporate catering and promotion of control, narcissism, and entitlement has recreated the spiritually malignant behavior of the elite within the general public. And, those generations emerging from such early programming will believe that "self-love" is an egotistical, narcissistic construct, which may or may not have a schema basis but is surely fed by materialism and narcissistic supply. Regardless, since this "self-love" is based on mental constructs, attention from others, and material goods, it will inevitably dissolve when reality contradicts the artificial sense of self, when narcissistic supply is not around, or after the novelty or effects of the product wear off.

However, whatever fears resurface can be projected onto others by means of the toxic tactics rooted in narcissism, entitlement, and domination. And there are ways to cultivate this within the general public, too.

"Social" Networking: Anti-social Conditioning

"Facebook gives people an illusory sense of being LIKED."

- Mokokoma Mokhonoana

In 1973, psychologist Kenneth Gergen conducted a group experiment which focused on behavior and anonymity. In this experiment, a group of men and women were introduced in to each other in a pitch black room without any furniture. After an initial conversational period, many began to touch each other and more. Almost ninety percent of the participants reported touching another person intentionally, half hugged another person, while one third ended up kissing.

The rise of social disinhibition through anonymity has been exponentially enhanced by the advent of the internet and electronic communication, and not just with regard to physical gratification. In the 1960s, Stanley Milgram conducted his now famous "Milgram Experiment" which measured the willingness of various subjects (acting as "teachers") to obey an authority figure. In following orders to administer an electric shock to the "learner" each time a question was answered incorrectly, the voltage of the shock was increased with each proceeding incorrect answer. Throughout the experiment, the teacher and learner were separated from each other by a wall. Thus, the teacher could not initially observe the direct effects of the shocks on the learner (despite receiving a sample shock at the beginning of the experiment.) Yet, as the number of incorrect answers and voltage increased, the learner would eventually start to scream and pound the wall from the other side. (The shocks were, in fact, fake and "received" by an actor who, after a certain voltage level, would feign agony.) The results of the experiment found that any resistance to following authoritative orders to inflict physical harm only came when the learner started to scream or pound on the wall. Thus, the teacher's ability to sense the distress they were (supposedly) inflicting upon another stimulated their conscience and their subsequent reluctance to continue.

Similar to the setup of this experiment, the harmful effects of words delivered though electronic communication will be felt by the recipient but not seen by the sender. At most, the sender will receive a response (negative, if the message was mean-spirited or offensive) but, since the recipient cannot be seen or heard, will not be fully aware of the extent of the emotional harm caused. Through anonymity, separation, and the inability to perceive effects, electronic communication diminishes such reservations against inflicting harm. Known as the "Online Disinhibition Effect," social restrictions, taboos, or inhibitions that would normally be present in face-to-face interactions are depleted or abandoned completely.

The results of this effect enables thousands to emotionally injure each other with little or no compunction, since being removed from the emotional harm they have caused makes it easier to carry out. This, however, gives rise to thousands of internet users employing a variety of spiritually malignant offense mechanisms toward each other with little reservation.

This can commonly be seen on any website featuring a news article accompanied by a comments section. Especially if the article is controversially charged, malignant "users" can scapegoat, debase, slander, intimidate, spin, lie, manipulate, shame, and more. Thus, the anger, frustration, resentment, anxiety, and self-judgment associated with the fears behind these tactics can be projected onto someone without remorse (since they can't see the harm they've caused) or accountability (because they are anonymous.)

Such offense mechanisms can be personal: "Not the brightest light bulb in the chandelier, are you?"; "Time to put on your tinfoil hat"; "Go take your crazy meds." Others are racist: "let's start targeting and executing mass murderers that shoot innocent people. here's the profile that fits most serial killers: WHITE MALE"; "I hate fkn *[sic]* black bas***ds *[sic]*."; "but really, what good are mexicans?";"I know some american sitizens *[sic]* in the military in germany of all places that speak non stop mexican *[sic]*. There *[sic]* english suck *[sic]* and they were born and rasied *[sic]* in TX." They can be homophobic :"If all you QUEERS/FAGGOTS/LESBIANS/FREAKS want a place ruled by homosexuality and wickedness...try hell....it has already been made just for you." Often, they are political: "I'm not a racist like you liberals"; "Show me someone the Tea Party supports and I will show you a racist." The use of such toxic "commenting" extends to social networking sites, which are used as comment sections for such articles as well.

Comment sections are thus conducive in establishing the spiritually malignant goals of narcissism, entitlement, and domination by means of offense mechanisms. Narcissism is enabled since the user becomes hyper-opinionated and feels self-important, often feeling morally, ethically, intellectually, or ideologically superior to those who disagree. The anonymous aspect to commenting fosters entitlement by allowing the user to feel that moral and ethical norms - especially the Golden Rule - need not apply to himself: it's okay for him to degradingly refer to someone else as a "libtard," "RepubliKKKan," or "freak." Subsequently, he is able to create a docile victim: he can incessantly inflict harm by hurling a litany of insults, potshots, and epithets or using virtually any offense mechanism without enduring much - if any - repercussions or accountability.

Yet, like consumerism, the fears behind the overcompensating and projecting offense mechanisms still linger after such mechanisms have been used. The comments of racial superiority used by the overly ethnocentric commenter will not tend to the core issues of the commenter feeling un-special, unlovable, vulnerable, or mistrusting. The blaring, dogmatic moral and ethical superiority of a comment will do little to address the guilty conscience and poor self-image of its author. The labeling of others as "tinfoil hat" wearers will do nothing to improve the commenter's own poor psychological health.

Thus, an internet population's fears not only go unresolved, they are infectious by means of a vast network as people lambaste, judge, condemn, insult, and manipulate others they do not know. But just because the "shock" is not seen does not mean it isn't felt. Others, adopting this negativity, are conditioned and prone to project their fear-based anger, frustrations, resentments, and judgements in the same manner as it becomes the apparent norm. The net result is an epidemic of spiritually malignancy and a nationwide stockpile of fear, hurt, anger, anxiety, and frustration.

Not only has electronic and internet communication catalyzed spiritual malignancy within the population, but narcissism in general. Websites and "social networks" have further enhanced the prevalence of hyper-opinionated, attention-seeking, self-involved, self-important, and self-promoting behavior.

Social networking sites continue this trend. Not only do they allow for self-promotion, but the user can promote or omit information to broadcast themselves as they please, which is typically better than they actually are in some capacity. By self-editing the blurbs, "tweets," comments, likes, pictures appearing in their profiles (which can be digitally enhanced), they can appear as perfect, beautiful, successful, cool, joyous, or however as they please, regardless of the departure from reality.

Yet this very trend of presenting a distorted self-image has caused many "social networkers" to become anti-social. The interpersonal distance provided by such sites becomes preferable when users fear the truth about certain aspects of themselves or their lives becoming known. The very fact that they are compelled withhold and even lie about personal matters with respect to others leads to decreased interpersonal intimacy and, in turn, socialization. It is less scary for some to distantly communicate with others and present to the world an alternate - yet happier - self-version than it would be to be in their presence, which could potentially expose the true lack of success, good looks, friendships, self-worth, happiness, abundance, wealth, and activity - in short, the fear - in their lives.

This partial (or substantial) personal removal will inevitably affect both their emotional availability and perception. Since they have socially distanced themselves from others, such reduced interpersonal intimacy will cause them to depersonalize their family, friends, and peers since the extent of their inter-communication is relegated to text-based comments, e-mails, and instant messages. Diminished is the ability to see the expression in their friends' faces when they speak, hear voice inflections when their peers talk, or feel what it is liked to be hugged. Thus, the conception of others in their lives becomes as virtual and impersonal as the communication between them.

Because others invariably appear less human (since they can no longer be heard, seen, or touched), interpersonal and emotional bonds weaken. As these bonds weaken, so does consideration of others as emotional beings. This will often reflect in lessened frequency and duration of the already impersonal electronic interaction: days, weeks, or months may go by without a response, if at all, resulting in the emotional abandonment of the other party. Since their hurt cannot be seen or heard, it matters less, if at all: the emotional and physical distance blocks out any noticeable anguish of the other party. Now, ironically, due to "social networking," they have now become more isolated and anti-social. Those relying on e-mail, texting, and instant messaging to communicate are prone to socially sequester in a similar manner.

Yet this concurrent inaccurate public portrayal and emotional, self-isolating aloofness is itself destructive, as this selective (or false sense of) social contact and avoidance become a means of diverting one's attention from one's own issues. It is often the very interactions we have with others which brings awareness to our own schemas. If such interpersonal interactions are avoided, so too will be the ability to notice our emotional wounds and heal them. In addition, the chance to just have somebody to talk to - to vent, to have a shoulder to cry on, to listen, to share a laugh with: all of which are therapeutic and healing - is lost.

Oddly, some psychologists (espoused as "experts") have suggested that not partaking in social networking is "suspicious" and anti-social.[14] This asinine diagnosis asserts that those who prefer to see and hear the person they're communicating with - that is, interaction that isn't "virtual" - are somehow more "anti-social."

If e-mail or instant messaging is relied upon as the preferred method of communication, the user will be confronted with the same "news" (mentioned before) on the main page of their webmail provider that manipulates and sways its readers' perceptions and opinions while diverting their attention from more pressing issues. In addition, such "articles" will avail comment sections to both view and post offense mechanisms on.

The modes of electronic communication themselves are prone to be more toxic and ineffectual than other personal means. Since the mode or transmission is text - and not involving facial expressions, voice inflections, body language, etc. - a large part of a conveyed message is lost. People will invariably find themselves "reading between the lines" of e-mails, texts, and other messaging, asking, "What did she mean by that?" Had they seen or heard her say it, they would most likely have a better idea. Moreover, since the method of communication is more oblique, passive offense mechanisms such as invisible insults and backhanded compliments are more permissible - if not, they're misinterpreted as such.

Cyber-bullying, online harassment, and internet scams are more examples of electronic spiritual malignancy. Despite the physical remoteness between the malignant personality and their victim, the effects can be just as devastating as if their interactions had taken place in person. Some cases have resulted in the victim being harassed or bullied to the point of taking their own lives.

In addition to fostering narcissism and entitlement, the anonymity provided by online interaction opens a trove of many other toxic tactics which can be used. Anyone can adopt an alias and, in doing so, use manipulative tactics such as invasiveness and constant surveillance, allowing them to extract sensitive, private information used to blackmail, extort, bully, slander, or inspire schadenfreude. Only persons with fears of vulnerability, mistrust, and the skeletons in their own closet would resort to such toxic behavior, as it is an obvious, shameless, and cowardly attempt to project these fears onto someone else.

Similarly, "phishing" scams exploit anonymity and use toxic tactics to victimize others, usually by stealing money. By means of e-mail, phone calls, or embedded web links, those behind phishing scams will manipulate the victim by claiming to be an alternate, false identity (e.g. financial institution, social networking site) and use some sort of fear creation ("if you do not respond, your account will be permanently blocked") to scare the victim into following suit.

The toxic dynamics that ensue from online anonymity are not exclusive to individual interaction. Groups, agencies, and organizations also exploit the ability to hide behind aliases to achieve various objectives. Such entities can make use of "megaphone" broadcasting to promote, influence, and manipulate public opinion - in short, propagandize. Anyone subscribing to a particular ideology, coverup, or agenda can become a "cyberspace soldier" by downloading software that provides "action alerts" to the activist about polls or articles pertinent to their cause. These alerts enable the activists to bombard relevant comments sections with messages, coercing the unknowing lay person to believe these posters are average people and that their opinions are authentic and reflect the majority. These notifications also allow these "soldiers" to use a wide range of offense mechanisms (evolving into bullying and harassment) toward those who disagree with their agenda. Moreover, they also allow for skewed polling results which were intended to reflect individual opinion. Since the effect is anonymous, one "soldier" can adopt multiple aliases to magnify the effect.

Often, the authors of such commented articles and blog posts are fictitious themselves, either providing an alias or no name at all. Unsurprisingly, a symphony of anonymously written articles are published with a similar bent or promoted agenda, reinforced by the biased and bogus comments of the arriving cyber-PR army. Such articles and comments can include rampant lies in the guise of "facts" or "experts" which unscrupulously attempt to manipulate public opinion. Lies, lies of omission, and half-truths can be expected.

"Shills" and "authors" need not be the only ones born in the world of make-believe. Profiles on social networking sites can also be manufactured, leaving anyone who interacts with them open to vulnerability. "Friending" such false personas (or the simple joining of a social network), can expose all sorts of personal information - and to whom is often a mystery. Yet everyone online, regardless of direct contact with such malignancy, will feel the fears of vulnerability and mistrust accompanying phishing and toxic anonymity.

If this does not conjure mistrust and vulnerability, the constant surveillance of the elite will. All electronic communications and activity - e-mailing, texting, social network profiles, blogging, browsing history, online and phone contacts - are monitored. This widespread, constant surveillance was spearheaded by the enactment of the Patriot Act, which not only abolished the need for a court order (and thus probable cause) to wiretap phones, but established fiberoptic connections between all the hubs of telecommunication companies and the National Security Agency (NSA). Now, in addition to conversational content by phone, the NSA has access to all forms of electronic communications and activity. The vast amount of electronic data stored, monitored, processed, and collected on the general public required the building of a spy-center in so large, it is more than five times the size of the Capitol. [15]

The 65 megawatt, one million square foot, $2 billion center, located in Bluffdale, Utah, requiring $40 million per year to operate, will be used to store, manage and mine data pertaining to the following: driving records, purchase history, medical records, internet browsing history, personal e-mails, text messaging, contacts, financial information and transactions, tax filings, location tracking records, DNA, criminal records, information derived from computer backdoor software, foreign travel, television viewing history, and more. Former NSA analyst Adrienne J. Kinne admitted, "basically all the rules were thrown out the window." When called before Congress to explain such mass spying, NSA chief General Keith Alexander claimed, "The NSA does not have the ability to do that in the United States...we're not authorized to do that."[16] This being accurate, this ability was enhanced by outsourcing the job to foreign agencies.[17] Ironically, this widespread, warrantless spying is conducted in the name of national security. Yet, most Americans have no idea this is taking place; by now, the reason behind this should be obvious.

If the torrential downpour of fear on the general population from central banks, corporations, the finance industry, government, media, entertainment, and advertising was not enough, it is both supplemented and amplified by electronic interaction. At this point, the public has developed fears of deprivation, vulnerability, and mistrust of the Federal Reserve. They have the same fears due to the finance sector as well, especially considering the multi-trillion dollar bailout. Corporations have imparted fears of subjugation, deprivation, vulnerability, failure, perfectionism, and entitlement. Our government has expanded on all of these and accentuates abandonment and exclusion. The corporate owned media, entertainment, and advertising lumped on much more of the same, yet underhandedly taught the public they were unlovable.

All of the tiers above have concertedly conditioned the public to do anything and everything toxic in "coping" with their fears, whether it be self or outward-oriented. It has been taught to deny, submit to, anesthetize, divert, consume, overcompensate for, project - anything but deal with the fears in a healthy manner by facing them. Instead, thanks to electronic social interaction, a litany of offense mechanisms rooted in narcissism, entitlement, and victimizing can be used to project schemas onto innocent others.

Someone with an issue of abandonment can be unavailable or abandoning, or a person with a deprivation issue can easily be aloof, distant, and ungiving toward another. Someone who feels unlovable can berate, insult, and judge with ease. A person with a mistrust or vulnerability schema can violate others. And, since they cannot see or hear their victim, all can be accomplished with less compunction and remorse or none at all. Yet, though the methods may be virtual, the effects are very much real. Some people walk away from their monitors feeling more unloved, violated, deprived, failing, and alone than they did when they logged on, while others build their narcissism, entitlement, and dominance. More often than not, they will experience both. All of them now require more healing and most have been manipulated. Everyone loses, and spiritual malignancy becomes the norm.

Yet, being at the bottom of the pyramid, any fear not transmuted cannot be pushed downward, nor can it be sustained for too long - especially by those most vulnerable and powerless within this tier: our kids.

9

The Fear Foundation

Fear Moves In: The Dysfunctional Family

"You, alright! I learned it by watching you!"

- A son to his father in an infamous 1987 Anti-Drug Public Service Announcement.

The beginning of this book explored the types and ways various maladaptive patterns in coping with trauma and emotional pain are adopted in early life. Children raised in healthy, loving, functional families have their emotional and physical needs met and are likely to grow into equally functional adults. They tend to their own needs as well as others, communicate effectively and in a healthy matter, and live lives reflecting self-awareness and authenticity.

Many of us, unfortunately, have been raised in families where our emotional needs, feelings, authentic selves, physical needs, aptitudes and limitations, boundaries, and even physical, psychological, and emotional safety were not honored. Some of us had hyper-critical parents who questioned, second guessed, denounced, or overrode our choices and abilities during our development. We may have been told that we were stupid, irresponsible, and not good enough during a critical learning curve which involved making mistakes and self-actualization. We may have been made to feel guilty for things which were not our fault. We may have been made to feel ashamed, unlovable, and unapproved for simply being ourselves. We may not have had any privacy, fearing that any emotional or personal sanctuary was fleeting and could be disrupted at any given time.

Many of us had parents who were aloof and distant, relatively uninvolved or uncaring about their children's lives or times their kids needed some kind of support. Perhaps our parental figures were emotionally unavailable due to being numbed out with alcohol or drugs and/or required being taken care of. Or, the self-absorption of our parents eclipsed our own wants and needs, or perhaps their way was the only way. Maybe they were physically absent or abandoning, completely disregarding their child's needs. Or, perhaps our parents were hyper-critical and had insatiably high standards - to the point of being unattainable.

Some of us may have had mothers, fathers, or other relatives who were verbally, psychologically, and/or physically abusive and grew up learning to fear rather than love. Too many tears, mistakes, and challenges of authority were met with yelling, epithets, slaps, punches, or another form of abuse. The converse may be true: we may have been enabled, spoiled, and overly-praised by mothers and fathers who refused to see their kids as anything but flawless.

Many of us who have had dysfunctional and abusive parenting continue through life not only bearing unresolved schemas, but the belief that this sort of negative upbringing is customary. Our parents, whether good, bad, or in between, were our role models, after all: how could we know any different? Consequently, because we grow believing the toxic environment we were raised in was normal, many of us will find life partners who compliment the familiar dynamics.

Depending on the frequency and severity of the abuse, neglect, and toxicity of our parental environment, we will naturally develop a complimentary set of maladaptive defense and/or offense mechanisms which we will carry throughout our adulthood. Unless resolved, healed, or kept at bay, these toxic and dysfunctional patterns will be passed onto and affect our children, as they inherit the "unwanted heirlooms" we had inherited. These heirlooms may be identical (an entitled parent may raise an entitled child; a subjugating parent may condition their child to grow up subjugating others) or complimentary (a parent with abandonment issues may foster fears of deprivation in the child; a perfectionistic parent may cause their child to feel they are a failure or not lovable.)

The types of offense and defense mechanisms manifested are not only shaped by the type of fear passed on, but the dysfunctional role played in the family's history. In dysfunctional families, the toxicity or dysfunction of the parent(s) requires other members to adopt maladaptive patterns which cultivate maladaptive roles. These roles, though spiritually corrosive, are taken on to maintain the family's operation. Abusive, toxic, or dysfunctional behavior of one parent is enabled by the other (or mutually enabled if present in both parents) due to a belief that family survival is dependent on it. In order to accommodate the dysfunctional parent(s) from experiencing the repercussions of his or her toxic behavior, the other family members must modify or abdicate their own emotional, mental, or physical health and needs. Children, being vulnerable and impressionable, will not only contort to such roles, but adopt them as their personality which extends into adulthood.

The roles which commonly emerge from dysfunctional families are: the Hero, the Scapegoat, the Lost Child, and the Mascot.

The Hero is usually, but not always, the eldest, attempting to save the family by personifying its ideals - be it personality, performance, achievement, appearance, vocation, success, etc. By living a life and adopting a persona that contradicts the family's own dysfunction, inadequacy, shortcomings, failings, codependence, and underperformance, this role accommodates the family's narcissism. Thus, dysfunctional parents derive from their "pride and joy" the false sense of being capable, since the Hero's "success story" is indicative of good parenting - however inaccurate. The attentiveness, dutifulness, and appeasement the hero displays toward his parents derives positive affirmation from outsiders, seeing the Hero as "the good kid." Yet, underneath the facade of success and well-adjustment, the hero feels much guilt, inadequacy, and pressure to appease, as nothing they do is good enough to save the family, no matter how hard they try. They may never be independently happy with themselves since others' approval is required for their self-worth. Moreover, since it was their job to make the family look good, they will feel responsible when it does not. The Hero will also feel an sense of resentment or emptiness inside: their entire identity and life decisions were based on the ideals, standards, and expectations of others. Since they can lack such self-knowledge and awareness, they may lack in their own spirituality as well.

The Scapegoat, resentful of the positive attention the dysfunctional parents gave to the hero or themselves, acts out in various ways in defiance and for attention. The acting out will involve irresponsible, deviant, delinquent, or rebellious behavior, which is often a cry for help and love. This will take the form of self-destructive of self-sabotaging behavior, such as drug use, truancy, poor academic performance, harm against self or others, and early parenthood. Subsequently perceived as the "black sheep" or the family's "problem child," the Scapegoat becomes the antithesis of the Hero. Whereas the Hero represents and is valued for all that is "right" with the family, the Scapegoat absorbs all the blame for what is wrong (hence the moniker.) After being branded as "no good" after so much effort to "be good" for so long, they stop trying. The result is rebellion, which can enable the Scapegoat to develop more deviant anti-social traits involving scheming, manipulation, and criminality. Narcissism can also result as compensation for their low-self image. As such, the Scapegoat tends to become out of touch with both their spiritual and moral centers.

Since all of the attention - positive or negative - has been assigned to others in the family, the Lost Child is forgotten. Those in this role will learn to be distant and isolated, since dysfunctional parents will teach them that their care is limited and to draw on attention is burdensome and meaningless. As a result, the Lost Child will feel like an outcast as they are often overlooked and excluded. Although lonely, those in this role will soon prefer isolation, since it is less painful to be lonely and alone than it is to be lonely and in the company of others; at least in isolation, they are not directly reminded that they are disregarded by others. Yet, this solidarity does not rid the feelings of depression, rejection, sadness, and abandonment. Since they are accustomed to aloneness, they will have difficulty connecting with others later in life and may take a "loner" lifestyle. Thus, they may bond with a pet as opposed to a marriage partner. Yet this aloneness, if not impeded by low self-worth or delving into a fantasy world, can enable the Lost Child a rich inner-life. Since they are alone with their own imagination, they may develop their creative skills. Or, this could enhance their spirituality, since the time spent in seclusion could be used to understand their inner-selves - and derive significant self-knowledge and expanded perception in the process. Yet, this preference to "go at it alone" may prevent the Lost Child from seeking necessary assistance as they "suffer in silence."

The Mascot, also known as the Jester, is usually the youngest child. The humorous, animated, and entertaining demeanor of the Mascot serves both to provide an escape for everyone to feel better and to gain attention and "love." Yet, like the Hero, this role will be relied upon to compensate for the family's negativity; the Mascot, too, will be pigeonholed with unrelenting expectations to "keep things light." When falling short of their duties, this role often bears the brunt of potshots, humiliation, and ridicule - the thought process being, "If you don't make us laugh, we'll laugh at you - and you'll regret it." (Here, the jester image becomes poignant.) Humor then becomes a means of defending and preserving self-worth. While they can be a pleasure to be around, this conditioning to use humor to counter fear will carry over into adulthood where the Mascot may not be taken seriously. Yet, they carry with them a deep anxiety that, if they cannot diffuse tension with humor, conflict will ensue within the group or they will be emotionally (or physically) targeted. Moreover, they will use humor (or some distraction) to divert attention from anxiety and negative feelings in general - including their own issues. In doing so, they can develop poor concentration or even mental illness.

A child may also become what is know as the "Little Parent." This role serves as a surrogate for the duties and traits neglected or underperformed by one or both parents, leaving the child to adopt adult responsibilities to ensure the functioning of the family. This role is usually taken on by the first born if the duties are logistical, i.e., the parent has passed out in a stupor and the child needs to feed her younger brothers and sisters. Any child, however, can be placed in this role if there is a "role-reversal" between the parent and child. Here, the child become the parent of the parent. A child of a tantrum-throwing parent with anger-management issues may take on a composed, rational, and stern maturity. Or, the child of an insecure, needy mother may be nurturing and emotionally grounding. These children, although typically wise beyond their years, may grow up rigid and cold. Inside, they feel resentment at being overburdened at such a young age, particularly at inept, irresponsible authority figures. They will often take on the role of caretakers or gravitate to a service-based career path as adults, yet the Little Parent will resent the lack of mutual consideration and reciprocity.

From this, schema manifestation takes dimension. The fears of deprivation, abandonment, and perfectionism become more apparent in the Little Parent. A Hero's fears of subjugation, unlovability, deprivation, and perfectionism stand out. Unlovability, failure, vulnerability, and entitlement accompany the Scapegoat as the Lost Child feels abandoned, excluded, deprived, and unloved. The Mascot harbors fears of vulnerability, exclusion, mistrust, subjugation, and unlovability. The fears may be more (or different) for each depending on the precise upbringing.

The roles may also shape the types of defense (and offense) mechanisms used in response to schemas. A Little Parent, accustomed to managing the household, may use offense mechanisms geared as establishing control. Since their self-worth is based on the expectations and ideals of others, a Hero may develop mechanisms rooted in narcissism. A Scapegoat, with an air of rebellion and defiance, can manifest offense mechanisms which reinforce entitlement and other mechanisms which mask low self-worth. The Lost Child, being alone, would be prone to defense mechanisms of avoidance and internalization. The excessive and perhaps inappropriate use of humor would certainly cause the Mascot to be susceptible to diverting defense mechanisms and perhaps offense mechanisms based in narcissism, since an alternate self was needed in order for self-preservation and attention. Of course, the defense and/or offense mechanisms would reflect both the toxicity imposed and the child's wherewithal for withstanding trauma.

Also, although these roles are exclusively described, it is often the case that more than one role is acted by a child, depending on the toxic, codependent dynamics at play. Some may even identify with all five to some degree. Whatever the case, these roles - in additional to the dysfunction and codependence of the parent(s), be it toxic behavior, substance abuse, ideological fascism, and physical and/or emotional abuse - thwart the family from functioning in a healthy manner. As such, feelings will not be expressed openly and honestly; members will fear "rocking the boat"; vocations, ideologies, and religious beliefs will be assigned rather than authentically expressed; parents will not lead by example ("Do as I say, not as I do"); members will only think of themselves and not the group as a whole; members will not communicate directly; and fun is rarely experienced.

Not only do these roles take different variations and combinations, but with changing cultural mores and norms, new roles may be created. One would be the "Little Boss," who is, in fact, the one consistently enabled by the parents. This role comes about when parents spoil their children and/or impose no boundaries out of fear that their kids will not love them. Or, conversely, a Little Boss may be the product of a parent (or parents) who recreates their own megalomaniacal image - based in dominance, entitlement, and narcissism - in their child. The child, after all, is a narcissistic extension of the parent: a "mini-me." The Little Boss grows up always in control, always expecting to be praised and respected, always getting what she wants whenever she wants, and wildly disregarding others' needs and well-being. Unlike the Little Parent, this role is a little tyrant. Because of their self-centeredness and pre-conditioning to disregard others at all costs, he or she is likely to be spiritually bankrupt at a young age. If not nipped in the bud, repeat offenses will conjure ire in others who will eventually teach the Little Boss that they are not in charge. If not, the Little Boss will grow to become paranoid, knowing on a subconscious level the harm he has caused others, which can lead to severe psychological disturbances.

Whichever the role (save for the "Little Boss"), they are all created by imposing fears - fear of being subjugated, unloved, deprived, abandoned, excluded, violated, failure, not being special, not being perfect, and catastrophe. Again, they are passed on from parental figures who developed their own roles and schema defenses from their past. The parental expectation is for children to accommodate their inherited issues by sacrificing their own emotional, psychological, physical, and spiritual needs. With this in mind, dysfunctional families act as "little pyramids" where pre-existing fear at the top is dispensed toward the bottom while power and control is centralized at the top. Moreover, if the parental presence is spiritually malignant, the goals are identical to the other pyramid models: domination, establishing narcissism, and reinforcing entitlement. In essence, they are miniature versions of the other pyramid models described previously.

Keeping in mind that schema reactions are created and triggered by stress (more appropriately, imposed fear), *the family which has pre-existing dysfunctional, toxic dynamics will find it exceptionally difficult to cope with and manage the additional fear being imposed on them from outside the home.* A father with a subjugating schema and a Hero history working at an excessively domineering and demanding corporate job will inevitably bring the triggered negative feelings home, where he will be more likely to superimpose this negativity onto his children, who will feel more abandoned, emotionally deprived, unloved, etc. A Lost Child mother whose self-worth is based on her appearance, feeling pressure from idealizations from the media, advertising, and entertainment, will neglect her daughter's own need for self-image support. Her daughter, in turn, will develop increasing fears of unlovability, failure, mistrust, abandonment, and/or perfectionism, to be handed down to her children at a later time. Examples of such dynamics are plenty.

Yet, *it is precisely this conditioning to dysfunctionally mismanage fears - and establish it as the norm - which is capitalized on by central banks, corporations, financial institutions, and government sectors.* A population bearing subjugation issues will not challenge the will of a central bank to create a debt based system. Nor will they stand up against an abusive, insatiable work environment. A population of mistrust will not address being violated by its own government when it takes its rights away, robbed by the trillions by investment banks in the form of bailouts, or poisoned by chemicals and additives in food produced by corporate manufacturers. A vulnerability issue permeating mass consciousness will prevent it from addressing (or knowing about) the fact that mass spying is taking place. They will not address any of these issues and more since they find them customary. Rather, in each case, they will "put up with it," anesthetize via consumption or activity, justify the behavior or believe an alternate reality, or project their angst onto others - anything but address what is occurring and confront the source.

Basically, *our mismanaged fears - and those of our children - are being exploited by powerful others to get our money, our rights, our power, and - most of all - our self-worth.*

Not only are these fears being exploited but *more fear is being cultivated through the incessant and underhanded programming of media, entertainment, and advertising - which allows their powerful operators to take even more advantage.* Whether subliminal or not, the general public, as perviously outlined, is being conditioned to behave dysfunctionally. Corporations need consumers to not only feel unlovable, but to learn to purchase products to anesthetize such unlovability. Thus, commercials and entertainment are used to manipulate the public into believing that nice clothes, status symbols, and beauty are essential for self-esteem. A malignant government requires its citizens handle subjugation dysfunctionally: they would not have the power they have otherwise. As back-up, the media is used to culturally condition the populace by slandering and vilifying protesters. And, like spoiling a bratty child, companies exploit the entitlement of the masses by giving them what they want, when they want it, how they want it, with as little rules and regulations as possible. In the meantime, their money, power, and rights are being extracted as they "feel special." Such cultural conditioning to ensure the general public remains fearful, dysfunctional, and exploitable is accomplished through the elite owned media, entertainment, and advertising.

The incessant bombardment of fear from corporate, finance, government, media, advertising, and entertainment agencies onto the dysfunctional family will not only strengthen its dysfunctional, unwanted heirlooms, it is liable to create more. In doing so, upcoming generations can expect even more toxic endowments.

Now, not only are dysfunctional families responsible for creating and passing on fear, but the elite conglomerate itself. *Consequently, this passing on of fear, trauma, and abuse from an authoritative, powerful few onto the whole while maintaining and reinforcing a norm of dysfunction renders the nation - if not, the world itself - a macroscopic version of a dysfunctional family.*

The very reason the elite has passed on so much fear onto the public and ensure its mismanagement is to exploit it. The more fearful the public is, the more powerless they will be. The more powerless they are, the less of a threat they pose to the elite's agenda of establishing control, narcissism, and entitlement. Again, these goals are sought by the elite to compensate for their own fears.

Sadly, the mass production of fear, trauma, and abuse will affect the lowest tier of the pyramid the most: the kids. In addition to inheriting fears (involving frustrations, anxiety, depression, low self-worth, and anger) from their parents, they will be exposed to exponentially more as they watch TV, go online, interact with their peers, go into debt, and lose their civil rights. Since they know nothing otherwise, they - like many of us - will continue the trend believing that toxic, spiritual malignancy is the norm.

It's no wonder that upcoming generations are growing more entitled, narcissistic, numb, depressed, impoverished, suicidal, criminal, anti-social, toxic, irresponsible, uneducated, self-absorbed, materialistic, medicated, bullying, violent, self-destructive, addicted, drone-like, and spiritually malignant. They learned it from watching us and others.

From this, not only are wars overseas apparent, but also the war going on right here at home, and it is one we are losing. It's hard to notice since it is both psychologically and spiritually based. Why are we putting up with this?

Groupthink = Grouped Fear

"The American decent into Marxism
is happening with breathtaking speed,
against the backdrop of a passive, hapless sheeple.

- A quote featured in the Russian newspaper, Pravda

As dysfunctional dynamics are reinforced and enhanced by external forces, families preconditioned to them will serve as building blocks to create a society which will be collectively dysfunctional. Such "little pyramids" that trade fear for power will combine to form a large one that is a civilization. The merging of such units will reinforce their own maladaptive patterns in coping with fear (along with its derivations of anger, depression, anxiety, panic, abuse, etc.) by interacting with others. "Victims" raised in one family will interact with "criminals" from another, and vice versa, thus calcifying collective dysfunction. Add to this infectious, reinforcing quality the mass conditioning to handle fear through internalization, avoidance, overcompensation, and projection and spiritual deficiency, malignancy, and even bankruptcy becomes the norm. Simultaneously, the percentage of the population accustomed (or grown to) handle their fears in a healthy, functional manner becomes less - to the point of being a counterculture seen as uncooperative, "paranoid," and rebellious.

Yet, as dysfunction becomes more culturally commonplace, others are more susceptible to follow suit via the "zombie effect" described previously. This tendency of individuals to adopt behaviors, ideologies, and trends of the majority is a historic construct of human evolution. In the past, human beings needed to rely on a "strength in numbers" mentality: it was necessary to share common goals, ideals, concepts, customs, mores, and norms even if it required abandoning individual appraisal. Its purpose served to minimize conflict within the group and foster the cohesion needed for protection against outside threats - in short, survival.

However, this "groupthink" survival mechanism becomes self-defeating when the behaviors, ideologies, and trends are dysfunctional. Like the family that enables codependence, narcissism, entitlement, despotic control, and abuse, a dysfunctional civilization will produce role members who are addicted, lacking in self-awareness, toxic, enabling, withdrawn, anxious, entitled, narcissistic, and domineering. The flawed reasoning, like that of the dysfunctional family, is that such roles are required for group survival. This could not be further from the truth since such roles inevitably lead to the spiritual, emotional, psychological, and physical destruction of self or others - yet, this time, on a massive scale. Because such maladaptive roles are viewed as necessary by the majority, anyone who steps out of the role will be seen as "rocking the boat" or dangerous dissidents.

As mentioned before, this adherence to dysfunctional, maladaptive norms by the masses gives rise to the "herd mentality," or more commonly, the "sheeple" effect. Because the majority of society subscribes to dysfunctional behavior, others will too. The capacity to think, react, or behave independently is abdicated out of fear of not being part of a larger body; it abrades against the very survival instinct built into many of us. However, just because something is "normal" does not mean it is in one's best interest or healthy. The majority may believe a widespread, distributed corporate news story yet, if it is based on half-truths, lies of omissions, or complete falsehoods to avoid accountability from the public or condition its behavior, an individual would be better off seeing through the façade rather than joining the herd. Similarly, just because everyone they know has the latest cell phone model does not mean it is in one's best interest to upgrade, especially if one is in debt. Whether is it with regard to politics, norms, mores, ethics, religious beliefs, fads, ideologies, behaviors, attitudes, or news, many people will be prone to follow the thoughts, beliefs, and feelings of the masses as opposed to self-reference.

Yet, when people stop using their God-given minds to think and God-given hearts to feel, cult-like dynamics ensue. They lose their capacity to think critically and independently, ability to cultivate wisdom and emotional intelligence, and identity. They will lose the ability to rationalize, judge, and make cognitive assessments since it has already been done for them by a group of others. They will believe dogma, falsehoods, and manipulations just because everyone else does. They will believe doctrines or "facts" they would not ordinarily accept on their own simply because most others believe them. They will purchase things they cannot afford because they don't want to appear "different" from others. They will join in the mass adulating of a narcissistic, famous personality for the same reason.

They will endure harsh working conditions since everyone else does. They will pay into extraneous, unaccountable taxation (even though many do not have the money to give) out of fear of repercussion. They will not stand up to despotic legislature since no one else does; or, they will support it in order to belong to a group even though the group has been manipulated to do so. Since everyone else has been taught they should not speak up when being subjugated and violated, they won't either; rather, they will deny, project, anesthetize, or accept the frustrations like everyone else. Perhaps such sheeple exist not only out being accustomed to malignant authorities figures growing up, but as a sort of a large-scale version of Stockholm Syndrome. On a subconscious level, they may understand that they are being victimized, abused, and enslaved, yet bond with their captors to derive a sense of protection.

Many will gossip, throw potshots, and verbally attack others as opposed to addressing their own low self-worth rooted in unlovability: it's been done to them, and everybody else seems to. Since many others communicate infrequently and impersonally through e-mail and texting, they will join in the emotionally aloof and distant behavior as well.

The sheeple effect is essentially the antithesis of socialization. A socialized person acts with regard to the wellbeing of the whole as well as themselves whereas sheeple join the masses in ways that are toxic, malignant, defeating, and destructive to both themselves and others. The irony is, they conform to such behavior in order to not be "alone" or "vulnerable."

Yet it is this tendency to mimic the behavior of the majority which reinforces the widespread use defense and offense mechanisms in coping with the anger, depression, sadness, frustrations, anxiety, and restlessness that accompanies fear. As discussed before, this propensity to internalize, avoid, overcompensate for, and project fear has allowed a small percentage to compensate for such fears of their own. The compensation comes from the money, wealth, power, and prestige extracted from the public by capitalizing on its mismanaged response to fear. Since they have found ways to profit and usurp power from mismanaged fear, more fear is projected onto the public as their dysfunctional managing of such fear is enhanced: the cyclic trading of fears for powers ensues. And the fear projected on the public has been plenty.

To recap: The debt based currency system established by the Federal Reserve projected its operators fears of mistrust, subjugation, vulnerability, entitlement and deprivation (if not, more) onto the public. By circumventing oversight and avoiding an audit of any pith (though a variety of offense mechanisms of their own), its operators avoided accountability, established entitlement and narcissism, and created a willing/docile victim.

The financial sector projected similar fears of its own onto tiers the below it. By operating without regulation, it too extracted money and power to compensate for its own issues of entitlement, subjugation, deprivation, vulnerability, mistrust, etc. - fears which were inherited by its clients and the general public when they lost money to investment scams and multi-trillion dollar bailouts, respectively.

Corporations have imparted fears of subjugation, deprivation, vulnerability, failure, and perfectionism in many of the work environments they create. They passed on the same fears along with abandonment when jobs were outsourced. Payroll cutbacks added more fear of deprivation. The harmful effects many of their products had on the environment and the individual added more fear of vulnerability. The consumer culture they've helped to create added entitlement. All of this fear projection allowed them to gain money and power, which was used to establish more entitlement, narcissism, and dominance in order to cover up their own issues.

Our government enabled the previous entities while it projected fears of its own. Politicians have passed on their fears of deprivation, abandonment, mistrust, exclusion, failure, etc. onto the general public by accepting the bribes and agendas of outside organizations. Whether the agendas supported corporate, financial, or foreign interests, they systematically worked against the interests of the public - whom these officials swore to represent. Fears of subjugation, mistrust, and vulnerability were superimposed when Constitutional rights were retracted. And, succumbing to their own narcissism, entitlement, and dominance, tax dollars were spent frivolously and often unaccountably, which added more fears of vulnerability, mistrust, deprivation, and subjugation onto the general population.

Much of the corporate owned media has dispensed fear of mistrust by using blackouts, half-truths, lies of omission, spin, etc. onto the public. By bombarding the public with fear-inducing stories, they have imparted more vulnerability and mistrust. "Commentaries" and opinions accompanying "the facts" have manipulatively added more mistrust, vulnerability, and subjugation. Giving airtime to attractive newscasters reminded much the public of who they are not. Broadcasted, toxic pundits interrupting, belittling, and debasing their guests conditioned the public to mimic spiritual malignancy, as they emulate such offense mechanisms to project their own issues of subjugation, unlovability, deprivation, and vulnerability onto others. All the while, these pundits acted as propagandists.

Both entertainment and advertising have surreptitiously imposed every fear imaginable onto the public while simultaneously exploiting them for their corporate benefactors' profit. Along with the media, they have taught the public to handle its fears dysfunctionally by internalizing, anesthetizing, overcompensating for, and projecting them: all of which inevitably involved purchasing products and using offense mechanisms to remedy. Thus, they have, in tandem, dispensed fear to get money while teaching the public to be spiritually malignant. The money collected then goes to the tops of corporate pyramids, where it is used to lobby - to gain more power and wreak more havoc.

New technology has reinforced and magnified the use of offense mechanisms as electronic communication provided anonymity and separation, allowing for unaccountable, spiritually malignant behavior. Since many individuals now interacted with a significantly larger portion of the population, the infectious trend of spreading toxicity has been amplified. Cyber-bullying, cyber-fraud, online harassment, and mass-manipulation could be carried out will little to no compunction or accountability. The impersonalization and separateness of such communication has also led to a rise in narcissistic, entitled, and anti-social behavior, to the point where it has become the norm.

All of this has seeped into the family unit where, if the dysfunctional treatment of fears had not already been inherited, the outside world induced it. Whether this emotional mismanagement was preexistent or adopted, leaders of finance, corporations, government, and media exploited it to accumulate more money and power - to go deeper into spiritual bankruptcy.

Since dysfunction and spiritually malignancy spread throughout the general populace and permeated every known aspect of culture, it is assumed to be the norm. Any dissension is thus seen as unpatriotic.

If the culmination of fears was not directly felt when superimposed, it was internalized, diverted, overcompensated for, or projected, due the majority of the general population being raised and/or conditioned to do so. As such, many - especially those using offense mechanisms themselves - lack awareness of being manipulated, exploited, and victimized. Meanwhile, all of those above got away (and continue to get away) with it since the majority does everything except face its fears and tend to them in a healthy manner. And all of those above became more rich, exclusive, and powerful in the process.

The net results: A general population of many who, due to derivative trading, bailouts, outsourced jobs, a debt based currency system, inflation, wages not complimenting rising costs of living, incessant government spending, and endless wars, have lost their jobs, savings, homes, and loved ones. A population of many who, working stressful corporate jobs, eating unhealthy corporate-manufactured foods made with GMOs, and being conditioned to anesthetize its fears with eating and drinking, have become overweight, toxic, or ill. A population of many who, through media, advertising, and electronic communication, have been manipulated into being materialistic, wasteful, solipsistic, anti-social, narcissistic, conniving, aloof, ashamed, toxic, scapegoating, addicted, alone, entitled, misled, uninformed, misinformed, and/or spiritually malignant or bankrupt. A population of many who, forgetting about or not knowing anything different, considers all this "normal" as they do a family unit which enables, abandons, holds secrets, withholds feelings, panders to the wills of others, loves conditionally, ideologically and vocationally subjugates, and/or abuses.

Of course, there are respectful corporations, ethical bankers, benevolent CEOs, honest politicians, responsible journalists, conscientious advertisers, reputable actors, functional families, and people who will call you, visit you, and treat you in a way they would want to be treated. However, if you're old enough, think back twenty years: all of this has depleted.

So has the Golden Rule in general.

Yet, because many believe spiritual malignancy is the norm, they hold themselves (and their children) accountable for the repercussions. Because they can't sleep, can't relax, can't focus, and can't get ahead, they are anxious, depressed, and sick and swallow a pill to "take care" of it - subsequently experiencing side effects which may include dry mouth, constipation, headaches, diarrhea, heart palpitations, nausea, water retention, itching, dizziness, irritability, skin rash, chest pain, drowsiness, et al. The fear causing the malady which needed a pill is still there - it just can't be felt since it's been numbed. And, while all the fear is still there, the money used to pay for such medication and other material anesthetics no longer is. It's purchased those in high places $16 muffins.

Yes, this money has gone to the elite. Yet, instead of a pill, money and power are used to numb the pain they feel inside. But like a pill, the effects wear off to reveal the anger, angst, frustrations, depression, anxiety, and panic cropping from fears of abandonment, deprivation, subjugation, mistrust, unlovability, exclusion, vulnerability, failure, perfectionism, and entitlement. They certainly could afford a pill to cope, but what good would that inevitably do?

Regardless, the end result, by now, ought to be clear. The fear-for-power pyramidal system can be huge, or it can be small, but the projection of fear toward the bottom and the collection of wealth and power at the top does *nothing to absolve anyone within any tier of their fear. Everyone* **loses in this pyramid scheme.**

For a long time, the currency of money has been circulating with a reverse currency of fear: nobody wants it, so many pass it onto others. Nobody wants to feel or deal with it, so we project it onto others, overcompensate for it by denial or delusion, numb it with substance or activity, or adopt it into our reality so that we "adjust" to it. The very debt-based system of printing money simultaneously creates fears out of scarcity, and the additional printing of money not only inflates prices, but also the fear factor. Thus, not only has our national debt risen, but our spiritual debt as well.

It doesn't have to be this way. The currency of fear in circulation can be converted, but we cannot leave that task in the hands of our mistrusted elected officials. Since depending on them in the past has proved fruitless if not detrimental, it will certainly be the case in the future.

It is therefore up to each and every one of us to exchange the bills of fear we have been given for tokens of love. Since our whole dysfunctional system - economic, political, social, and cultural - is based on fear, *the whole game changes when we stop being fear-based consumers and start being love-based producers.*

Knowing this opportunity, there isn't just a silver lining on this dark gray storm cloud: *It's Golden.*

☥

Part II:

A Love Revolution

10

The Dharma Initiative

Starting with the Self

"Knowing others is wisdom, knowing yourself is enlightenment."

- Lao Tzu, Chinese Taoist Philosopher, in "Tao Te Ching"

The first half of this book examined how a fear-based system - comprised of the interconnected agencies of currency control, corporations, financial institutions, government, media, entertainment, and advertising - has allowed a powerful minority to derive wealth, power, and control from the majority by creating, reinforcing, and exploiting the fear within it. This was only permissible through the population's general mismanagement of fear, which caused them to accept victimhood, provide narcissistic supply, and enable entitlement. Whether such mismanagement was learned in a dysfunctional home, conditioned by a toxic society, or both, it allowed for the spiritually bankrupt few to usurp power by amassing a disproportionate amount of money. This money allowed for more power and control, which allowed for further creation of fear (and spiritual deficiency), which allowed for more victimhood, narcissistic supply, and enabling, which allow for more disproportionation - thus a vicious cycle.

Not only has this cycle been fed, yet the dispensing of fear from the top to the bottom and the public's mismanagement of this fear has to a disintegration of the Golden Rule. It has become more common for people to be greedy, entitled, spoiled, judgmental, materialistic, manipulative, deceptive, aloof, ungiving, anti-social, and self-absorbed - just like the many tiers in between and, most notably, the epicenter at the top. Through the zombie effect, the contagious properties of spiritual malignancy have caused it to spread across the nation, if not the globe, where it has become the norm - to the point of approaching spiritual bankruptcy.

Spiritual bankruptcy *always* leads to destruction.

In short, the problem the world is now facing - one that bears great potential in destroying it - is not political, economic, religious, socio-cultural, ideological, or military in nature.

These are just manifestations of a problem which, at its most basal level, is spiritual in nature. Specifically, it is *mismanaging and imposing fear, living in the ego, and violating the Golden Rule*.

As such, there are two ways to disrupt this trend. The first would require the epicenter of fear - that is, the pyramid's top - to stop producing and capitalizing on fear. Yet, since money is sought in an ego-driven manner to provide power and control over its own fears, this is unlikely - especially given the extent to which the top has relied on wealth-based power to counteract its fears. Unless the top could manage its own fears with love instead of spiritual malignancy, the avalanche of fear will continue since a foundation of fear is necessary for its survival.

The second option, naturally, would require the foundation of fear to disappear. If the general population managed its own fears with love instead of defense or, like the elite, offense mechanisms, the dysfunctional pyramid would sink. With cooperative victimhood, narcissistic supply, and enabling cut off, so too would be the money needed by the elite to amass power and control.

In the first half of the book, it was described that fear is the root of all evil, not money. Money, as mentioned before, is sought to alleviate fear. In this respect, money and self-love have something in common: they are both sought to ease the negative feelings associated with fear. While it may seem that both attempt to accomplish the same thing, only self-love is effective as a long-term solution. Money, in essence, is an artificial, man-made, ego-based, and ineffectual surrogate for self-love. Only self-love absolves us from our fears; money (or the material goods it buys) simply overrides the negative feelings of our fears, and usually does so temporarily. Self-love is also free of charge and always accessible, whereas money needs to be earned, swindled, or stolen.

Thus, the more the general population transmutes its fears which form the foundation of the dysfunction pyramid, the more the pyramid will lose its support. And, the more the public transmutes it fears into love, the more likely a new system will emerge. Instead of being based on a fear-based currency which is limited, centralized, and finite, it could be based on love, which is unlimited, abundant, and infinite.

Since a widespread deficiency in spirituality is the problem, building up our own spirituality is the solution. The more each of us does our own part, the sooner this will happen. The more people who address their fears with love, the sooner this new reality will manifest.

Since each and every one of us form the foundation of this pyramidal structure, *we need to start with ourselves first.* Not doing so can be like putting the cart in front of the horse; we can't tend to those who are sick when we ourselves are bedridden. While it is possible to tend to the needs or issues of others without taking care of our own, we are likely to burn out in the process. And, more importantly, we cannot teach something we don't know. Yet, in taking care of and transmuting our own fears, we provide to others a personified display of healthy functioning from which they can learn through interaction and by example.

So what does someone with self-love look like? As mentioned, a person with authentic self-love would need to have an inner foundation based on love, transmute any fears they may have had, and mindfully tend their emotional, physical, and psychological needs. To get an idea, it is first helpful to assign attentive perspectives to the various schemas:

Table 6:

1) **Abandonment:** At peace during times of solitude. Satisfies needs for emotional, moral support and interpersonal interaction appropriately.
2) **Deprivation:** Tends to and satisfies one's own emotional, psychological, and physical needs as needed.
3) **Subjugation:** Vocalizes/asserts one's will in a healthy, respectful manner. Self-referring.
4) **Mistrust:** Feels safe around and trusts others in one's life. Ensures and reinforces personal security.
5) **Unlovability:** Unconditional self-acceptance; accepts and likes who they are. Has confidence, self worth, and self-esteem. Self-affirming and self-approving.
6) **Exclusion:** At ease in group settings; social. Satisfies needs of inclusion, yet unafraid of accepting individuality or being different within a group. Honors individuality/being different.
7) **Vulnerability:** Content with emotional, physical, and psychological safety. Tends to and at peace with one's safety and health.
8) **Failure:** Unafraid of making mistakes, taking on challenges, striving for goals. Confident and aware of abilities, talents, and attributes.

9) Perfectionism: Content with personal aptitudes, talents, and achievements. Self-assured. Accepts and embraces personal shortcomings, limitations, and deficiencies.
10) Entitlement: Abides by rules and laws. Self-accountable.

Yet, as mentioned before, in many of our homes growing up as well as the culture in which we live, we have been conditioned in ways which impeded the above. We may have been alone at times when we needed somebody, or we may have been been excluded from others for one reason or another. Our emotional, physical, or psychological wellbeing may have been violated, or our wants and needs may have been eclipsed by those belonging to others. Whatever the case, the fears which replaced the self-loving traits listed above were compensated with defense and/or offense mechanisms.

In order for us to reclaim a self-loving state, our defense or offense mechanisms must be addressed as well as the issues behind them. Otherwise, the fears and associated negative feelings these mechanisms attempt to resist will persist if we do not acknowledge them. Not only will the fears persist, but the mechanisms which were taken on to defend us against the fears will as well. Mindfulness, as mentioned earlier, is a tool that can help us navigate our own reactions to the negative emotions which accompany fear.

Mindfulness, again, is about seeing things as they are, without trying to change them. When we observe the negative emotions that arise from a triggered schema without trying to change them, we can dissolve our reactions them. Stilling the mind allows for a more aware mindset to observe such emotions, an objective vantage point with regard to the situation, and provides us with the ability to buffer our reactions to these emotions. Thus, mindfulness can help us mediate our defense and offense mechanisms.

Mindfulness comes much more easily with meditation. Meditation and mindfulness are similar in that both involve stilling the egoic mind, raising awareness, and observing without attachment. The difference is, mindfulness is applied during moments of a schema reaction (or other moments of everyday life), whereas meditation is a regular practice and does not necessarily involve observing negative emotions.

With regular meditation practice, mindfulness comes much more easily since the mind is trained to observe without identifying, analyzing, or reacting to what is taking place. Meditation usually involves sitting in a dark, quiet room with eyes closed (some prefer them open), relaxing, allowing the mind to quiet, and simply being observant, present, and aware.

I'm sure many of us have heard ourselves and others say, "I keep telling myself..." So, if we can tell ourselves things which we can listen to...which one are we? Are we the ones who are "telling" or are we the ones listening to what we are saying? The one who is "telling" is the ego which, if observed, can be managed. The one who is listening is the same as the one observing in meditation and mindfulness; this is our *core self*. As we observe the activity of the egoic mind - or the "me" that is "telling" - it begins to quiet. Just the process of bringing our *attention* to the mental activity causes it to dissipate.

This is especially important when it comes to our fears. Simply drawing this sort of attention to fear helps to both manage it *and* alleviate it. However, getting to that point of "stillness" can be difficult who those of us who are "mental" and "live in our heads" a lot. For many of us, this is due to working demanding jobs which involve a lot of multitasking; all of that mental activity can make it difficult to slow down enough to observe what is going on. For others, this sort of high mental activity exists to divert our awareness from our inner selves. Have you ever met someone who can't stop talking? It's almost as if they cannot cope with "being in the same room" as their inner selves. Chances are, if they allowed both their inner and outer voices to stop talking, they would come into contact with the emotions and issues which the internal and external chatter served to circumvent.

For those of us who are very "mental," starting a meditation practice that involves slowing down mental activity can be like slamming on the brakes of a car traveling at eighty miles-per-hour. In this case, it is best to start off with reducing external stimuli rather than eliminating it. Techniques involving staring at a flame, focusing on breath, or focusing on relaxing one body part at a time can be helpful. In general, keeping a mindful state of mind throughout everyday life is highly beneficial.

And sometimes it is the case that such egoic activity protects us from the negative feelings that exist at a deeper level. If the negative emotions are too much to handle at once, this mental activity may be necessary. Yet, if we are to transmute our fears, it is necessary to face them. In this sense, meditation can be a proactive step in allowing our issues to surface so that we can address them. When the mental activity (incessant talking, not being able to sit still, overactive mind, etc.) quiets, the issues which were covered up by such diverting mental activity often surface. Sometimes repressed emotions or even a repressed memory will "come up." In such instances, it is best to simply release the emotion by letting it run its course. Harboring repressed negative feelings, as we will see later, can cause dis-ease in the body. Meditation brings up such emotions because the quieting of mental activity allows ourselves to become *aware* of them.

It is this very awareness that shines a light into darkness. As with our pent up or repressed issues, fears, and emotions, once light is shed on darkness, shadows can no longer exist. This isn't just true for our fears: bringing awareness and attention to any sort of toxicity - whether it belongs to us or others - makes it go away, as we will see later.

Yet, once we are able to notice the negative feelings that arise from schemas, we have greater control in how we respond to them. A person prone to slipping into docility when being subjugated can handle things differently. When in the presence of someone else who monopolizes a conversation by asserting their own ideologies or opinions as they interrupt incessantly, instead of being docile and quiet, such a person can establish a boundary by saying, "I can't have a conversation with you if you continue to interrupt me." A person with an unlovability schema now has the ability, by noticing the negative feelings associated with low self-esteem, to avoid overcompensating for their low self-worth with manufactured bravado. In these cases, noticing the schema helps to realize and honor authentic self-worth and thus self-love ("I have a will, too," "I'm okay with who I am.")

This awareness that comes with meditation and mindfulness not only increases our awareness to our schemas, but our free will as well. The "moment before" we choose to act out of fear or love - and the moment we choose to abide by or violate the Golden Rule - becomes more apparent. Consequently, dysfunctional or malignant patterns and behaviors which have become habitual to the point of being automatic become more manageable.

And, not only does the attention that comes with meditation increase our awareness to our schema reactions and free will, but perception as well. This can open a door to a whole new world as we discover intuitive and extra-sensory perception we never knew (or forgot) we had. More about this and the many other benefits of mediation will be discussed in greater detail later.

Whether or not we have issues or negative emotions covered up by mental activity, meditation is paramount for self-knowledge. We can only truly understand ourselves through objective observation, and this is key in meditation and mindfulness. Authentic self-love cannot exist unless we know who we are. Self-respect cannot exist unless we respect who we are. And, unless we know who we are, our highest selves cannot manifest.

This self-knowledge comes about since mindfulness allows us to distinguish between what we "tell ourselves about ourselves" and what is truly the case. This in itself buffers against both narcissism and low self-image. With self-love, the motto is "I love who I am" whereas with narcissism, it is "I am who I love." The difference here is that the latter bases self-concept on an egoic, mental construct ("As long as I keep telling myself that I'm sexy, smart, talented, etc., that means it's true") whereas the former sees the self for "who they are and what they are for better or for worse" through objective observation and without bias. The same is applicable to low self-worth. In this case, the person identifies with that which they are "telling themselves": "I'm no good," "Nobody loves me," "I can't trust anybody" and so forth. Although such thoughts can *affect* reality and are certainly real themselves, it does not mean that they *are* reality: reality is what is really going on. (Obvious though it might be, many accept their perception *as* reality, regardless of its departure.)

So, if we were not raised in a household or later environment which honored our needs of safety, trust, self-worth, attention, involvement, attentiveness, socialization or have not learned to do so on our on, both mindfulness and meditation are excellent tools to get us on that path. The more we understand ourselves and our reactions to fears - depression, anger, worry, resentment, anxiety, etc. - the more we become self-loving. The more we become self-loving, the less we feed a fear-based system which causes scarcity and more fear. The more this fear-based system erodes, the closer we will be to personal, national, and world peace.

Of course, whether or not we were raised or conditioned to honor self-love, anyone will find their self-love, self-respect, self-worth, and self-knowledge challenged by

168 • The Toxic States of America

spiritually malignant influences they encounter in everyday life. Therefore, ways and means of self-preservation and self-protection must be adopted in order for a person to maintain their self-love.

And, a person with self-love based on self-knowledge will have substantially more reservations against doing harm against others in comparison to someone who does not. Since the knowledge they have of their selves allows them to tend to their fears and treat them with love, violating the Golden Rule becomes impossible. Recall that spiritual malignancy - violating the Golden Rule - is based on offense mechanisms of overcompensation and projection. These offense mechanisms, as illustrated earlier, arose out of maladaptive responses to fear. A self-loving person, since they were aware of and thus tended to their fears, could not have any such fear-based mechanisms. (They would not have any internalizing or diverting defense mechanisms either.) Since they do not have any offense mechanisms to counter their fears, they cannot be spiritually malignant. Since they are not spiritually malignant, they do not violate their conscience. *They would have no need to overcompensate for or project their fears since they are no longer afflicted by them.*

As such, for a self-loving person to violate the Golden Rule would go against their own grain. Not only would they have no need to do so, it would simply feel odd and unnatural. Since they have a foundation of self-awareness and love, violating their conscience would stand out substantially more than someone who harbors fears and relies on overcompensation and projection to (mis)manage them.

As mentioned before, the most effective way to counteract fear is to shed light on it by bringing awareness to it. This is true whether the fear is within ourselves or being imposed on us by others. If someone is consistently subjugating, the fastest and most effective way to "nip it in the bud" is to call it out: if a guilt trip is being used, stating "I'm being made to feel guilty" will buck it; if favoritism is being used, the coercing of one to mimic the behavior of someone else more favored or idealized, ie., "Why can't you be more like..." or "Well, so-and-so does it," can be countered with "I'm not so-and-so." Thus, by bringing attention and awareness to malignant behavior when it occurs, we can protect ourselves. Notice that such self-preserving mechanisms are neither defensive nor offensive: rather, they are *truth mechanisms*.

Moreover, someone who is self-loving would not only find much internal resistance in violating their own conscience and use truth mechanisms for self-preservation, they would find it morally abrasive not to uphold others' wellbeing as well. For their own honor to remain intact, they would feel compelled to address instances of other persons bearing the brunt of spiritually malignant behavior. In such cases, they would shed light on the toxic behavior by bringing attention and awareness to it to preserve their own conscience and self-love.

Now that it is apparent that a self-loving person has transmuted their internal fears, has gained self-knowledge, calls out spiritually malignant behavior for preservation of self and others, and maintains a clear conscience, we can derive a clearer portrayal of this type of individual. What does a person who is self-attentive, self-knowing, self-accountable, and uses truth mechanisms - in short, self-loving - look like? Consider the following:

1) **Abandonment:** Honors and understands one's own needs for company and solitude as well as others'. Abides by empathetic, moral obligations to be present for others in times of need while maintaining their own wellbeing. Speaks out for self and others when abandoned in times of need.

2) **Deprivation:** Aware of, respectful of, and attentive to the emotional, psychological, and physical needs of self as well as others' without sacrificing own. Emotionally honest toward self and others. Mindful and considerate of one's own physical, emotional, and psychological wellbeing as well as others'. Vocalizes instances where one's own psychological, emotional, and physical needs were ignored or disregarded as well as those of others.

3) **Subjugation:** Vocalizes/asserts one's will in a healthy, respectful manner. Acknowledges, honors, and respects the wills of others. Does not subjugate, control, or dominate. Speaks out against being subjugated, controlled, or dominated. Speaks out when others are being subjugated, controlled, or dominated.

4) **Mistrust:** Trustworthy; does not violate, lie to, or manipulate others. Trusts others, yet with healthy awareness and discrimination. Does not tolerate being violated, lied to, manipulated, etc. Speaks out when others are being violated, lied to, manipulated, etc. Ensures and reinforces personal safety for self and others.

5) **Unlovability:** Accurately self-assessing. Aware, but not condemning or judgmental, of one's own flaws and shortcomings and those of others. Has confidence, self-worth, and self-esteem rooted in realistic assessment. Self-affirming and self-approving. Sees others for who they are and not what they claim to be; regards them as such. Has integrity: says what they mean and means what they say. Respects others' dignity, self-worth, and self-esteem. Stands up to being insulted, debased, belittled, etc. Stands up for others when they are insulted, debased, belittled, etc. Eschews and does not provide narcissistic supply.

6) Exclusion: Social and at ease in group settings while maintaining individuality. Honors others' individuality and being different. Includes and involves others; does not discriminate or shun without just cause. Speaks out when being excluded or ostracized. Speaks out when others are excluded or ostracized.

7) Vulnerability: Content with, tends to, and mindful of one's own emotional, physical, and psychological safety as well as others'. Addresses threats - environmental or interpersonal - against one's own or others' safety.

8) Failure: Aspires to reach a self-referring, soul-fulfilling level of success or has attained it. Encourages similar success in others while remaining respectful and caring. Unafraid of making mistakes, taking on challenges, reaching for goals. Allows others to make personal mistakes, challenges, and goals. Confident, content with, and aware of one's own abilities, talents, and aptitudes as well as others'. Does not berate self or others for not being good enough. Does not tolerate being told they are inept, not good enough, or is a failure. Does not tolerate others being told they are inept, not good enough, or failures. Does not compare oneself or others to others as a measure of inadequacy.

9) Perfectionism: Content with personal aptitudes, talents, and achievements of self and others. Self-assured. Accepts shortcomings and deficiencies of self and others. Does not tolerate insatiable or unattainable expectations of self or others. Does not hold self or others to unreasonable or insatiable standards.

10) Entitlement: Abides by rules, moral codes, and laws; self-accountable. Addresses others when they behave with entitlement, holds others accountable for disobeying or disregarding laws and rules. Does not consider oneself to be "special" nor anyone else; considers everyone to have intrinsic value and worth.

Whereas the goals of spiritual malignancy are domination by creating a willing/docile victim, reinforcing entitlement, and establishing narcissism/narcissistic supply, the goals of *spiritual wealth* are the opposite; they are: honoring freedom and wellbeing of oneself and others, ensuring that rights and rules apply to everyone, and respecting and loving oneself and others at the same time.

When considering the disparity between the two sets of goals, not only is the dichotomy of "good versus evil" apparent but, at a deeper, intellectual level, "true versus false." It is inaccurate to believe that one is more "special," is endowed with more rights and less rules, and is more powerful than others. At a fundamental, spiritual level, this is not true. Moreover, both offense and defense mechanisms cover up our truth and that of others whereas truth mechanisms reveal it.

Also on a deep, yet emotional, level arises the dichotomy of "love versus fear." The first half of this book described how dominance, entitlement, and narcissism are outcroppings of offense mechanisms, which initially arose in response to fear. The converse arises from spiritual wealth, which produces freedom, accountability, and love of self and others - which, of course, are the products of truth and truth mechanisms which arose out of love.

Getting to know You

"Verily, that which is Dharma is truth.
Therefore they say of a man who speaks truth, "He speaks the Dharma,"
or of a man who speaks the Dharma, "He speaks the Truth."
Verily, both these things are the same."
- Brihadaranyaka Upanishad, 1.4.14

In practicing mindfulness and meditation, we cultivate self-love through self-knowledge and self-awareness, which allows us to observe and address the negative feelings that arise out of contact with fear. The light which awareness brings to this fear - whether it is observing it within ourselves or bringing attention to it during our interaction with others - counteracts the negative effects of the fear. In doing so, we can maintain a clean "system" where our emotional and mental - thus spiritual - bodies are free from the anxiety, worry, anger, frustration, resentment, grief, guilt, jealousy, depression, and any fear-based negative manifestation.

The process of transmuting/converting fear through attention and awareness can be depicted as follows:

Figure 2: Wheel of Dharma

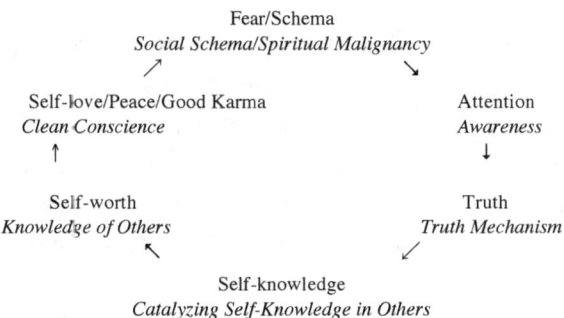

Fear/Schema
Social Schema/Spiritual Malignancy

Self-love/Peace/Good Karma   Attention
Clean Conscience   *Awareness*

Self-worth   Truth
Knowledge of Others   *Truth Mechanism*

Self-knowledge
Catalyzing Self-Knowledge in Others

This process starts when fear and its associated negative feelings are encountered. This may occur when such feelings arise during mediation/mindfulness or interactions with others (in which case, the dynamics are italicized in the diagram above.) First, attention is brought to the negative feelings (or awareness through mindfulness when the interaction is with another person.) Then, the truth which is occurring within ourselves *mentally and emotionally* is acknowledged, ie."I'm feeling sad because I'm telling myself I'm a failure" (or, if the fear is being felt in the presence of or imposed by another person, a truth mechanism is used: "I feel agitated because I'm being/I feel like I'm being subjugated right now.") Acknowledging the negative content that we are "telling ourselves" brings about self-knowledge. (And, addressing the negative content others are sending us brings their own toxicity - and, hopefully, self-knowledge - to their attention.) Knowing our own negative "mind talk" allows for it to be healed, which brings self-worth (as it will for others who, after having their own toxic behavior brought to their attention, become more aware of the fears behind their behavior and, hopefully, heal them.) Honoring our self-worth after realizing self-knowledge brings authentic self-love, since the inhibiting fear(s) have been addressed and tended to with love and compassion. Also, since fear has been transmuted into love, the prevalence of our own fear-based defense and offense mechanisms decrease, which fosters inner-peace (and a clean conscience as well, as we are less likely to hurt others. Hopefully, others who have had their spiritually malignant behavior brought to their attention will follow the same path.) And, this sense of self-love, peace, and a clean conscience will strengthen our ability to address and transmute additional schema-based fears (or spiritual malignancy) we come into contact with.

Personally, I like to refer to the above cycle as the "Wheel of Dharma." The term "dharma," used in both Hinduism and Buddhism (in Sikhism, it is known as "dharm;" in Zoroastrianism, "daena"), refers to adherence to Natural Law, or that which respects, upholds, and sustains the natural, moral, and cosmic order of the universe: which is truth, which is love, which is good. Dharma thus conveys (or is interpreted as) *the duty one has to social order, right conduct, and decent behavior; specifically, the duty one has to honor truth.*

As shown above, honoring our own truth about what it is we tell ourselves and who we truly are leads to true self-knowledge, true self-worth, and true self-love, which leads to inner peace. It thus aligns us to cosmic or universal order. Honoring the truth we experience in relation to each other not only reinforces this, but enables others to do the same. By honoring our truth, we dissolve our fears. By the dissolving our fears, we dissolve the defense the offense mechanisms which cause harm to ourselves and others, respectively. By dissolving the harm we cause ourselves and others, good dharma leads to good karma.

Karma is commonly thought of as "what goes around comes around." This is true in a sense, yet it is often thought that a certain misdeed brought against someone else will "come back" for us to experience. For example, it is thought that if someone steals from someone else, they will later experience theft. Although the potential certainly exists, this isn't necessarily the case with karma. Specifically, karma refers to the *action or deed performed in relation to our adherence or disregard to Natural Law, which results in a cycle of cause and effect* - in other words, the actions taken in relation to dharma, or truth.

Again, since the practice of dharma involves building self-love and dissipating fear through awareness, the foundation of offense and defense mechanisms which respectively cause harm to others and ourselves dissolves. The more this foundation dissolves, the more love prevails. The more prevalent love is, the more it will emanate outward from ourselves into our environment. This will inevitably effect those whom we come into contact with, which is *good* karma.

Notice that karma refers to the *action* occurring in relation to our dharma practice. "Action," in this case, is not excluded to physical behavior: *thoughts, demeanors, wishes (good or bad), and words in addition to physical undertakings are all actions in that they affect ourselves, others, and the outside world psychically, mentally, and emotionally as well as physically.* With this in mind, karma refers to the *energy* we send to ourselves and others, typically resulting from our practice (or lack thereof) of dharma. The directed *energy* in our actions - our thoughts, demeanors, words, etc. - is our karma.

During my acting training, one of the best pieces of advice I received regarding how to "land my lines" on another actor was to focus on how I wanted to make them feel. The literal content of the lines was one thing, but the intent of the words and how they were delivered could mean something completely different. In both acting and real life, we add energy to words - to make someone else feel loved, guilty, ashamed, safe, threatened, etc. In real life, that energy is representative of our karma.

As described, the more dharma - or acknowledgement of truth - is practiced, the more loving we will be to ourselves and others. This is likely to influence our karma for the better. Conversely, the less dharma is practiced, the resulting lack of truth we shed on our fears enables them to thrive, which results in defense and offense mechanisms that cause harm to ourselves and/or others. This, of course, leads to bad karma.

Since karma is directed energy, we concurrently give out ours and receive others'. Not only do we affect others positively or negatively with our karma, we are affected by others' karma to some extent or another. In this sense, we are all connected. Yet, because we have free will to acknowledge our own truth and can manage our own personal energy, we have domain over our own dharma and karma, respectively. In this sense, we are separate and self-accountable.

By practicing good dharma and karma, we reap spiritual wealth. The benefits of spiritual wealth are plenty: self-awareness and self-knowledge not only dissolves our fears and creates self-love, it helps us to create a life which can bring happiness and self-fulfillment in our relationships, vocations, and activities. Positive karma creates harmony within our lives and, as we will see, good health. Spiritual wealth, as we will see later, brings a host of other benefits as well - to the point of experiencing an entirely new and wonderful existence.

Since we are, to some degree or another, affected by the karma of others, we can unwittingly absorb their negative energy. This is not just the case with bearing the brunt of others' offense mechanisms, but being in the presence of (and usually receiving) others' anger, depression, anxiety, fear, worry, animosity, etc. whether accompanied by words or other actions. In this case, the energy is transferred emotionally. The negative karma we absorb may even come in the more insidious form of what is known as a "psychic attack," where we absorb the negativity someone is psychically sending to us, as when someone wishes us harm. As such, the ways and means of some toxic people in our lives may be less noticeable. We may feel drained by them without readily perceiving the reasons behind feeling sapped. Of course, the opposite is true: we also experience the loving energy emanating and the "good vibes" sent from others emotionally and psychically.

Whether the karma we absorb from others (as well as our own) is negative or positive, the effects can and will be felt psychically, emotionally, mentally, and physically - regardless of the way in which it was received. Therefore, karma invariably affects our mind, body and spirit since all are interrelated.

However, the "negative" emotions affecting karma arise when the intrinsic and natural foundation of self-love is challenged - and this is *fear*. Derivative emotions with respect to fear and love are grief, anger, and envy. Grief is the emotion we experience when we lose something or someone we love; it allows us to emotionally recognize the loss of love. We feel anger when we are treated in ways in which we are not loved or do not like to be treated; it teach us to say, "No." Envy is experienced when someone else has something we love but don't have; it teaches us to aspire. Fear, in essence, is the absence of love. The repressed emotions of grief, anger, envy, and fear give rise to depression, rage, jealously/obsession, and panic/paranoia, respectively.

Thus, love and fear are akin to being to sides of the same coin.

These emotions - in fact, every emotion - will impact our physical being. However, if our negative karma - whether a product of a lack of awareness, a repetitively "bad" attitude, or exposure to others' negative karma - is not tended to, the effects it can have on the mind, body, and spirit, can be detrimental. If consistently experienced, the negative feelings of anger, grief, fear, and envy - and especially their repressed manifestations of rage, depression, panic, and jealousy - can lead to dis-ease. People who are depressed or stressed out tend to get sick more often, and those who are angry or anxious often have high-blood pressure. People who are happy tend to be more energetic, and those who are in love have a certain "glow" about them and feel healthy.

An interesting set of experiments designed to observe the effects of psychic energy on matter was conducted by Dr. Masaru Emoto and David Sereda. As detailed in *The Message from Water*, different mental stimuli were directed to samples of water through prayer, blessings from a monk, or labeling its container with an emotion-inspiring word or phrase, such a "chi of love" and "thank you." Photographing the resulting crystals, in comparison to the control water samples, yielded structures which were noticeably more ornate and beautiful. The crystals from water samples subjective to negative thoughts or words appeared more haphazard and aesthetically unattractive. Considering the amount of water within the human body, one can imagine the effects of karma on the individual.

Since both dis-ease and health are influenced by the energy of the spirit-body which inevitably affects the physical, meditation and mindfulness can do wonders in converting fear-based negative energy into love-based positive. Moreover, repressed emotions of anger, envy, grief, and fear (and their repressed, enhanced versions of rage, jealousy, depression, and panic) can lodge within our physical bodies, wreaking havoc on our health.

I want to make it very clear that, although it is good to remain as impenetrable to negative energy as much as possible, this is absolutely not to suggest that we should not feel the feelings of fear, anger, grief, envy and their derivatives when they arise and address and/or express them accordingly. Life circumstances and others' toxic behaviors are likely to conjure anger, frustration, fear, grief, and other negative emotions. When someone berates or steals from us, we are certain to feel hurt and anger. Quite possibly the worst thing to do is to override strong feelings by going into some sort of "happy place." Not only will this energy in the form of anger be stored in the system (as we will see in the next chapter) and potentially cause dis-ease, but this is an excellent way to become deluded. Imagine someone getting punched in the face and giggling in return. We're human and the emotions we feel - good or bad - connect us to our humanity and our hearts. Not honoring the negative energy we receive by avoiding the relative emotions is likely to stockpile negative energy within us since it is not released.

However, the idea that our attitudes are the sole determining factors affecting our happiness has become increasingly prevalent in recent years. Many have come to believe that illness, misfortune, failure, financial strain, joblessness, or any other affliction is a product of a bad attitude and that, somehow, the individual is at fault when they face such distress in their lives. That is, if the person just had a better attitude, things would "go better" in their lives. While our thoughts and attitudes certainly affect our reality, they are not the sole cause of it. Such belief systems disregard the fact the many of the misfortunes and distressing circumstances we face are the product of others' free will and, consequently, exonerates them from their spiritually malignant behavior. The following quote by author and Pulitzer Prize-winning journalist Chris Hedges summarizes this well:

> *"Those who fail to exhibit positive attitudes, no matter the external reality, are seen as maladjusted and in need of assistance. Their attitudes need correction. Once we adopt an upbeat vision of reality, positive things will happen. This belief encourages us to flee from reality when reality does not elicit positive feelings. These specialists in "happiness" have formulated something they call the 'Law of Attraction.' It argues that we attract those things in life, whether it is money, relationships or employment, which we focus on. Suddenly, abused and battered wives or children, the unemployed, the depressed and mentally ill, the illiterate, the lonely, those grieving for lost loved ones, those crushed by poverty, the terminally ill, those fighting with addictions, those suffering from trauma, those trapped in menial and poorly paid jobs, those whose homes are in foreclosure or who are filing for bankruptcy because they cannot pay their medical bills, are to blame for their negativity. The ideology justifies the cruelty of unfettered capitalism, shifting the blame from the power elite to those they oppress. And many of us have internalized this pernicious message, which in times of difficulty leads to personal despair, passivity and disillusionment."*

Also, many are of the belief that we choose our tribulations prior to our incarnations as human beings. Although this belief can be useful in establishing some context of our lives, this, like the previous belief, completely eradicates the notion of free will - provided the condition is not congenital in nature. Whether or not we chose to be born to a certain set of parents, hired by a certain employer, or born in a certain place and time, this does not absolve the parents' choice to be abusive, a boss' choice to engage in toxic behavior, or a political system's collective decision to become corrupt and despotic. That is not to say that there is nothing *to learn* from such dynamics: whatever conditions we face in our lives - negative or positive - teaches us something of value. Yet, oftentimes, spiritually malignant behavior is practiced because the person believes they can get away with it. The lesson to learn in such cases is to remind the malignant that they have a conscience and ought not to.

While I personally believe the "Law of Attraction" has value, interpretations of such doctrines can ignore the existence of free will in others and inhibit accountability. While we are responsible for our own happiness or unhappiness, we are not responsible for *all* the happiness or unhappiness we encounter. Much of the unhappiness we face is a result of others' free will, usually in the form of toxic behavior. A person who feels unhappy after being robbed did not create their unhappiness nor are they responsible for it. The robber created the unhappiness and is certainly responsible for it since the robber *chose to* steal, regardless of the potential of some sort of pre-life agreement the two parties might have had. However, the person who was robbed *is* now responsible for tending to and healing their unhappiness of being robbed, whatever that might entail. So, although the person is not responsible for the onset of the unhappiness, he is responsible for converting or dissolving it for his own wellbeing and thus happiness.

Likewise, much of the negative energy (or karma) we take on is not our own creation, yet we are ultimately responsible for transmuting it. Whether the negative energy we have harbored is a byproduct of unattended fears or absorbing others' negative energy, it is vital for our emotional, mental, spiritual, and physical wellbeing that we tend to it. Also, in order to be a positive, helpful influence to others, we need to prioritize this first before assisting others. Fortunately, in addition to meditation and mindfulness, there are other ways for us to "detox" from this negative energy.

‡

11

The Fear Detox/Karma Cleanse

*"Let's not forget that the little emotions
are the great captains of our lives and
we obey them without realizing it."*

- Vincent Van Gogh

The previous chapter touched upon ways in which karmic energy can influence our physical, emotional, and mental health. This usually happens simultaneously as the states of wellbeing of the mind, body, and spirit are all interconnected. Anyone who has stubbed their toe or had an earache knows they didn't feel happiness or bliss as a result. Or, anyone who has had a severe cold or flu knows it is more difficult to concentrate than when they are healthy. And, anyone who has left a toxic relationship or work environment, I'm sure, has felt happier, healthier, and more energetic.

Since negative energy affects our mental, physical, emotional, and spiritual health - and each one of these affects the others - the methods for clearing out the negative energy in our system can be based on the mind, the body, or the spirit. Although the methods described below will be based on one of the three, they will tend to influence all of them. And, while healing all three is the goal, you may choose one type of method over another on the basis of the area which needs to be tended to the most. The good thing is, we can start with whichever area is most appropriate for us at the time.

Meditation:

It was previously described how meditation and mindfulness can dissolve our reactions to the negative feelings and emotions associated with our schemas. The attention we give to our negative feelings not only helps us manage our reactions to schemas, but helps dissolve them as well. When we observe and honor our truth, our dharma improves, and this influences our karma for the better. Not only does meditation assist in all this, the calmness and relaxation which it brings affects our physical bodies. The stress-based tension we hold in our muscles starts to relax, affecting our circulation and blood pressure. We may even start to appear and feel younger and healthier with sustained practice.

The focused, though relaxed, awareness of meditation also sharpens the mind. As our mental processes slow down in our focus, we are mentally and physically prepared to address any negativity the overactive mind and physical tension shielded from our attention. Thus, our ability to now be attentive to our negative thoughts and emotions allows us to manage and heal them.

In addition, memory recall heightens. The calm, relaxed state helps repair neurological pathways, and often causes us to remember or recall events in our past which we had not thought about for years. These past events may be as innocuous as remembering a toy we used to play with, or they may involve some past trauma. If the memory involves the recall of some emotional pain, we now have the ability to tend to the repressed emotions as they surface. In this sense, meditation can help clear any embedded, unwanted emotions which we have stored for years. With such emotions cleared, we feel lighter, more alert, and carefree. The clearing of stored emotions may also alleviate some recurring physical condition we have; it may even cure it completely.

As mentioned during the beginning of this book, routine practice of meditation has a physiological effect on the brain. Meditation increases grey matter density in certain areas of the brain, which enhances learning (in addition to memory), emotional regulation, self-referential processing, and perspective. The gyrification or "folding" of the cortex which occurs as a result of routine meditation allows the brain to process information faster.

The one side-effect which may be experienced initially are headaches. I would assume this is due to the physiological changes taking place in the brain. If headaches are experienced at the beginning, they will subside over time.

Guided Meditation/Self-Hypnosis:

For those of us with overactive minds and new to meditation, guided meditations and self-hypnosis are excellent places to start. Both can be helpful in both slowing mental activity and stress reduction. There are a variety of techniques which can be used for guided meditations. One is autogenics, which involves the practicer imagining their limbs and body parts relaxing, becoming warm, or becoming light, etc. one at a time. Another technique involves repeating and focusing on a soothing word or phrase (or what is known as a mantra) in one's mind. Focusing on breath is another technique.

With *guided imagery*, the practicer imagines or is guiding through a calm, soothing scene, such as walking through a garden, on a beach, or through a forest as they visualize the environment, feel the air on their skin, and smell the fragrance of the air. Not only does guided meditation relieve stress and overactive mental activity, it can help improve our karma. Even though the calming energy is induced by imagination, its positivity compensates for any negative energy which may be in our system. Those who come out of a guided meditation session feel calm, refreshed, and rejuvenated.

Also, guided meditations can be of great help in developing the psychic senses. Developing the senses of sight, hearing, touch, smell, taste, and emotion on an imaginary level improves and strengthens our ability to sense messages of the same medium when they are "inspired" through intuition. Many mediums I know will visualize different fruits or vegetables just to keep their clairvoyance sharp. Also, it helps to distinguish between imagination and inspiration, which is vital in understanding which impressions are psychically received rather than imagined.

Self-hypnosis using *creative visualization* is an excellent technique used for stress management as well as manifesting positive personal or lifestyle changes and build up our own energy. The principle behind this is using thoughts in a productive manner to affect reality. Like guided imagery, the practicer will visualize a scene. The difference is, the scene is something they would like to manifest in their lives. They may envision a party if they wish to increase their social contact, or they may picture themselves delivering a wonderful speech if they wish to improve their public speaking. Just like guided imagery, the practicer sees, feels, hears, and creates the atmosphere they wish to experience. And, the more they feel their wishes energetically - or, the more it is karmically realized - the more the scene permeates the practicer's existence.

Reparenting:

For those of us who have had dysfunctional upbringings or early traumatic, abusive experiences, reparenting is an excellent, proactive tool to heal the wounds from our early years. If we didn't like the way we were raised, reparenting provides us with the opportunity to do the job as we needed back then: if it wasn't done right the first time, we can self-customize and do it right the second time. Since nobody could know us better than ourselves, the job done a second time can deeply and effectively compensate for the "mistakes."

With reparenting, we revisit the moments in our early years where we were abandoned, made to feel guilty for something that wasn't our fault, violated in some way, or any instance where we were hurt, harmed, or mistreated. The purpose is not to re-open wounds, assign blame, reinforce victimhood, or reinvent history: it is to emotionally tend to the fears our "child-selves" experienced during the episode. As we revisit these painful scenes, we provide the child with what they needed emotionally. If we were abandoned, we make sure we are present for the child and ask what they need and ensure the child they are loved. If they are told they are "no good," we send them the message that they are lovable just the way they are. We may even introduce our "adult self" in the scene. If our child-self is being abused verbally, psychologically, or physically, our adult self may step in the scene between the abuser and the child, admonishing the violator as we protect and care for the child who is being victimized.

Since reparenting involves healing the early moments when we learned to respond to fears in maladaptive ways, this sort of reconditioning helps to dissolve our current defense and offense mechanisms originally adopted to cope with them. Thus, if we had been accustomed to inflate our ego during times when we felt unlovable or unsuccessful, this will become less likely to occur (or substantially diminished) with this sort of practice. If we were prone to slip into self-pity during times when we needed someone, this too will become less likely. Since we have proactively addressed the schemas when they manifested during the original episodes from our past, they will affect our present and future much less.

Because of this sort of "deep cleansing" of our wounds from the past, we excise the negative emotions which have been harbored for years - and this may involve a good deal of emotional release. Yet, by absolving this emotional "freight and baggage" at an energetic level, we will feel the effects physically. Years ago, on a popular daytime talk show syndicate, the topic of the day was about "aging brilliantly." Prior to watching this episode, I was considering reparenting on my own intuition, yet this show confirmed my instincts. One of the guests mentioned that, in addition to walking regularly and eating healthy, she decided years ago that she did not like the way she was parented, so she combed through her earlier life and reparented herself. This woman, over seventy years old, appeared to be in her mid-forties - literally almost half her age.

Reparenting need not only be applied to earlier moments when we were not treated with the love we needed from our parents. Tending to our younger selves during any sort of traumatic or painful experience which may have occurred outside the home can also be accomplished by reparenting. Also, we can revisit *any* stage in our life when we experienced trauma or abuse and tend to any emotional issues which were not healed at the time. Whatever the case, reparenting is an excellent, assertive method for "clearing house." In time, attitudes, self-knowledge, self-worth, and physical health will all improve with the practice of reparenting.

Therapy, Self-help, and Understanding Dysfunctional Family Role:

One of the most unfortunate stigmas present in our culture is that against therapy. Many people avoid seeking help or assistance from a professional to protect their pride, as they are afraid of being seen as weak or "crazy" or feel that "nothing is wrong" with them. Ironically, a person who is truly crazy will not know that they are crazy and will therefore not seek help.

Not benefitting from therapy, to me, is like saying that some people would not benefit from practicing yoga. I have yet to meet anyone, regardless of their experience, who would not benefit from regular yoga practice. Everyone - whether they are a beginner or teacher - benefits from doing yoga. It is when a yoga practice is ceased that liabilities begin.

Therapy is no different. Whereas yoga addresses the stressed areas of our bodies, therapy addresses the stressed areas of our souls. While yoga stretches our bodies and breathes oxygen into areas in which we carry stress, therapy stretches our emotional selves and brings awareness to the areas in which we carry anxiety, sorrow, anger, or any fear-based emotion. Therapy is therefore like yoga for the soul: to say that no one would benefit from therapy is akin to saying that no one would benefit from yoga. And, like yoga, once we stop the practice is when problems start to arise. When we stop practicing yoga, our bodies store toxins and become stress ridden, leaving us susceptible to physical illness which will affect our whole being. When we stop practicing therapy, our emotional selves store toxicity and stress as well, leaving us susceptible to mental un-health which will affect our whole being. Like yoga, I have yet to meet anyone - whether they are a beginner or a professional - who would not benefit from therapy. The very fact that it has been stigmatized has reinforced spiritual deficiency, emotional rigidness, and a lack of self-knowledge within the general population: no one benefits from this.

Like yoga, is it possible to practice self-psychoanalysis independently once a foundation of understanding is laid. While it is helpful to have a professional and objective observer during practice (like it is having a yoga instructor), some of us have financial or time constraints. In this case, many excellent books have been written - and many which include individual exercises - which allows someone to work on their own and at a pace which is convenient for them. The other benefit to independent self-care is that it can help to avoid professionals who are incompetent. Just like any profession, there are some professionals who are excellent and some who are not. If outside assistance is preferred, a recommendation from a trusted and respected friend who has sought therapy is highly beneficial.

Many books and professionals focus on childhood-origin issues, similar to reparenting. In this case, not only can we gain insight into the origins of our schemas, but we can obtain a better idea of our own "role" within a dysfunctional family. Understanding our dysfunctional role can further assist with healing as the personal needs we had be taught to abdicate and the expectations imposed on us during our early years become more apparent.

Whether independent, one-on-one with a professional, or in a group setting, therapy brings awareness to our issues. In each case, the goal is the same: to bring our attention to our emotional "tight spots" so they can be eased through awareness.

Venting/Support System:

Many of us, regardless of our upbringing, will face trying moments during the course of daily life. Whether these emotionally taxing moments are due to toxic personalities or the trials and tribulations we encounter through life, just having someone to talk to is therapeutic.

By venting our fears, anger, frustrations, and sorrow, we release the pressure valve on our hearts and feel better afterward. As mentioned before, holding onto such negative emotions can be toxic and, if stockpiled enough, can lead to dis-ease.

Many people feel "guilty" if they vent, feeling that they're being "negative" and a burden on the listener. However, the alternative - to keep the fear, anger, and grief inside - is likely to repress such negative emotions to the point where they manifest panic, rage, and depression. Worse, they may take the form of offense mechanisms, if not dis-ease. In any case, not allowing the release of these emotions will negatively affect both oneself and others.

Choosing dependable support systems involves some discernment as well, as they require sympathy and compassion: unfortunately, not everyone has these qualities. Some people view anything "negative" as bad and something to avoid. These types - since they avoid acknowledging and tending to uncomfortable emotions at all costs, including their own issues - are usually not the best to rely on. It is likely that their own unaddressed schemas and negative feelings have caused them to be toxic and lacking in self-knowledge themselves. Such people will eschew anything "negative" - whether it's venting or news they do not want to hear - even if it involves information which requires their attention for their own safety and best interests. They don't want to hear about their "house being on fire"; they prefer an alternate reality to remain intact. Their repetitive denial of (or overcompensation for) the negative things occurring within and outside themselves will, unfortunately, cause their house to burn down. No one will be a viable support system if they can't even acknowledge that their own "house" is on fire. If they do not show themselves sympathy and compassion when they need it, they won't with you.

Therefore, it is best to seek out those who understand that dealing with problems often includes talking about them, even if it is just at an emotional level. Besides, such people will sympathize with the need to have a listening ear. If they truly love and care about you (as they do about themselves), they will be there for you when you need someone to listen.

Personally, I love being there for other people when they need to vent. Being able to help someone feel better, to me, is one of the most spiritually fulfilling things anyone can do. It's a win-win situation: the other person feels better, and we feel good for helping them.

Of course, we must avoid using venting as a "crutch" and set boundaries with others to do the same. At some point, venting about the same issue over and over again stops being therapeutic and becomes codependent as the venter is enabled. Repetitively expressing their negative feelings about the same situation becomes their "solution" to the problem instead of addressing the problem itself. Thus, the venters' problem continues to bring them unhappiness as the listener becomes exasperated and drained.

Also, a distinction needs to be made between venting and gossiping. Venting involves a person expressing emotional distress after the Golden Rule has been violated against them. Gossiping involves broadcasting another person in a negative light when the other party did no harm. Whereas venting is healing, gossiping is toxic: the person superficially (and ineffectively) makes themselves feel better by putting someone else down or placing themselves above them. Since the other person is absent, gossiping as also quite cowardly. Many of those who gossip will exonerate their behavior since the other party cannot hear what is being said. The other party may not be able to hear the words but, on a sublime and energetic level, the are likely to feel it, even though they may not be fully cognizant of what is occurring.

But, with venting, saying a person shouldn't feel or express negative feelings when they have been hurt is like saying a person shouldn't feel pain or scream when they are burned: it's heartless. Being a good listener when someone needs to vent, to me, is following the Golden Rule: all of us would like to have someone to be emotionally available when we need them, so, if we can, we ought to avail ourselves to others when they need us.

Journal Keeping:

Another exercise - and one which has gained popularity in recent years - is keeping what is known as a "gratitude journal." With this practice, five things are written down everyday for which one is grateful for in their lives - be it a good friend, good health, recent success, etc. This is a great practice in that it boosts our energy and allows us to acknowledge the positive aspect of of lives.

In addition to logging sources of gratitude is to list five things to manifest in life, be it a more active social life, better health, a more satisfying career, etc. The purpose is not to focus on what we lack, but to *feel* our wish list into being. If we want to have more close friendships, it is best to *feel* these relationships as we write them down. This is an exercise of karma at its basal level: as we cultivate this energy within, we will inevitably emanate it outwardly, attracting those who gravitate to that energy.

Also a good practice is writing down five things which had "blown our fuses" during the course of the day. By looking at the day in retrospect and writing down moments when we felt anxious, nervous, frustrated, angered, etc., we can use hindsight to reexamine these episodes with a more clear, objective, and rational mind. Doing so helps us to gain insight to our own emotional patterns and reactions. If we weren't successful in applying mindfulness at the time, we can go back to assess these situations and cultivate self-knowledge.

Self-praise journaling is another great practice. Because many of us can be our own worst critic, taking some time to reflect on the day and positively reinforce the good things we've done is an excellent morale booster. It also keeps us acquainted with our highest selves.

Journal keeping is an excellent alternative for those facing time constraints which inhibit more intensive therapeutic methods. And, if five items can be written down for each of the above categories, the improved energetic effects will be felt over time. The things we are grateful for, proud of, and wish for will develop good karma, while the awareness we bring to negative karma helps to convert it into positive. This helps us understand that we learn from both the things we do right and our mistakes. This sort of journal keeping not only accentuates the positive and coverts negative into positive, it helps us track our progression.

Diet:

The adage "you are what you eat" not only applies to our physical bodies, but our mental, emotional, and spiritual health as well. Since the body, mind, and emotion are interconnected to such a appreciable extent, the food we ingest will invariably affect our overall wellbeing.

I am sure everyone can relate to this to some extent or another. Anyone who has consumed a good deal of sugar or caffeine knows the sudden rush of energy followed by a "crash." We are likely to be mentally or emotionally stimulated at first as a result, only to feel sapped a few hours later.

Just like our own physical bodies, food has its own energy. The energy of the food we consume, in turn, affects our own energy, for better or for worse. Therefore, to maintain optimal mental and emotional health, it is important to consume foods which reinforce it on a physical level.

Maintaining a healthy diet is becoming increasingly difficult for many with the greater prevalence of processed foods, pesticide use, genetically modified organisms (GMOs) and seeds, fast food, etc. Many of us are often pressed for time and need to grab a "quick bite" which usually does not involve food which is necessarily healthy. Some of us gravitate to "comfort food" as a means of anesthetizing or diverting our attention from our emotional issues. Still, others may feel they simply cannot afford the higher cost of healthier foods during these difficult economic times.

There are solutions to all of these dilemmas and usually just involve some lifestyle changes and developing new habits. If we feel strapped for time, it may simply be the case that some pre-planning is needed. Before we start our day, we may need to remind ourselves to bring some healthy fruits or snacks along with us. If we tend to cave into comfort foods, examining the issues behind the tendencies would probably be a better place to start. If we cannot afford healthier foods, we may just need to reassess what is available to us or recalibrate our spending in other areas of our lives.

We can only do our best with establishing a healthy diet yet, the better we do, the better we will feel physically, mentally, and emotionally.

Yoga:

While any exercise - provided its not overly strenuous on the body - is good for our overall health, yoga is an excellent practice in that it incorporates mental and spiritual discipline in addition to physical exercise. In this sense, yoga as exercise is in a class of its own in that detoxes our entire system, not just our body.

The term "yoga" encompasses many types of practices, which can be mentally, spiritually, or physically based. In western culture, yoga tends to pertain to the physical practice with some basis in Hatha yoga, which focuses on asanas (body positions), breathing, a quiet, focused mind, and - most importantly, remaining outside of the ego. The most prevalent schools are Iyengar Yoga, Ashtanga Vinyasa (or "Power") Yoga, and Viniyoga.

As the body experiences the various asanas, deep breathing and attention allows areas of physical stress to be oxygenated and dissolved. Subsequently, and since the body tends to become warm during a yoga practice, stored toxins are released. Those who practice yoga feel healthy, relaxed, calm, and focused as a result.

Sometimes, the emotions stored in our bodies are released during a yoga practice. It is sometimes the case that a person may start to cry or experience a surge of anger as they breathe into certain areas of the body that tend to store stress. Other times, a repressed memory may even accompany the release of such emotions. When this occurs, not only is the body cleansed of physical toxins, but emotional and mental ones as well. Thus, not only does yoga benefit the body, but the clearing of negative energy at the physical level also detoxifies the mind and the spirit. And, since our own energy - our karma - affects our body, this symbiotic, psychosomatic relationship is natural. Since the body is cleansed and strengthened, so too will be the spirit.

190 The Toxic States of America

Amanae:

If any proof is needed to verify that the body stores repressed emotions, look no further than Amanae. Founded by Christine Day in 1987, Amanae is a hands-on bodywork technique that focuses on releasing physically stored and repressed emotions. In my opinion, Amanae is one of the best kept secrets of today; hopefully, it will become less of a secret in the future.

I first learned about Amanae several years ago when I had met someone in passing who recently had his first Amanae treatment. He told me about this type of massage he had just received that caused him to release an enormous amount of repressed emotions. After the practitioner pressed on certain areas of his chest, he told me, he started to scream, cry, roar, laugh - in short, release all of these pent up emotions which just sort of "came out." He emphasized that, afterward, he felt like he was on cloud nine and that this feeling lasted a few days.

Having been a firm believer in psychosomatic relationships for a while, I was intrigued by this and decided to give it a try. I met with a practitioner who, like the man I had met, worked on my heart area. My experience was identical. After getting on the massage table and laying on my back, the practitioner gently pressed one of his fingers on the middle of my chest bone and began to move it around a bit. He soon asked me if I could feel a slight pinch (which I confirmed) and informed me that the pinch indicated a channel which had been closed. After instructing me to breathe deeply through my mouth into the "pinch", it wasn't too long before the emotions blocking the channel began to emerge. Before I knew it, I began to scream, yell, sob, laugh, shout - all of the emotions I had held onto were being liberated as I found myself heaving into my chest, which only released more of the stored emotions.

I couldn't believe all that I held onto. I also couldn't believe how good it felt to get all of that "off my chest" - literally. Although I felt spent and a bit light-headed immediately afterward, I felt a strange calmness. And, like the man I had met, I felt amazing the next day and the week following. I literally felt lighter to the point where I felt weightless - like I could float off into the air at any given point. This profound experience cinched it for me: we store emotions in our bodies and, after we honor and release them, we feel exceptional.

As mentioned before, Amanae is a fairly young practice, so locating a practitioner in your area may not be a possibility. However, if the opportunity is available, Amanae is an exceptional method to emotionally detox. When negative, pent up emotions are released, the effects they had on the body subside. With renewed emotional and mental clarity, Amanae allows for better karma and feeling physically amazing as well.

Reiki:

Like Amanae, Reiki is a hands-on healing technique. Yet, instead of involving any sort of pressure or massage, Reiki is a technique in which the healer introduces "ki" (also known as "chi" in Chinese) into the body of the recipient.

This ancient system of hands-on healing was sought out during the mid-nineteenth century by Mikao Usui, believed to have been a Christian minister and principal of the Doshisha University in Kyoto, Japan. After taking residence in a Zen Buddhist monastery, he translated ancient texts describing this healing method from their original Sanskrit. Because the material did not reveal the ways in which this healing energy was activated, Usui set off on a three week period of meditation, fasting, and prayer on Mount Koriyama in 1922 in order to uncover greater understanding. It was at the end of this twenty-one day retreat that the information regarding this ancient healing method was revealed. Since then, Reiki has been passed on to others as they receive "attunements" to practice on others. Today, this ancient healing art has become more widespread.

About a decade ago, the gym I had enrolled with was offering free Reiki sessions to its members. Having heard a bit about Reiki, I decided to experience it for myself. At the time, I was feeling a lot of stress due to a number of changes - a new job, a new living situation, and a new relationship - within a short period of time. As a result, I was feeling severe stress pains in my neck and shoulders.

The session I had with the practitioner lasted for about an hour. After the session started, I soon found myself very relaxed, yet I noticed that the practitioner's hands became very warm. I could also feel energy seeping into the areas where I had felt stress;

this is hard to describe, but it felt like a tingling warmth permeating through my body. As the session progressed, I found myself becoming more and more relaxed - to the point where I felt like I was in a trance and lost my sense of time.

When I returned home, I felt incredibly relaxed. Oddly, and much to my surprise, I had a strange emotional release: it was like I was experiencing the *release* of my emotions without exactly *feeling* them, almost like I had an objective perspective on my emotional release. I wasn't feeling grief or sadness, yet I was crying. I decided to just let things take their course and release the emotions as needed.

After this release, all the pain stored in my neck and shoulders had gone. The resulting relaxation allowed for one of the most restful night's sleep I've ever had. And, the next morning, I felt amazing. The emotional weight on my shoulders had been lifted and I felt completely rejuvenated.

Since then, I have become attuned as a Reiki Master/Teacher. I know much skepticism surrounds Reiki, and I can certainly understand any doubts others might have. Personally, since my second attunement (there are three), I've had various experiences which have been both profound and surprising. Yet, I would never suggest that anyone accept anything without some discernment; I believe a certain degree of skepticism is both healthy and wise. However, there is a difference between being skeptic and formulating an opinion without any kind of exposure or experience. I truly believe if one is to be convinced one way or another of the healing power of Reiki, they must at least receive it once.

Much of the skepticism is rooted in the lack of scientific evidence regarding the effectiveness of Reiki. This, unfortunately, will continue to be difficult to resolve since such empirical evidence requires the need of a realistic placebo. Also, the healing method is based on chi or universal life energy, which in itself has not been verified by science. Other healing methods such as acupuncture or practices such as Tai Chi are based in increasing the *flow* of chi within the body, yet that cannot be proven either. Also, since Reiki involves channeling this mysterious life energy, the results are not always the same: sometimes the healing may be physical, psychological/spiritual, or mental or any combination - and such variables can be difficult to measure. However, simply because we cannot measure or calibrate chi does not mean that it can't be perceived and doesn't exist.

It is also worth mentioning that we cannot quantitatively or qualitatively measure the negative energy we receive from others who are toxic or spiritually malignant, but we can certainly experience its effects on a emotional, mental, or even a physical level. We also can't measure the surge in positive energy we feel around others who liven us up, for that matter.

Regardless of the lack of proof or means to assess its effects, Reiki, for those who are interested, is a remarkable method which heals the negative energy we may have stored in our system.

Nature Walks:

Taking walks - even if it is on a treadmill - is great exercise, yet when we walk in areas of nature, we immerse ourselves in a special kind of energy. Whether you believe nature was created by God, "the Universe," or evolution (or any combination thereof), simply being in the presence of this energy is soothing and rejuvenating. Since all of us are creations of nature, we reconnect with this powerful, primordial essence and absorb its energy.

Many of us can relate to this. Whether it is taking a path through a forest, hiking along a mountainside, or walking along a beach, there is something calming and even cleansing about reconnecting with nature. Since everything (including ourselves) is energy, we take in the grounding, nourishing, and revitalizing energy nature produces. As we walk through nature (or swim, if in a lake or an ocean), we gain clarity and insight into our own nature and our lives.

Taking nature walks is a great way to decompress and reunite with the same essence which gave us life. Like a child bonding with her mother, taking time to revisit areas of natural growth and scenery is like bonding with our Mother. It helps us reconnect with who we really are. Absorbing and embracing her energy inevitably affects ours, so this is a wonderful way to replenish and cleanse our own energy.

Chakra Cleanse:

When we absorb the negative energy of others, it can collect in various energetic regions of our bodies known as chakras. The concept of chakras originated in the Hindu and Buddhist traditions and, although they may be correlated to a particular gland or organ, are thought to be a part of our subtle or spiritual bodies. It is believed that blockages or imbalances of these chakras give rise to physical or emotional illness and that "cleansing" our chakras alleviates such distress and restores physical and emotional well-being.

There are multiple chakras, yet the seven chakra system is typically the one followed in a chakra cleanse. With a chakra cleanse, any negative energy which has been stored in each of the energy centers is cleared, usually through a visualization technique similar to a guided meditation.

The first chakra is known as the Root Chakra, which is located at the base of the spine. It is associated with the color red and influences our basic instincts and influences - including those of survival - as well as issues of sexuality, stability, sensuality, and security. Physically, it is related to the gonads and the adrenal medulla.

The second or Sacral Chakra is located just below the navel and is associated with the color orange. The key issues involved with this chakra deal with basic emotional needs, relationships, addictions, self-gratification, and pleasure. It is correlated to the testes and the ovaries.

The Solar Plexus Chakra, the third chakra, is situated at the base of the rib cage. It is associated with the color yellow and involves personal power, self-control, issues of self-acceptance, opinion formation, and anxiety. This chakra is related to metabolic, nervous, and digestive systems; physically, it affects the muscles, stomach, pancreas, adrenal glands, liver, and gallbladder.

The fourth or Heart Chakra is located at the center of the chest and is associated with the color green (sometimes pink.) This chakra involves issues of compassion, trust, forgiveness, empathy, unconditional love, rejection, and well-being. The Heart Chakra is related to the thymus, which helps regulate the immune and endocrine systems. This chakra is also linked to proper circulation.

The fifth chakra, the Throat Chakra, is associated with light blue and is situated at the base of the neck in the throat. This chakra influences proper communication, dreaming, artistic expression, independence, fluent thought, clairaudience, truthfulness, good judgement, and a sense of security. The thyroid gland is linked to this chakra, and it affects the throat, mouth, teeth, and immune system.

The Third Eye or Brow Chakra is the sixth chakra, located is the middle of the forehead just above and between the eyebrows. The color indigo is related to this chakra, which involves intuition and intuitive clarity, spiritual wisdom, clairvoyance, concentration, and awareness. Linked to the pineal gland, this chakra affects the eyes, nose, and central nervous system as well as sleep regulation, since the pineal gland produces melatonin.

The Crown Chakra, located at the top of the head, is associated with the color purple or violet (or, sometimes, white.) This chakra serves as the foundation of the spiritual body and connects us with divine or highest guidance and inspiration. The Crown Charka is thought to be related to the pituitary gland; physically, it affects the cerebral cortex, the endocrine system, the central nervous system (particularly, the hypothalamus.) (Some sources maintain that the Third Eye Chakra is related to the pituitary gland, whereas the Crown chakra is associated with the pineal gland.)

One correlation I found interesting when researching physiological brain abnormalities in psychopaths is that such affected regions correspond to the Third Eye Chakra area. The ventromedial, anterior rostral, and orbital pre-frontal cortices - all of which have abnormal functioning or structure in psychopaths - are located directly behind and above the eyes. (Perhaps this insinuates that the psychopathic Third Eye is "blind?") Also interesting is the reduced connectivity between these areas and the amygdala, which sends impulses to the hypothalamus - a region that is related to the Crown Chakra.

There are various techniques used to cleanse the chakras. One is to sit upright yet comfortably in a chair with the feet flat on the floor. This is followed by imagining a silver cord coming down from the sky, connecting to the crown of the head, and traveling downward through the body as it exits from the base of the spine going down deep into the earth. Then, a brilliant red ball of light is envisioned traveling up this cord until it reaches the base of the spine where the Root Chakra is located. Its color and warm, healing energy are sensed as the ball spins in this chakra region. Then, an orange ball of light is envisioned traveling up this cord until it reaches the Sacral Chakra, where it spins and cleanses this area. This same pattern is repeated with the other chakras, as a ball of light with a corresponding color is conceptualized traveling up the cord to the area where the chakra are located, as it spins, cleanses, and heals its respective chakra region.

After performing this exercise for about a month, the practicer should feel lighter and more centered. With continued practice, intuitive (or even extra-sensory) perception may be enhanced as well.

Establishing Boundaries:

Sometimes we have relationships in our lives which are consistently taxing and draining. The reasons for this may be obvious: we might be in the presence of others who consistently berate, dominate, subjugate, or use other toxic tactics on a regular basis. Or, the reasons may be evasive: others may drain us with insidious, passive offense mechanisms or may routinely send out bad energy. Other times, it can be an organization, group, or workplace which consistently drains us with its negative synergistic atmosphere.

In some cases, there is only so much we can do. Other people or groups of people can be bound and determined to remain toxic, regardless of how we interact with them. Again, my definition of a "toxic person" is anyone who believes the Golden Rule should be applied *to* them, but they do not believe they ought to abide by it. In other words, toxic individuals expect to be treated a certain way, but they do not treat others in the same fashion. Some expect to be listened to, but they do not listen to others. Some may demand attention while they ignore others. Some expect things but give little in return. Others expect to be respected while they disrespect others, and so on.

While we can speak our truth, stand up for ourselves, and treat others in ways in which we would like to be treated, we cannot change others. In truth, this is not our responsibility: we are ultimately responsible for our own happiness and how we treat others. However, if we are consistently being drained by toxic tactics and offense mechanisms, we may need to establish distance or even sever relationships or jobs with those who are spiritually malignant out of self-care and self-preservation.

Whether it is a hyper-critical in-law, a verbally abusive boss, or a toxic partner, too much interpersonal contact or intimacy with these types can erode our own sense of emotional, physical, or energetic wellbeing. Such people are often referred to as "emotional vampires" or "energy parasites." If given sufficient opportunity, they will drain others of their energy and will have no reservation in doing so. There is no benefit to being subjected to this, for either party. If others are a source of our unhappiness, we are responsible for taking care of ourselves by learning some healthy and appropriate discrimination.

Such boundaries will, of course, depend on the situation and the severity. If another person's toxicity is stimulated by discussing our personal lives, we may need to reinforce a relationship which is more superficial. Or, if someone else makes us feel bad or worse when we need to vent, we may need to remind ourselves to rely on someone else. However, if we consistently feel drained by others or that they jeopardize our emotional, mental, or physical wellbeing, it may be necessary to cut ties with such people completely.

If there are others in our lives who are consistently toxic, part of the detox process will inevitably involve establishing boundaries. Many of us feel obligated to maintain such relationships and experience subsequent guilt after distancing ourselves from (or severing ties with) others who are toxic. It must be remembered that such dynamics benefit no one: the recipient feels sapped (which can eventually lead to bad mental, emotional, or physical health) while the toxic person usurps energy in an unhealthy manner. Also, perhaps the greatest benefit to give to such toxic people is solitude, since it provides them the opportunity to be alone to address their own issues which caused them to be toxic in the first place.

Humor:

I'm sure every reader has experienced a time when someone has cheered them up when they've been sad, scared, frustrated, or angry. Humor, by far, is the best tasting medicine for our energy bodies. Being able to laugh does wonders in replacing negative energy with joy.

I'm convinced that having a great sense of humor has wonderful affects on our bodies and as well as our minds. Consider comedians for a moment. More often than not, they look younger and healthier than their age would suggest. They also tend to be mentally sharp as well. The energy that comes with laughter - especially being able to make others laugh - feels great. When we feel great energetically we will certainly feel the effects physically and mentally.

Personally, the more I become familiar with spiritual practices, the more I see the connection between our "vibrations" and spiritual outcomes. Not only are the vibrations of love and peace conducive to enhancing our own spirituality and spiritual experiences, but *humor is huge*. Not too long ago, I starting meeting up with a small group for what is known as a Reiki share, which is a group of Reiki practitioners who take turns performing Reiki on each other. I really liked the Reiki group at first but, as we began to be more social and enjoy each others' company during our practice, the energy the humor brought seemed to raise the effects several octaves - even psychically. There have been times when I literally felt a high after the meet up which lasted a couple of days.

These techniques are excellent ways to heal ourselves from past wounds, cultivate self-knowledge, gain insight into our own maladaptive patterns in response to fears, build our energy, and cleanse our systems of unwanted, negative energy. It should be emphasized, though, that these are practices and not necessarily "cures." While practicing such techniques can be excellent preventative measures for dis-ease and oftentimes heal certain mental, emotional, and physical conditions, stopping the practice stops the healing. Just as the body begins to atrophy when an exercise regimen ceases, it is possible for the spirit body to accumulate negative energy when such practices are discontinued. Also, it should not be expected that the positive effects of these techniques will be felt overnight. Although each will have noticeable results after every practice, the true benefits of these techniques will be felt after a certain period of time.

However, just like exercise, the more we devote ourselves to these techniques, the sooner we will see results. And, although each detoxing practice directly impacts a certain area, we will be likely to notice results in other areas as well. For instance, after practicing reparenting, not only will we understand ourselves more and become more compassionate and understanding toward others, it is very likely that we will feel physically healthier as well. A regular yoga practice will certainly allow us to feel more physically relaxed, yet we will tend to be more flexible, at ease, and grounded with others as a positive side effect.

In general, the overall positive effects of these practices are improved physical health, increased cognitive ability and self-awareness, an overall positive sense of self and wellbeing, patience and understanding of self and others, rejuvenated self-worth, increased intuition, and even extra-sensory (or psychic) perception. The increased self-knowledge cultivates better dharma while converting negative energy into positive generates good karma. Most importantly, these techniques enable us to manage and understand our fears in a healthy manner.

As we strengthen our ability to manage our fears and the anger, frustration, angst, sadness, worry, jealousy, and hopelessness that comes with them, we will become less likely to indulge the various fear-based systems described earlier. As social beings, each one of us will also influence socio-cultural dynamics for the better. Since self-knowledge and good energy have been cultivated, we strengthen our ability to cope with and buffer spiritual malignancy from the outside world while we impart good energy onto others.

⊕

12

Soul Defense

GRACE: So I'm "arrogant." I'm "arrogant" because I forgive people...

THE BIG MAN: My God, can't you see how condescending you are when you say that? I mean, you have this preconceived notion that nobody can't possibly attain the same high ethical standards as you, so you exonerate them. I cannot - I <u>cannot</u> think of anything more arrogant than that. You - my child, my dear child - you forgive others with excuses that you would never in the world permit for yourself...and that is extremely arrogant!

- From Lars von Trier's Dogville

The more we tend to our selves, clear out negative energy while amassing positive, and speak our truth while respecting others, the more at peace we will feel. In time, we develop a new respect and understanding for ourselves and others, a new awareness, and possibly new spiritually-based sensing capabilities.

To ensure that our positive energy remains plentiful, safeguarded, and intact, it is useful to adopt certain practices that defend against any toxic behavior that contaminates and/or saps it. In doing so, not only do we preserve and protect our well-being, but we immediately set a boundary with others who are toxic. This not only nips spiritual malignancy in the bud, but it brings others' awareness to their own toxic behavior.

It is most important to emphasize that, with respect to others, such practices are best accompanied with *an intention of compassion*. Since fear and its negative emotions are behind all toxic behavior, including an element of compassion is highly worthwhile as it assists the other party in tending to their fears.

By adopting means of soul defense, we avoid enabling the spiritually malignant goals of dominating a willing and docile victim, reinforcing entitlement, and establishing narcissism. In turn, we uphold the goals of spiritual wealth: honoring freedom and wellbeing for ourself and others, ensuring that rights and rules apply to everyone, and loving and respecting ourselves and others at the same time.

By shifting both our reactions and our perspectives, we can deflect and nullify the effects of spiritually malignancy. Fortunately, there are several ways to do this:

Protective Disengagement:

This technique simply involves not "letting things get to us" by adopting a state of non-reactiveness. Part of the reason malignant personalities persist with toxic behavior is due to our vulnerabilities being triggered and exposed. Allowing others who are toxic to "get a rise" out of us only encourages them. If we allow them to succeed in eliciting an emotional reaction (to whatever degree), it reveals our "Achilles Heel," indicates to toxic individuals that the potential to create a willing/docile victim exists, and increases the likelihood of them persisting. By avoiding a victim mentality, the fodder for malignant behavior is deprived. Plus, doing our best to remain impermeable to negative energy is in our own best interest as well. By not being too sensitive and allowing others to "bring us down" or ruin our day, we take measures to keep our own energy centered and positive.

At times, remaining non-reactive is easier said than done, especially if our own energy is low or we face circumstances where toxic behavior is incessant, unrelenting, or extreme. More assertive means of defense will most likely be necessary in such cases. However, Protective Disengagement is most appropriate as a first step or in dealing with rare or isolated incidences, as it psychically sends the message, "I'm not going to indulge your behavior to any extent." The inherent pitfall, however, is that the malignant may interpret the non-reaction as a green-light to being enabled.

Truth Mechanisms

Truth mechanisms were mentioned previously, but they are worth mentioning again since they are probably the most effective, proactive, and immediate defense against spiritual malignancy and projected negative energy. In short, truth mechanisms involve "calling it out when you see it." If someone is using a guilt trip, simply stating, "I'm being made to feel guilty right now" will buck it. If someone is controlling a conversation, saying, "I can't get a word in edgewise" is likely to influence the other party to relent. If someone is playing the victim, expressing that "it sounds like you're feeling sorry for yourself" will bring awareness to their behavior. Truth mechanisms are effective in that they shed light to the spiritual malignancy that is transpiring. *Darkness cannot exist in light, and ignorance cannot exist in awareness.*

This method of defense is not only useful in addressing toxic tactics, but in any instance when fear is being imposed. If we notice we are being abandoned, deprived, subjugated, violated, threatened, excluded, or made to feel unlovable, less than, or a failure in ways which do not involve noticeable toxic tactics, it is best to recognize it as such and, if applicable, bring it to the attention of the other party (or parties.)

Sometimes such fears can be imparted in drastic ways which cannot be readily addressed or acknowledged in the moment, since they can take place without immediate awareness (that is, covertly, underhandedly, manipulatively, or behind one's back.) If this is the case, is it imperative to become aware of what is occurring. And, depending on the situation, we may need to confront the perpetrator, disengage from the relationship if possible, or appeal to a higher power. Not all of the options will be available nor will all worthwhile, yet it is important to proceed accordingly.

Whatever the case, when using truth mechanisms, it is essential to speak the truth, the whole truth, and nothing but the truth. Not addressing or diluting the entire truth will depreciate the defense's effectiveness, while going "overboard" by stretching, over amplifying, or overly admonishing will assuredly result in a battle of egos and counter-productivity.

Many people fear "confrontation" as they believe it is adversarial. However, if handled properly - *by simply raising awareness by stating the truth* - such anxiety need not be. There is nothing wrong with speaking the truth: just because another person may have an adverse reaction to it doesn't mean we have to.

Compassionate Exposition

Sometimes the medicine of truth can be bitter, and a spoonful of the sugar of compassion helps it go down. This method raises awareness to toxic behavior without inspiring defensiveness or offensiveness by adding a dose of sympathy. For example, if we were to see a frustrated parent admonishing their child to the brink of being abusive, we may say to them, "I bet it's hard being a parent." This brings awareness to their conduct without permitting them to feel like their being judged. Stating something along the lines of "You're being mean to your kid" will get the point across, but it is likely to conjure a nasty response. This approach is a good first step to take in raising awareness to toxic behavior, especially with people we don't know. The downfall of this approach is that its tactfulness may cause the message to be dismissed. The parent in the example might respond, "You have no idea!" and continue to lambaste her child, in which case a more forthright approach may prove appropriate.

Overcoming Denial

Denial is a powerful force, and it one heavily relied upon by malignant personalities. Many times when a truth mechanism is used, the spiritually malignant person will deny accountability or the existence of their toxic behavior. In doing so, they attempt to reinvent history and disturb others' sense of reality. For this reason, it is imperative to stay grounded. However, if the cycle of "Yes, you did" versus "No, I didn't" becomes repetitive, it is best to disengage from a potential battle of wills and proceed with a more assertive response, be it distancing from, avoiding, severing ties with, or setting some sort of boundary with the malignant. Trying to get another person to acknowledge the truth is inevitably not your responsibility and will only result in more crazy making - *and you can't fix crazy*. Save yourself the time, energy, and sanity. If the other party is determined to enforce their flawed version of reality, there is no need to indulge, enable, or coerce them, whether they believe this false, alternate version of reality or not. We are responsible for our own understanding of the truth, not others'. Simply move on to the next step. Otherwise, we will find ourselves in a situation similar to a crazy person calling another crazy - after a while, both will be.

The best way to avoid the potential for denial is to state the truth rather than vocalize an interpretation of it. By saying, "I'm being subjugated" as opposed to "I feel like I'm being subjugated right now," it reduces the likelihood of the malignant to distort perception. With the latter, the malignant person will capitalize on the potential that the victim sees subjugation as their *perception* and not necessarily reality. With the former, the victim asserts that the subjugation is true, conveying a firm stance which the malignant is less likely to challenge.

Confronting denial becomes especially difficult after some time has lapsed, so it is best to address it as soon as possible. This is not always an option, since the evidence of toxicity may not be readily apparent. For instance, a person may lie about something which later proves to be untrue. Thus, we may realize that we have been subjugated, violated, deprived, etc. in a manipulative manner after the fact. Nevertheless, it is important to address such malignant behavior as soon as possible. However, if it gets to the point where you wish you had a tape recorder or a journal of some sort, it is probably best to take further action with respect to the relationship.

Repetitive Reinforcement

Sometimes, a malignant personality will continue their toxic behavior even after a truth mechanism is used. As an alternative to denial (or as a back-up plan), they may assert themselves by rationalizing, justifying, explaining, exonerating, or persisting in their toxic behavior. A means of defense to this is to keep repeating the truth mechanism over and over again.

Take, for instance, someone who was berated for making an honest mistake and made to feel like a failure. When confronting the malignant, the person states, "I was made to feel like a failure." The malignant may subsequently justify her harsh and condemning words, exonerate her behavior due to having a bad day, rationalize the "reasons" such behavior was "necessary," etc. By repeating "I was made to feel like a failure," it renders all the excuses rightly ineffective. It sends and reinforces the message that, no matter what is said, no exoneration will vindicate the toxic behavior.

By repeating truth mechanisms, we also save ourselves from becoming embroiled in more toxic tactics and ego battles. When the malignant "explains" his toxic behavior, restating the truth is much less emotionally and mentally draining than it is to counter the "explanations." When he switches to exoneration, the burden of holding him accountable is eased by repeating the truth. If he starts to rationalize his behavior, we can save our energy from attempting to explain how irrational the "rationalization" is; instead, we can just reinforce the truth by restating it.

Avoiding defensiveness

If justifying their own toxic behavior proves ineffective, a spiritually malignant person may try to get others to justify theirs. This "turning of the tables" attempts to shift the focus from the malignant to the victim as the malignant begins to interrogate the victim. The most effective way to counter this is to ignore and disregard such questioning and repeat the truth mechanism. By indulging the interrogation, power is given to the malignant which can lead to exoneration, avoiding accountability, and reinforcing victimhood. It is imperative to stay on course to prevent the malignant from dodging the topic at hand.

Shock Defense

Many of us have found ourselves in a situation where we bear the brunt of an offense mechanism which comes out of nowhere. Whether it is a potshot, undeserved blame, a guilt trip, or another toxic tactic, the fact that it came out of the blue left us stunned, tongue-tied, and briefly disoriented. We later wished we had said something or even knew what to say at the time.

This sort of shock tactic is a common practice by aggressively (or passive-aggressively) toxic individuals. If we are around them enough, we may feel as though we always need to be on guard. This is a torturous way to exist and, fortunately, it isn't necessary. To counteract this without constantly preparing ourselves to react, we simply need a little self-conditioning.

If we frequently find ourselves in this situation, it would do wonders to get into the habit of having the malignant person repeat themselves in that moment of disarray. Once we feel that stun, saying "What did you just say?" or "Excuse me?" buys us time to snap out of the shock and adjust so that we can react accordingly. Often, it will shut the other person down immediately. Other times, they'll respond with, "You heard me" or move onto another toxic tactic. It doesn't matter: now that they are aware that the shock did not create docility, they are instantly disempowered. They no longer have the upper hand and, by proceeding to address their conduct with truth mechanisms, they won't be allowed to.

Protecting Personal Privacy

Most of us want to trust other people and appreciate intimacy, especially when we open up about things that are personal. By "letting someone in," we allow them to hold our hearts in their hands, providing a true "gift of intimacy." Many of us feel honored when another person opens up to us and appreciate being trusted. We value the closeness and treat another's vulnerability with care and compassion and cherish these gifts of intimacy by protecting them. When we or others open up, we entrust others to love us as we are. We also demonstrate great courage and self-love in the process.

While it is great to be honest, many of those who are toxic will use personal, sensitive, and trusted information against others though emotional blackmail, shaming, guilting, judging, debasing, or any other means to make them feel "less than." They will often ask personal questions regarding information which is in no way relevant to them, only to violate our trust by using it against us in some way. Afterward, we regret being open and honest and become more reluctant to be emotionally intimate with other people.

Such gifts of intimacy truly are gifts. In fact, they are probably the most meaningful gift we can give to anyone. If someone else does not respect, appreciate, or takes advantage of the gift for what it is, it is best to stop giving them such gifts and save them for someone else who does. Also, if we consistently find ourselves in a position where we don't want to lie and telling the truth has undeserved repercussions, it is probably best to allow for some sort of distance from relationship. And, if we find that we're always giving while another is always withholding, it is probably best to rescind the gift giving.

If our trust has been violated, it is imperative to heal from the hurt and anger. We all deserve to have others whom we can open up to, and healing from past wounds will allow us to trust others in the future. It may be necessary to exercise some discrimination, though. We're inevitably responsible for own hearts, so we should be careful about choosing who gets to hold them.

Cutting Off The "Supply"

There are times when we come across relationships or meet people who only talk about themselves. Inquiring about how they are doing will illicit not a response, but a dissertation. "Ask them for the time and they'll build you a watch" is a commonly used phrase to describe this. Such people will continuously talk about themselves but will never ask how others are doing. After some time, we realize that conversations with such people are very much one-sided. When we attempt to bring up something in our lives or going on with us, they steer the conversation back to themselves even after we had spent an appreciable amount of attention listening to them.

They may even ask you a question and, while you are answering, interrupt so that they can talk more about themselves. When you ask them a question which does not involve them, they'll interrupt and provide a litany of impertinent information about themselves.

Such self-absorbed persons are narcissistic at its most basal level. They're only concerned about themselves, as it's their world and others are living in it. In addition to demanding undivided, uninterrupted attention, they may seek others' adulation, expect others to always be their audience or to be enabled by them in some way. Whatever the case, they won't ask about others with any genuine interest because, in truth, they don't consider it.

When we find ourselves in a position where we're constantly being expected to listen with no reciprocity, we give out our energy without receiving any back. If "one hand is always giving while the other never receives," the relationship is imbalanced. Common courtesy and symbiotic interactions involve give and take. If boundaries aren't set, we will be depended on as narcissistic supply and, sooner or later, we will feel sapped by such self-involved individuals.

The solution to this is simple: cut off the supply. *Since they are unwilling to give, they are not owed anything.* Cutting off the supply may require stating the truth: "You only talk about yourself and never listen to me." While it good to be respectful, don't feel obligated to spare their ego: it's the truth. Besides, it brings their toxic behavior to their awareness, which they can now address.

Or, cutting off the supply may require creating boundaries, up to and including avoiding them, depending on the severity of the situation. If it becomes evident that they never reciprocate by asking how you're doing, stop asking them. Otherwise, a codependent relationship is being enabled.

Such boundaries should not be intended to punish or retaliate against such persons. Clearly, this sort of self-involved behavior is ego-based and has a basis in some sort of unattended inner-void - and this is certainly deserving of compassion, which we ought to feel and, if possible, give. However, while this is sad and while we can assist, it is not our responsibility to rectify. Rather, it is mutually beneficial to maintain some distance: for ourselves, we defend against someone else depleting us of our energy; for them, they will experience greater solitude. This solitude may provide them with the opportunity to employ some introspection into the very issues which caused them to become self-absorbed in the first place. Also, it allows them to experience what it is like to have nobody care about them, since they haven't cared about other people. Again, this is not meant out of vindictiveness, but merely as a reflection to foster some self-awareness and, hopefully, self-knowledge and resulting self-love. However, that is inevitably their choice.

Confronting in Person

When speaking truth mechanisms with honest and appropriate emotion, it is best to do so as directly as possible - preferably in person. By having the other person in our presence, we will be much more able to assess the appropriateness of our emotions since the degree of interpersonal contact is at its highest. We can see the direct effects of our words by noticing the other person's reactions as much as possible. This can help us from expressing too much or too little. Also, the other party can witness the effects of their behavior with greater sensory perception since they can see body language and facial expressions in addition to hearing voice inflections and words.

Also, this eliminates (or, at least, reduces) the potential of the malignant disengaging from confrontation or avoiding accountability by hanging up the phone, not returning a call, or not responding by e-mail or text message. Sure, the person could leave the room, yet they will be more reluctant since this is more brazen.

Confronting in person may not always be a possibility. If toxic behavior is used over the phone, it is probably best to address it immediately. Also, some of our relationships may be long-distance, which makes confronting in person impossible. In some cases, we may have no direct contact with spiritually malignant others who affect us directly or indirectly, such as dishonest politicians or corrupt financial leaders. However, if the potential exists, addressing in person is worthwhile. If not, the more direct, the better.

Honoring Your Feelings

When confronting a toxic personality on their spiritual malignancy, we owe it to both ourselves and to them to be emotionally honest. This means we communicate our feelings as well as the intellectual content of the truth mechanism. Whether we state the emotion we are feeling or display it, this is vital to our own emotional health and appropriate for the malignant to understand the repercussions of their behavior. Being stoic or non-feeling when confronting spiritual malignancy will not honor the negative emotions inspired by others (which, as discussed previously, body often stores and can lead to dis-ease.) Moreover, not expressing the negative feelings will dilute the message received by the malignant.

For instance, it is understandable for someone to be upset or angry when they've learned their partner or spouse was unfaithful. Therefore, there is no reason to approach confrontation with a demeanor which is overly calm and devoid of emotion. If we feel resulting hurt and anger and do not honor it by letting it out, it will stay with us. By not acknowledging or letting out the negative emotions associated with fears of mistrust and vulnerability in this example, harboring them can cause dis-ease or we may take it out on someone else at a later time. We will also be likely to regret not allowing ourselves to honor our emotions in hindsight. And, by withholding such negative emotions from malignant, it deprives them from experiencing the emotional effects of their actions. Not realizing the full effects of their actions enables their behavior, which they will be more likely to repeat with others including ourselves. Also, by withholding the emotional component of confrontation, it lessens the contact the malignant makes with their conscience since the results of their actions are withheld.

Oftentimes a malignant will use the emotional state of the recipient of their behavior as an excuse to escape confrontation and accountability. A cheater may tell their lover, "I can't talk to you until you've calmed down." This is absurd. If they didn't want to deal with someone who was upset or angry with them, they shouldn't have cheated in the first place. If they had abided by their conscience and followed the Golden Rule, they wouldn't have to deal with anyone angry or upset with them. Learning that a violation has taken place isn't calming, and they certainly wouldn't be calm if it happened to them. Refusing to acknowledge the negative emotional effects their actions had on others is the epitome of entitlement. They deserve to experience the repercussions of their spiritual malignancy; after all, they chose it.

Karma Plus Dharma

Of course, the degree of negative emotion is entirely dependent on the situation. "Going overboard" or over-amplifying the negative feelings when confronting is not only counterproductive, it violates our own conscience as it can be abusive and malignant itself. (This can take the form of "kicking others while they are down.")

Having someone, say, monopolize a conversation is different from having ten thousand dollars stolen. Screaming at someone for hours after putting us on a guilt trip is clearly flying off the handle. In confrontation, it is best to approach the situation with a balance of reason and passion, appropriate to the situation.

As such, a distinction needs to be made between "non-feeling" and "non-reaction." When we're mistreated, is it a natural human reaction to feel hurt, anger, upset, frustrated or any negative emotion. We are emotional-thinking beings, not thinking-emotional beings. We are ultimately responsible for our own happiness so, if we have been hurt, we owe it to our selves to release the negative energy we have inherited in the form of emotion. We owe it to others to hold them accountable and remind them of who they are - beings capable of loving themselves and others. After doing so, we feel better and others learn about themselves from the repercussions their actions.

Honoring our negative feelings in a healthy, appropriate manner is essential to maintain our own humanity as well as address the anti-social behavior in others. If we do not, the negative energy not expressed becomes stockpiled within us as spiritual malignancy goes enabled and condoned. Nobody wins by keeping the hurt inside.

To gauge emotional appropriateness in confronting with truth mechanisms, the best approach is to be mindful of dharma and karma. With dharma, we speak truth yet, with karma, we do so in a way in which we would want - or deserve - to be told. Again, this is not to suggest that we should not express anger, be upset, or establish a boundary when we've been hurt; not expressing such emotions would be a disservice to others as well as ourselves. Rather, it is perhaps the worst thing to do: it enables others to disregard their conscience and continue down a path which harms other people in the process. If we did not receive a good, healthy dose of disciplinary emotion during times in our lives when we disrespected or mistreated others, we would likely be entitled, anti-social, and malignant today. Not doing so for others would endorse the same to happen.

Knowing When To Let Go

Similar to ensuring that our emotional response to malignant activity is appropriately balanced with reason and passion, it is appropriate to know when to let go of negative emotions or at least keep them at bay. Oftentimes when we are hurt, violated, or harmed in a certain way, we can stew in the fear, hurt, or anger long after the episode. After a while, such dwelling on the negative feelings only breeds more toxicity within us. It is therefore essential that we learn to distinguish healthy emotional release versus chronic rehashing.

I'll be the first to admit: this isn't always easy, and this certainly involves some subjectivity depending on the nature of the misdeed itself as some are more impacting than others. Yet constantly reliving, analyzing, or rehashing the event and its emotional aftermath will become self-injuring after a certain point. Our goal is to heal from being hurt, not reopen wounds. Once we realize that we are "going in circles," it is probably best to move on and forgive the situation, as in leave it in the past - for our own sake.

This can be especially difficult for those who are aware of the many violations, crimes, and toxic activity within government, corporations, media, the financial sector, etc. Learning about such malignant behavior, while important to be aware of, can catalyze much anger, fear, despair, and worry. Such emotional responses are appropriate yet harmful if we dwell on them too much or too long. We must learn to respect our own capacity for taking on this negativity and, for our own well-being, know when to emotionally disengage from it when it becomes excessive. If not, we can become chronically enraged, depressed, or even paranoid, which does neither ourselves nor the situation any good. No one is productive when they are debilitated, so we cannot afford to "lose ourselves" when dealing with this sort of malignancy. We are most productive in logistically dealing with these situations when we have some emotional grounding, which may require backing off at times. It's beneficial to know that "the house is on fire" but we must be careful not to get burned while trying to put it out.

Not letting go of a situation (or at least backing off from it) can be like venting about a certain problem over and over again: after a while, it becomes draining and little to no remedy is realized. If we find ourselves stewing about something without finding improvement within ourselves or the situation, it is best to let go. If we cannot let go, we may need to take further action by addressing the situation and doing something *both transitional and productive* as an outlet for this energy. We may need to do this either independently or, if dealing with issues on a larger scale, alongside and with the help of others who feel the same way. The latter, in fact, can be empowering and comforting at the same time.

Calling Out Bad Behavior: Condoning Versus Forgiveness

Whether we come across a toxic tactic or witness other spiritually malignant behaviors which attempts to victimize, establish narcissism, or reinforce entitlement, it is imperative to call it out. This may involve vocalizing a truth mechanism immediately or after the fact, or subsequently acknowledging to ourselves what had occurred and understanding that it was not okay. Whatever the case, it is important to honor the negative emotions such transgressions inspire in a healthy manner.

While it is very important to reach a place of forgiveness, it is necessary that the emotional acknowledgment of the hurt, grief, anger, or any negative emotion that arises after being subject to spiritual malignancy be honored. More still, and if possible, it is important that we share with others' how their misdeeds made us feel. Doing so honors our own emotions and brings awareness of such behaviors to others, which allows them to reflect upon and, hopefully, address the core issues behind them.

However, many bypass the step of acknowledging their emotional wounds and avoid addressing the perpetrator on their actions by instantaneously moving into a manufactured intellectual state of "forgiveness," attempting to convince themselves that they are "okay" with what had occurred. Believing this to be forgiveness, they abandon their own wounded hearts and, by not calling out the bad behavior, enable and thus condone it. Not only is victimhood accepted and condoned, but the perpetrator is more likely to repeat the offense, causing more harm to the recipient or others at a later time. The more harm the perpetrator causes, the more they violate and become distanced from their conscience. The more this occurs, the sooner they will reach spiritual bankruptcy.

If such "forgiveness" exists solely as a mental construct, it is phony. True forgiveness is based in the heart and requires emotionally releasing the hurt as well as the situation - after which, we can truly *for-give* and move on since there is no longer any residual emotional or mental attachment. Whether we do this in the presence of the perpetrator or not, this step is essential in order to truly forgive. Our emotions are real things; if we ignore them, it doesn't mean they do not exist. Repressed emotions, in time, usually come back to haunt in some way or form.

Moreover, we learn how to treat others by being emotionally honest in how others treat us. If someone hurts, abuses, or mistreats us and we override, disregard, or preemptively "get over" the negative feelings of hurt, anger, frustration, and more, we miss out on the lesson completely. Learning how to do unto others as we would have done unto us requires that we emotionally acknowledge the pain that results after times when we've been harmed.

When we allow ourselves to experience such pain, we not only provide an opportunity to heal ourselves, we know from acknowledged experience how another person would feel were we to do the same thing to them. *Doing so cultivates empathy which maintains the conscience.* Not doing so causes us to miss out on knowing ourselves, which is imperative for true, authentic self-love. And, not calling out bad behavior while vocalizing our hurt separates the other person from their conscience, and what good does that ultimately do for them? Or, others they come into contact with in the future, for that matter?

Therefore, *not* emotionally and intellectually acknowledging times when we've been hurt not only makes true forgiveness more difficult, it prevents our own healing as well as others'. Also, not calling out bad behavior - whether we recognize it ourselves or bring it to the perpetrator's awareness - condones it. It is much easier to forgive *another person*, whether or not they accept accountability, after bringing their attention to their misdeed since we have "spoken our peace."

Nowadays, the Golden Rule bears the connotation that we should always "be nice" to others and treat them with kindness. With this, it is believed we should always forgive. While this is important - as we would all want to be forgiven for times when we've hurt others - it is vital that this not be interpreted as an endorsement for enabling bad behavior. If we were mistreating others, wouldn't we want this brought to our awareness? Wouldn't we benefit as human beings to be made aware of our own behaviors which hurt others? Wouldn't we have an opportunity to better ourselves by examining the reasons behind our toxic behavior? Do we not deserve to witness the emotional harm we've caused others when it occurs - for our own good? If you have answered "yes" to these questions, then it is owed to others - out of love.

Besides, when we do not hold others to an ethical standard to which we ourselves abide, it makes us arrogant. Like the quote from the film *Dogville* at the beginning of this chapter, it is condescending to believe that we are capable of abiding by a certain moral code of conduct and not others. This insinuates that we are "better" than other people which is not only false, it is smug and condescending.

Forgiveness Versus Absolution

We may not always receive acknowledgement or an apology from the other party after raising awareness to their malignant behavior. While it is helpful, this is not necessary for forgiveness - at least for the situation. By being emotionally honest with ourselves and others, we have done our part by respecting our hearts and the path to forgiveness opens. It just may be necessary to establish some boundaries going forward. After some time, we will be able to forgive as in "move on" from the situation since we have honored our truth.

Hopefully, time will allow for any resentment toward the other party to dissolve. If the other party did not accept any accountability, it is in our best interest to move on from harboring resentment or ill will. Clinging onto such negative energy will only do additional harm to ourselves. And, after all, we do not need their approval or acknowledgement of our hurt feelings in order to feel better; we just need to take care of them.

Inevitably, however, the other party will need to address their transgressions and, in fact, judge themselves. It is only when such remorse is experienced and expressed that they can be *absolved* from their spiritual malignancy.

This was something I learned during a mediumship class I had taken. The turnout for this class was small - it was just myself and another woman. After we were taken through a guided meditation, we were asked to share our experiences with each other. I had a pleasant experience, yet the woman I had taken the class with had one which was quite heavy. During her channeling, she was visited by her ex-husband who had been deceased for decades. When she met with him, she described him as being flanked by two beings of light who were supporting him as he was hysterical in tears, as he had come to apologize for molesting their daughter about forty years before. The woman seemed taken aback by this, since she had forgiven both him and the situation long before (and good for her!) But she couldn't understand why he had come, saying "I don't get why he came to me; I haven't thought about this for the longest time - I forgave him years and years ago. Why would he come to me with this?"

We were then asked to do a reading for each other. Immediately, her husband came to me with the answer - and I'll never forget the sense of grief and sorrow that came with it. Although she had done her part by forgiving him years ago, he had not done his. In order for the process of *absolution* to take place, not only does the victimized party need to forgive, but the perpetrator needs to feel and share their remorse with those they hurt. Both forgiveness and remorse can happen on their own, but absolution requires both to take place. Only then is the transgression truly resolved.

I share this story for two reasons. First, it is much easier to ask for forgiveness from those we have hurt while we are still alive, and it is in everyone's best interest that we do - even if we are not forgiven. Our conscience is not something we can escape from and, really, why would we want to? Second, if we are approached by someone who has hurt us and is truly remorseful, it is in everyone's best interest to forgive both them and the situation. This is probably the most beautiful way to honor the Golden Rule. If we were *truly* sorry for a time when we had hurt another person and understood the pain we caused, wouldn't we want forgiveness? Of course we would. Although what her ex-husband did was horrible, I couldn't help but feel compassion for him after feeling the extent of his heartache, penitence, and regret - I felt incredibly bad for him. But since he had expressed his remorse to both his ex-wife and his daughter, true and thorough healing could take place.

Knowing Others' Truth

Recall from the first half of this book that those who are spiritually malignant and engage in offense mechanisms do so out of unresolved and mishandled fears of their own. This in itself is proof positive that such persons are, in a sense, living their own hell. Only a person with issues regarding their own appearance will put down others. A person who lies, cheats, and manipulates to swindle money and belongings from others clearly has inner demons of some sort. Those who gossip or talk about others behind their backs do so to compensate for their own poor self-image.

Deep down, those who are spiritually malignant are miserable themselves. Although bearing the brunt of toxic or spiritually malignant behavior is not pleasant, understanding the truth behind such behavior adds some perspective. This perspective can help ease the blow, not out of schadenfreude or taking pleasure in their misery, but out of understanding what it is they're dealing with. This may even inspire compassion.

Knowing the truth behind others' malignant behavior can also make for a powerful truth mechanism. If someone is constantly invading others' privacy to "dig up dirt," informing them that they "must have a lot of skeletons in their own closet to want to expose those of others" can be extremely potent. Telling someone who puts us down because of our clothes, weight, hair, or other physical attribute that "only someone with a poor self image would feel the need to put others down; it must be sad to be you" can be very effective.

Truth mechanisms - whether calling out bad behavior or addressing the truth behind toxic behavior - are used to bring awareness to the transfer of misery, not fix it. That is not our job. We responsible for our own happiness, self-worth, and self-preservation, and how we treat others. While it is important to be helpful, available, and assisting, it is not our responsibility to transmute others' negativity. In fact, we can't; only they can. And it certainly is not our responsibility to adopt their negativity. However, the light we shed on their toxic behavior is perhaps the best way to show such people love.

Critical Thinking

In order to preserve our own well-being, it is essential to be self-referring and impermeable to the manipulative toxic tactics which influence our emotions, beliefs, and behaviors. All behaviors are based on beliefs and emotions, and those who are spiritually malignant often coerce others into behaving in ways which are contrary to their own well-being or the well-being of others by playing on their emotions and beliefs. They accomplish this by instilling emotions and beliefs in others which contradict true circumstances.

While it is a gift to trust and believe in others, many violate this gift through manipulation and deception. Those who are susceptible abdicate their own ability to think rationally by readily adopting a false belief because an "expert" or "leader" told them so. As a result, their subsequent behaviors are no longer based on self-reference; rather, they reflect the will of a spiritually malignant or egotistical person or persons who conned them into behaving in a certain fashion.

God (or Nature, depending on your beliefs) endowed every human being with their own heart and mind, allowing them to feel and think on their own without anyone else's help. The very moment that the ability to think and feel on one's own is forgone, that person is liable to be brainwashed, manipulated, and susceptible to toxic tactics such as spin, lies of omission (or blackouts), half-truths, or outright lies.

This is the very principle behind propaganda, and it exists in many arenas as any type of cult - religious, political, cultural, or ideological - thrives on this. Whether it is a minister who inculcates his parish with messages about a wrathful, angry god or a politician who spins mass spying on the public as necessary for its own safety, the effects of mass manipulation can be devastating. The individuals who allowed themselves to ignore their own reasoning and emotional intelligence will, at some point, regret doing so - that is, if they're ever willing to come to terms with reality.

With critical thinking, we honor our own ability to rationalize and cultivate our own beliefs and feelings about various matters, protecting ourselves from being deluded, exploited, or taken advantage of, which ultimately will affect our own rights and well-being. Doing so is self-preservation at its most basal level, as we maintain and cultivate our own cognition and wisdom.

Critical thinking requires the ability to observe pertinent evidence, assess relevant criteria, perform contextual analysis, employ logic, address and resolve doubts and discrepancies, evaluate circumstances based on present and absent factors and information, gauge and recognize probabilities, assess cause and effect, and understand human nature and psychology. Most important, critical thinking involves formulating questions. This questioning not only applies to our own beliefs and the feelings behind them, but others who claim or are portrayed to be experts, leaders, and sources of information.

Just because something was said on the news does not make it true: the only thing true in this scenario is that something *was said*. The *likelihood* of it being true is based on evidence, probability, potential, motive, and logistics, to name a few. Just because a number of outlets reported it does not make it true: the only thing true is that a number of outlets reported it. There was a time when the majority of leaders, experts, and authority figures maintained that the earth was flat; just because there were many who believed it did not make it true.

Therefore, in order to develop a belief system - political, religious, spiritual, cultural, ideological, etc. - free from imposed bias, manipulation, propaganda, dogma, and inaccuracies, it is imperative to be self-referring. While it is fine - and good - to be open-minded and consider others' opinions and vantage points, once we take another's word or succumb to dictation, we literally lose our sense of self. When our sense of self is lost, we lose self-knowledge. When self-knowledge is lost, we not only stop authentically loving ourselves by denying our own truth, but we become prey to toxic tactics as well. However, when we use our own hearts and minds as the sources of our emotional and intellectual intelligence, we remain safeguarded and authentic.

Satire

The most effective way to bring malignant behavior to a screeching halt is to make fun of it right in front of the toxic personality. This works especially well for narcissism. Satire whips out the pedestal the narcissist placed themselves on; it's the pin that pops the inflated ego. Satire exposes the parody of a human being that the toxic personality is and, since the ego is crushed, they will think twice about repeating the behavior.

The more we gain self-knowledge, self-cleanse, and learn self-protection, the more we cultivate and preserve authentic self-love. The more we enhance and preserve the love we carry within ourselves. the more peaceful and joyous our existence will be. The more peaceful, truthful, and joyous our existence is, so too will be our presence and affect on others. The more of us who do this, the sooner we can manifest true change in this country, if not, the planet.

☀

13

Spiritual Activists and Soldiers of Love

Shine Your Light

_"However vast the darkness,
we must supply our own light."_

- Stanley Kubrick

During a recent service at the Spiritualist Church I attend, one of the regular guest speakers provided a wonderful metaphor describing how we as human beings relate to and affect each other as a whole. She discussed how each one of us - whether in the physical or spiritual plane (if you believe in such a plane) - is a bundle of energy. She described our own individual energy as being like a drop of water in a lake: while each of us has our own energy, all of our energies combine to form the lake of mankind. Each of us therefore contributes our own energy to mass consciousness, and this mass consciousness is a sum of all its parts, just as drops of water make up a lake.

Now, imagine two drops of water coming together: one of them clean and pure, the other dark and dirty. What happens? The resulting volume of water is twice as large, yet it is half as clean as the pure drop and half as dirty as the other. But, considering there are still two drops, the pure drop is now more dirty and the dirty drop is more clean.

Our own "drops" affect each other in the same manner when our energy comes into contact with another persons. We are likely to absorb others' energy - good or bad - when we merge with them. But, unlike drops of water, we have the ability to remain clean, cleanse ourselves, or remain (or become even more) contaminated. We thus have a good deal of ability to be as clean or as dirty as we choose.

Although living in a culture which is becoming more toxic makes it increasingly difficult to keep our "drop" pure, it is not impossible. By being honest about ourselves through self-awareness and self-knowledge, we become aware of the pollutants of fear in our "drop," which we can purify through love. By knowing the toxins we have in our droplet, we can detox our water by any of the methods described before.

And, unlike water drops, we can choose whether or not to merge with other "drops" or not. We can also let other "drops" know that they are polluted and, hopefully, they will purify themselves and help keep the lake clean. If not, they can merge with other drops as dirty as they are, if not more. Then, hopefully, they will discover that it's better to have a clean drop than one that is dirty.

Now, take a moment and look at the energy that is in your "drop." Notice how you typically feel on a daily basis. Are you usually tired, frustrated, worried, resentful, or angry? Or are you rested, proactive, calm, energized, easygoing, and pleasant? Are you looking forward to starting each day or are you dreading it? Do you usually feel stressed, frazzled, and dispersed? Or are you calm, focused, and collected? Is your mind in a million different places and always running or is it present and in the "here and now?" Are you gentle and compassionate with yourself or are you harsh and your own worst enemy? Are you absorbing the pollutants from other drops, or worse: do you allow - or even plan - for other drops to take on your contaminants?

What are your political, moral, ethical, cultural, ideological, and religious beliefs? Did you formulate them on your own or were you told to believe them?

How do you generally interact with other people? Are you patient, courteous, and respectful, or are you curt, short-tempered, and impatient? Do you set boundaries and vocalize when you are mistreated by others or do you bite your tongue? Are you afraid to "rock the boat" or are you willing to "push the envelope" with others, including authority figures?

Do you notice changes in your energy when you encounter certain people, relationships, or environments? If so, how did your energy change? For the better or for the worse? What brought the change on?

If we notice any negative energy within our "drop," we owe it to ourselves to do what we can to cleanse it. Whether is it due to something internal (such as unhealed emotional wounds or negative thought patterns) or external (such as a job, certain relationships in our lives, or current events) we must face it and recognize it for what it is in order to cleanse the negativity. Then, we can work on transforming it, whatever that might entail. We are, after all, responsible for what is in our own drop and for what we contribute to the lake.

Many of us believe that world peace is an objective which is political in nature: if the governments of all nations could get along, we could have peace worldwide. If this were to happen, it would realize harmony within global politics, yet it would not ensure world peace. In order for peace to thrive uniformly and thoroughly at a national or global level, each person would have to do their part; that is, each person's drop would need to be purified. Relying on our governments to manifest peace worldwide has not only proved to be futile, it is personally disempowering. The "lake" can only be pure and peaceful once all of its drops are cleansed of any fear-based negativity, and we all must do our part since we all are co-responsible for the energy here on earth.

This may sound like a lofty - if not impossible - goal, but in order to make true, positive change, there really is no other way. Fortunately, by amassing spiritual wealth within ourselves while transmuting negative energy, we can - and will - affect others in a positive way. By acting with courage, authenticity, integrity, and love, we will inspire and influence others to do the same.

And, truly, every human being on the planet does not have to be on board at the same time for this to happen. After enough of us make a conscious, determined effort, a critical mass will be reached and will permeate the population at large. It is this infiltration and influence of mass consciousness which makes propaganda so successful. Yet, instead of manipulating on a massive scale, the more of us who express ourselves authentically, speak the truth, and follow the Golden Rule, the sooner we can be just as affecting but in a positive manner.

When we do our part to face and replace our fears with love, we send out that energy to every other "drop" in the lake we come into contact with. The more mindful and proactive we are, the more consistent our positive influence on others will be.

And, naturally, the greater the positive energy of truth and love we carry, the more potent our influence on others will be. We are all units of energy, and this energy we carry can be positive or negative and it can be weak or strong. We each have the ability to increase our energy and for the better - and it is our *choice* to do so.

After we build up our own positive energy through self-knowledge and self-love, detox from any fear-based negative energy we have harbored, and learn to protect ourselves from spiritual malignancy which either saps or contaminates our energy (or both), we can embark on letting our light shine upon the outside world. Truth mechanisms, as mentioned before, can convert the domination, narcissism, and entitlement that comes with spiritual malignancy by bringing such behavior to awareness or, in short, spreading truth. As spiritual activists, we must not only shed truth on ourselves and others, but love as well.

As mentioned in the first half of this book, spiritual deficiency is caused by the mismanagement of fear. It was also described how spiritual deficiency has enabled the toxic political, social, cultural, financial, and economic climates we currently face both on a nation and global scale. The spiritual deficiency we experience on a personal level, as mentioned before, can be compensated by practicing good karma and good dharma, both of which are enhanced by regular practice of mindfulness and meditation. By replacing unattended fear with truth and love within ourselves, we become spiritually wealthy. When we emanate the truth and love cultivated in our spiritual wealth to the outside world, we become spiritual activists.

The increase in spiritual malignancy - the violation of the Golden Rule - has given rise and strengthened these toxic, destructive climates. Therefore, the most effective way to counter the negative energy supporting these toxic manifestations is to impart the positive energy of truth and love from our own spiritual wealth. We must counteract and override the many violations of the Golden Rule not just with truth, but loving others by treating them the way we would want to be treated.

In our spiritual activism, we will have countless opportunities to spread love and kindness on a daily basis. We can hold a door open for someone, smile at somebody, say a kind word, or let someone in our highway lane when traffic is heavy. Simple things like saying "hello" to someone who walks by, or "how are you?" and "thank you" and "have a nice day" to a cashier all help to transmute the negative energy which has permeated our population. It will also help to transmute our own: it feels good to be good.

And this positive energy - like all energy - is transferrable. If you want to observe this firsthand, notice the next time you are waiting in line at a store and the person in front of you is rude to the cashier. When you approach the counter, you'll be lucky to be greeted even if it is obligatory, since the cashier absorbed some of the previous customer's negative energy. Be kind and pleasant to the clerk. Genuinely treat them the way you would want to be treated and, as you walk away from the counter, listen to how the cashier interacts with the person who was behind you. I guarantee that the cashier will say "Hi, how are you today?" and be pleasant with them.

The good thing is, the Golden Rule is boundless. We can spread as much joy, kindness, compassion, and love as frequently or as potently as we want. If we know someone who is lonely or has suffered a loss of some kind, we can call them and be emotionally present and supportive. If someone is down, we can cheer them up; or if they're hard on themselves, we can help them gain a new perspective and ease up. We can feed someone who is hungry or help someone in need. We can literally be a godsend to others. Some refer to such spiritual activists as "Light Workers."

When we impart kindness, love, truth, and joy to those around us, we help to transform the synergy of the world around us. The light in our drop expands to the larger pool it is in. The more of us who commit to the Golden Rule - and the more frequently we practice it - the sooner the lake lights up and we see some remarkable change.

This potential for positive synergy is crucial for productive and collective transformation. To get a better understanding of synergy, consider shopping experiences you've had in the past. Recall a time when you walked into a store and noticed that the workers were cavalier, downtrodden, and miserable. The store itself probably appeared haphazard, sloppy, and unkempt. Chances are, the physical and emotional environment was attributable to a toxic, inept management, but remember the energy you felt while walking around. You probably felt sapped, frustrated, irritable, and tired, just like the staff. Consider a shopping experience when you were constantly inundated with questions from type-A salespersons asking if you needed help, what you came in for, or if you were "finding everything okay?" (as if you could find anything without being constantly interrogated.) You probably felt tense due to the over-ambition or fear factor imposed on the staff about meeting personal sales goals. You probably also noticed barely any other shoppers there, or that they left as soon as they came in. I doubt you went back unless you had to. Now, think of a time when you were shopping and the staff seemed to be having a good time, joking with each other and the customers, enjoying what they were doing and everyone's company, and having fun while getting things done.

You probably left the store looking forward to shopping there again (and, chances are, you have.) It literally felt good to be there, right?

Whatever energy you feel when coming into contact with a group of people reflects its synergy, and that synergy is the sum of all the energies of the persons within the group. Now, I'd like for you to consider the present synergy of our country. Really take into account the cultural, political, economic, and social climate we're experiencing. It kind of feels like a combination of the first two shopping experiences, doesn't it? For a good part, we're stressed, fearful, angry, frustrated, worried, apathetic, and hopeless. We're also more distant, aloof, antisocial and, in some cases, loopy. Sure, there is a lot of good going around but, depending on your age, consider the synergy that was present twenty, thirty, or forty years ago. Notice both how and how much it has changed.

As detailed in the first half of this book, the reason for this is due to an increase of mismanaged fear amongst the general population, allowing a small yet malignant percentage to obtain disproportionate power, and this small percentage to extract more power by cultivating more fear to exploit.

Spiritual activists counteract this trend in a variety of ways. Though meditation and mindfulness, we can identify our inner fears and transmute them into love; in doing so, we deplete the amount of fear which is exploitable by those who are spiritually malignant and/or bankrupt, for which exploiting fear is a source of power. This is aided by spiritually detoxing, which converts our own dark energy into light, and the various spiritual defense methods, which both preserve our light while simultaneously shedding light on others' darkness, or truth onto spiritually malignant behavior. This not only preserves our selves, but the truth shed on others' malignant behavior allows for it to be converted since it has been brought to the forefront of their awareness. In addition to spreading truth, the positive energy of love, joy, and kindness can also be spread as a remedy to the pre-existent and cultivated fear-based negative energy which has permeated our population. By influencing local synergy toward the light, we will influence it nationally. Then, the darkness which has permeated our country has less of a chance of surviving, since the fear which gave rise to it no longer exists. The most potent way to realize this is to abide by the Golden Rule and practice doing "unto others as you would have done unto you" as much and as often as possible, which is a win-win situation: it makes others feel good and we feel good doing so. Besides, although it is great to feel unconditionally self-loving while being unabashedly self-honest and possess an abundance of positive energy, *we can only influence the outside world by interacting with it.*

By now, you may be thinking, "Okay…meditation, reparenting, truth mechanisms, dharma, karma…will this really affect the political corruption, economic turmoil, souring international relations, and the socio-cultural downturn facing the country?" Absolutely it will. By converting the negative energy in your system into positive, you are most certainly being a part of the solution by transforming fear and falsehoods into love and truth: your drop makes the lake more bright.

You might respond, "But I'm just one drop in a huge lake." The truth is, you're not the only drop, and you don't have to go at it alone. There are many drops elsewhere in the lake currently working on purifying it: you just need to find them, but you need to find your own light first before you can appreciate theirs. Plus, the amount of influence you have on the outside world depends on the amount of light of truth and love which emanates from your own beacon.

Although we are each a drop in the lake and each one of us is unique, we have a certain, personalized way of shining our light. The light we shine authentically reflects our passion and love, and this varies from person to person. Some of us may take the Golden Rule to the next level. We may join others in healing and caring for those who are physically, emotional, or mentally disabled. We could enlist with an organization which builds homes or join another group which performs charity work. We may enroll in a program to act as a mentor to a child who could use one. We could help to provide sanctuary and safety for battered wives. We may find homes for abused, abandoned, or orphaned children. We may do something to care for those who have lost their homes.

Or, the light we shine may be truth-based, confronting large-scale spiritual malignancy. We could courageously address corporate, political, and financial corruption by advocating truth, demanding transparency, calling out toxic behavior, and demanding justice. We could do this by creating our own broadcasts, writing a book, starting a blog, or creating films to inform others. Or, we may raise awareness by protesting with others in a certain activist movement. Some of us are whistleblowers (quite possibly my favorite people), and some will offer their services to protect whistleblowers.

There are so many ways to join others to amplify love and truth in the world around you. After you determine what it is you're passionate about - that is, what your soul is speaking to you - you must act on it in order to influence the outside world in a positive way. Your light will shine as much as you allow it to and it will shine brighter when it merges with others who are like-minded and like-hearted. Whether you're a Truth Seeker, a Freedom Fighter, or a Light Worker (or all three), the brighter your light shines, the greater our synergy will be. The greater the synergy, the greater it will illuminate the world around it. The more love and truth illuminates the world, the closer it will be to world peace.

A "You" You Never Knew But Always Were

The more the general population transmutes its fears, the less prevalent maladaptive responses to fear will be, including offense mechanisms in the form of toxic tactics. The more toxic tactics disappear, the more spiritual malignancy will as well.

Yet, the more each of us do our part in being mindful, dissolving our own negative responses to schemas, detoxing from any negative energy we harbor, replacing this negative energy with positive, and preserve this positive energy with truth mechanisms and other means of soul defense, the greater we will realize our own spiritual metamorphosis and its influence on the world around us. These changes will be emotional, mental, physical, interpersonal, and spiritual in nature.

As we bring awareness to the fear-based emotions involved with our schemas, we provide ourselves with the potential to navigate our reactions to them. The self-knowledge enhanced by mindfulness allows us to heal unattended emotional wounds with authentic self-love. The more this is practiced, the better our general emotional well-being will be. If we had suffered from depression, anxiety, restlessness, panic, chronic anger, or any other emotional malady, we will notice these conditions dissipate as the core issues behind them are brought to light and healed.

Not only will mindfulness assist in dissolving our own negative "internal chatter," the self-love we shed on the corresponding issues will inevitably generate more compassion, understanding, sympathy, and empathy toward others. The increase of self-knowledge, self-worth, and self-love in ourselves increases the knowledge we have for others and their suffering. We will know such suffering in others since we have acknowledged it within ourselves and can identify with it. We can then treat others with compassion, empathy, and understanding provided we treated ourselves in the same manner, since we will then know what that is like, too.

Naturally, the more we tend to our emotional selves, the more at peace we will be. The increase in self-knowledge, self-love, and self-worth is bound to influence both our sense of self and others' perception of us, as is highly likely that our personalities and behaviors will change. Those of us who had been docile, passive, or unassertive will begin to unearth a powerful, vocal side to them which had been dormant for years, while those of us who had been domineering, controlling, and inflexible may develop a personality that more amicable, empathetic, and considerate. Those of us who may have perceived themselves as victims will no longer do so, and many of us ruled by guilt and obligation will grow to be more self-honoring. Those who had been highly inhibited are likely to behave with greater abandon whereas those who had been inconsiderate will be more mindful of others, and those who have been self-exonerating may find themselves accepting accountability. Whatever the case, the result will be growing more and more comfortable in one's own skin and an increasing sense of inner peace. People may even comment on how we seem to be our "own person."

As we heal and grow, a probable side-effect will reflect in the pre-established personal relationships in our lives. As we change, so will our interactions with the other people in our lives. Our internal changes may not be readily embraced or welcomed by others in our lives whom have known us for some time. This is almost always the case if the relationship has a history of being dysfunctional, codependent, or toxic. When we break the inner mold of enabling, providing narcissistic supply, or acquiescing to others' control (or when we stop demanding such from others), we change the dynamic. The other party is likely to find themselves in a state of anomie, to which they may respond with assertive measures to keep the dysfunctional characteristics intact. Or, the dysfunctional relationship may dissolve completely on its own. Or, hopefully, the relationship stays intact while the dysfunction itself disappears.

Many readers can relate to witnessing a relationship "go sour" after their participatory role had been altered so that they stopped engaging in dysfunctional, codependent, and toxic dynamics. Some of us may have lost friends when we stopped enabling them. Or, we may have seen a romantic relationship dissolve when we "stopped putting up with the crap." Still, some of us may have had ties severed when we "rocked the boat" by speaking the truth against ideological or political "taboos." At times it can be rueful to see such relationships dissipate. (Or, if the relationship is toxic enough, it may be a breath of fresh air.) However, as we heal, evolve, grow, and gravitate to our higher selves, we must understand that others may not be "up for the ride" and evolve with us. This is not something we can force upon others. Rather, it is helpful to perceive such severed relationships as a tree that is being pruned: the branches which have been cut off served their purpose, yet staying attached to them will impede fruitful growth. Hopefully, with time, it will become evident that such interpersonal separations were mutually beneficial.

The more we dissolve the internal and external toxicity in our lives, the more we will notice the effects in our physical reality, both internally and externally. As mentioned before, the energy we contain affects our wellbeing either positively or negatively. When we transmute our own fears into love, this will assuredly reflect in out physical wellbeing. The lethargy. pains, and aches that accompany chronic depression, anxiety, panic, and exposure to toxic personalities will lessen as the internal root causes behind them are dissolved. Many will find that they are sick less often. Some of us will even find that we physically appear healthier, even younger.

The same effects will take place when we distance, counteract, or sever ties with toxic personalities in our lives. Think about a highly toxic personality you used to know, and remember how tired and physically drained you felt after interacting with them. When this sort of toxicity disappears from our lives, we notice a boost in our energy as well. Just like transmuting our own negative or fear-based energy, addressing toxic dynamics with others will bring about a more energetic, upbeat, and calm state of being as well as feeling more healthy in general.

Any addictions or bad habits we may have carried are likely to dissipate as well. This is almost certain to be true for those of us who have been accustomed to anesthetizing as a means of defense against our schemas. When we observe and transmute the fears behind our addictions, they can no longer thrive. For instance, someone who relied on "retail therapy" by shopping for clothes in order to make themselves feel more attractive is less likely to do so after tending to their unlovability schema.

Also, with some effort and healthy discrimination, any voids left by relationships which had fallen to the wayside can be fulfilled. With greater understanding, respect, compassion, and authentic love for our selves, we will naturally resonate and identify with others who are similar. These new relationships allow for dynamics which are mutually respectful, supportive, and uplifting. Rather than sapping our energy, these relationships uplift it.

After garnering enough self-knowledge, understanding our souls, and discerning between that which feeds them from that which drains, many of us will also seek to pursue a vocation which is more fulfilling. Those of us stuck in the daily grind, going through the motions, and performing soulless work in order to pay the bills are likely to grow restless. As we unearth our authentic selves, we may discover or rediscover passions and aptitudes which can translate into a more fulfilling career. Those of us who have tolerated a toxic or unpleasant work environment will be less likely to do so. Chances are, change is inevitable: reflecting our self-respect, we will either become more vocal against any workplace mistreatment or leave altogether. Whatever the case may be, practicing this sort of work will catalyze a drive to improve our lives on a daily basis. Since our work occupies the majority of our waking consciousness (for those of us who are employed), it will certainly be no exception. The pursuit of our external happiness will reflect our own internal fulfillment as we gravitate toward a career calling which has us waking up every morning looking forward to the day ahead instead of dreading it.

With this sort of work, it is likely that the list of metamorphoses will expand beyond our personas, relationships, vocations, and mental, emotional, and physical health. With regular practice of mindfulness and meditation, we may notice some other changes as well. Since both practices involve detaching from the ego through awareness and expanded perception, mindfulness and meditation can unveil a sensory perception set normally blocked or overridden by the ego. This set of "right-brained" senses tends to be received intuitively and, in some cases and if developed enough, psychically. Whether such information is received from another plane that is spiritual in nature, I will leave to the discretion of the reader.

Since meditation involves a still, aware, quiet, and relaxed mind, many - if not all of us - will begin to perceive stimuli we never noticed before with practice. This "extra-sensory perception" may occur during or outside of meditative practice, as our intuitive senses become more apparent. We may start to have gut feelings (good, bad, or anything in between) more often, or we may simply "just know" information without supporting, corporeal evidence that later proves to be valid. This occurs because the quiet, awareness of meditative practice allows for the information received by the subconscious to be perceived. This may also occur due to the physiological change in brain tissue. If practiced enough, the psychic senses of clairsentience ("psychic feeling"), claircognizance ("psychic knowing"), clairvoyance ("psychic sight"), clairaudience ("psychic hearing"), and clairaugustine ("psychic smell and taste"; sometimes psychic smell is separated with the term clairscentrist) may emerge or become more apparent. Whereas the five physical senses help us perceive the physical world, the "inspired" psychic senses allow us to perceive the intuitive, which may bring a variety of messages, including those pertaining to our personal wellbeing, growth, and safety.

It is often considered that humans use only about ten percent of their brain capacity. I strongly believe this to be untrue: the mind has capabilities far beyond what is noticeable to most since the average person has grown accustomed to conducting their daily lives in a constant beta brain wave state. This constant mental state of multitasking, strategizing, planning, analyzing, conceptualizing, and sole reliance on the five basic senses and a mindset based in the ego not only leads to burn out, it prohibits the ability to observe, explore, and experience extra-sensory perception.

Since the norm of everyday life for many of us is to wake up at a certain time, shower, eat, get dressed, arrive to work on time, perform eight or more hours of mentally and/or physically prescribed and demanding labor, and return home after a commute to (attempt to) decompress from a stressful day - usually by watching the news or another television program - most of us constantly live in an egoic state of mind. Even when we "vacation," many of us are still mentally active.

Always being mentally "on-the-go" inhibits the potential of experiencing what the mind is capable of in a different state. With increased practice of meditation, we not only allow ourselves to become more familiarized with other sensory capabilities which had previously gone unnoticed, we strengthen them as well.

With increased practice, we learn that we are not only capable of creating thoughts, images, concepts, plans, emotions, analyses, or any sort of "active" mental process, yet we are equipped to receive information as well. We discover that in addition to our "active" senses of sight, taste, touch, hearing, and smell, we also have intuitive and psychic senses.

Whereas the physical senses are palpable, left-brained, and relied upon to carry out egoic activity, the psychic senses are intuitive, right-brained, and received rather than implemented. But we must learn to let go and "get out of our own way" in order to experience them. We must evacuate our own manufactured processes and intellectual input in order to allow such sublime and inspired information to be perceived.

Perhaps you can identify certain moments when you have had gut feelings about certain things which proved to be valid or dreams which accurately (if not symbolically) forecasted upcoming events in your life. Many of us have, although we may have written such occurrences off as coincidence or chance since we could not explain it. If you have received such intuitive messages in the past, think back during the times when they occurred - you were probably in a relaxed, focused, present, or centered state of mind.

Throughout my life, I have had similar curious episodes where I "knew" that someone would call just before they did (and what their call was regarding), prophetic dreams, and strong gut feelings one way or another. I could also "read people" very well, oftentimes knowing the content of what they were going to say before they did. For the most part, I wrote it off as being sensitive.

However, about a year and a half before writing this book, I realized that I was always "in my head" a lot. I had spent much of my waking-state consciousness always thinking, analyzing, mulling over, or worrying about things related to my past, present, and future. I had come to realize that it was non-stop, as my mind was always pre-occupied with *something*: when my next phone bill was due, who I needed to e-mail, how I got screwed over the week before - you get the idea. Something was *always* on my mind.

Simultaneously, many of my social contacts were either becoming more distant and ungiving or more toxic and self-involved, as were many of the people I became acquainted with. I either found myself being drained by others or witnessing escalating aloofness. This actually had been the case for some time, but the increased in toxicity and separateness had seemed to reach a crescendo.

In fact, it became so acute, it was hard not to notice. So was my realization that I was very "mental." For whatever reason, I examined my given state of circumstances and listened to my intuition, which seemed to suggesting that I needed a break.

Heeding what my intuition was telling me, I literally decided to give myself a mental vacation from all the intellectual activity my mind was processing. I also decided to become a hermit for a bit as I mentally detached from others whom I found draining or disappointing. "I'll be a monk for the next few days," I told myself as I decided to get in touch with my spiritual side. I had heard about Spirit Guides during my Reiki training (at this point, I was attuned to Reiki II); if they truly existed, perhaps they were the best company for me right now.

Over the next few days, I devoted the majority of my time to meditation and performing Reiki on myself. For exercise, I skipped the gym to either take a long walk around the neighborhood or practice yoga; in both cases, I made sure I was present and "in the moment" while I exercised. For recreation, I decided to read a book authored by a remote viewer who was formerly involved with intelligence in the US Army. Mentally, I did my best to remain in the "here and now," avoiding the tendencies to fret, analyze, worry, speculate, stew, and so forth.

After a couple days of this regimen, I noticed I was much calmer than usual and looked and felt healthier. I decided to keep going.

That night, I began my meditative practice. I was considerably calm, relaxed, and focused going into it, although there was still some mental activity still going on. First, I allowed myself to relax considerably with my eyes open as my mind quieted. After doing this for a while, I had the impression that I was not alone: it "felt" like others were in the room with me.

As I continued to meditate, I objectively brought my awareness to what was mentally transpiring. When I noticed any mental agitation, I simply applied mindfulness by observing it without trying to change it. I didn't "force" my mind to be quiet and still, nor did I judge or expand on what was occurring mentally. I continued to remain detached and observational with respect to any sort of averting mental activity while remaining calm and relaxed. Doing this, I noticed, allowed my mind to quiet even further and deepen its concentration.

After a while (for how long, I don't know; my perception of time was altered), the mental activity was incredibly still. Then, this *overwhelming* and incredibly palpable sense of bliss, joy, and love came out of nowhere. By maintaining my awareness on this wonderful state of being, it seemed like this bliss was the only experiential thing - and it seemed as though my own thoughts were no longer perceptible.

As I continued maintaining my awareness, this state of bliss decreased but did not disappear; rather it was accompanied by a sense of peace. This peace is hard to describe, but it was like a stillness, almost like a void yet peaceful in a zen-like way. Yet it was a peace was like no peace I had ever experienced before. Then, I progressed into a state where the bliss I had felt - or what remained of it - was gone and all that was left was this zen-like peace. Here, I noticed that I was so relaxed, I was barely breathing.

Then, subsequently, my sense of time, place, identity, personal and physical existence, mental activity - everything that was left of my egoic existence - has dissipated. This is very difficult to describe, yet it was like the sense of "being" was all there was. In this state (a sort of "ego-death", I suppose), it felt as though space, time, and consciousness (now no longer belonging to myself - or having that sense) converged and was infinite. I found this to be immensely calm and indescribably peaceful.

Then, I experienced a state of absolute "nothingness"; no sense of anything whatsoever: my existence, time, place, identity - even "nothing" itself.

After being in this state (I have no idea for how long - there was no way of telling), something incredible happened. This RUSH came over me out of nowhere. I suddenly became aware that I was not alone, as I could feel a presence which felt like it was both in and around me. It was like I had merged with and was in the presence of this entity, yet it was not "physically" there. And this entity's presence - and this is something I cannot underestimate - was *palpable and overwhelming*.

Whomever - or whatever - this was had the ability to project an *incredible and indescribable* amount of love onto me - love like I had never experienced before. It seemed to know, understand, and love everything about me *far* more than I did. I felt I recognized this being, too. In fact, this entity seemed so familiar, it felt like I couldn't tell how long I knew it for.

But it was evident that this presence was communicating to me through sentiments as it conveyed profound messages of unconditional love. Soon, I realized that the sentiments I "gave out" in response were immediately and thoroughly responded to by this presence. Apparently, I could transmit messages in the form of thoughts/sentiments/emotions toward this being telepathically, receive this being's telepathic responses (also in the form of emotional and intellectual content), and engage in a telepathic dialogue. Since my own mental activity had ceased prior to this point, it was exceptionally easy to distinguish my own thought processes and imagination from what was being received from this entity, *especially* considering how palpable its presence was. Communicating with this entity was not only very rapid since no words were needed to convey sentiments, but extremely - and beautifully - intimate. Imagine having a conversation with someone without saying any words while they instantaneously feel and understand the ideas and sentiments you intend to communicate to them, and vice versa. This sort of spiritual proximity is incredibly intimate: it's basically soul speak.

Whomever or whatever this entity was (or, is), coming into contact with it was - undoubtedly - the most beautiful moment of my life. I did not physically - or psychically - see this being, yet it was animate and its presence was undeniable. One indelible impression was that, although it did not seem to have a gender, this entity had a sort of maternal quality to it. And it was incredibly, incredibly, sweet - like a great, big, loving heart - and had a very distinctive innocent and pure feel to it.

After this, I came out of this altered state and back into consciousness a bit, yet I was still feeling the effects of what had just occurred - the bliss, the joy, the peace and, most of all, the love I had received as well as this strange sense of connectedness and unification - not just personally, but experientially. Although I was rather dazed after what had just happened, it still felt like I was not alone.

Still feeling some connection to this altered state and amazed at what had just occurred, I relocated to a different room. "Who else is here?" I asked myself. I quieted my mind again and, this time, when I felt that I was in that receptive state, I asked a question. I just sort of "put it out there" to see what would happen. This time, it was a bit different: I could now see clairvoyantly through my third eye the soul responding in addition to communicating with them telepathically. These souls, although I did not know them personally, I knew of. Their appearance and presence seemed to just "come into" my third eye. One of the souls whom I conversed with - a young man - appeared clairvoyantly although I had no prior idea as to what his physical appearance looked like. Interacting with these souls was not the same as interacting with the first entity I encountered, which felt quite omniscient and powerful ("potent" might be a better word.) What surprised me about conversing with these souls was how much of their personal identity remained intact after death.

Like the being I first met, I could communicate with each soul telepathically. Since no auditory words were used (or necessary), conversations which would normally require a minutes to carry out transpired in a matter of seconds. Since exact ideas and sentiments were directly transposed, there was no room for misinterpretation or ambiguity. I understood exactly what they intended as they did with me. And everyone I had "met" that evening was a pleasure to converse with.

Although clairvoyance, claircognizance, and clairsentience were the predominant "senses" used in communicating, there were some instances of clairaudience and clairaugustine.

To be honest, I still didn't quite know what to make of this after I "came out" of it. Despite of the profundity of the experience, there was still some confusion. Clearly, something happened...but what? Due to my calm and focused state of mind, I knew I wasn't imagining things. Yet, the novelty of this occurrence along with thirty-six years worth of acknowledging sensory perception based on five physical senses left me rather disoriented.

Fortunately, various events which took place during the following week resolved any doubts or confusion I had. For several days after this experience, I carried with me a consistent feeling of peace, joy, equanimity, compassion, and love - completely devoid of any worry, fretting, or ill will - and my mindset was continuously mindful and in the present. I found these mental and emotional states to be quite natural and effortless, as they seemed to be residual effects of the transcendental experience I just had. One thing was for certain: I had not reverted back to my previous state of mind during the week which followed.

Yet it was the multitude of experiences I had during this week which dissolved any skepticism or doubt. What followed was something I would refer to as "psychic puberty" due to the variety of psychic experiences I was having along with an uncanny synchronicity that accompanied them.

Whenever I would have a psychic experience during this week, I would inadvertently come across material which would explain it shortly afterward. It was basically the opposite of being taught in school: here, I would first experience the "lesson" that would then be described later in material of "the lecture." Much of this post-experiential material was presented in the book I was reading by the remote viewer. For instance, when I had an experience of what is know as "pre-reaction" (where the body or a body part acts automatically on it own for a reason unbeknownst to the person at the time), I would read the chapter on pre-reaction later that night. First I would experience it, then I learned about it - and accompanying this trend was an uncanny sense of confirmation.

Pre-reaction was one of many experiences. During this week, I had many episodes of pre-cognition, usually in the form of "knowing" beforehand when someone would call, who they were, and the reason they were calling. There were also countless instances were I would sense or feel that I would see or hear something moments before I did.

I also noticed my ability to "read" people was enhanced considerably: not only could I pick up on unexpressed thoughts, emotions, and concepts others were having during our conversations but, if their minds wandered, I knew where it went. In general, my sense of telepathy was substantially heightened.

During my daily, hour-long walks around the neighborhood as I listened to music, I would know if someone was walking behind me, how far they were behind me, and something about the person - usually their age and gender - without seeing them first.

Some people can see auras (I have only a couple of times) yet, during this week, I could "feel" them quite easily. It became readily apparent that I could simply walk by someone to get an idea of their energy and what it was about. For example, while taking care of some grocery shopping during this week, I passed by three people who were shopping together in the cereal aisle. I didn't pay much attention as they walked toward me, as they were barely in my peripheral vision. As the first two walked passed me, I got a sense of their "energy" - their personality, their emotional state, etc. - as they walked behind me. They seemed pretty normal to me, so I didn't pay much mind to it. Yet when the third person walked behind me, I felt this *surge* - and it did not feel good.

It was so overwhelming, in fact, I spun around to see where it was coming from. The energy coming from this person's aura was, well, awful; to say that he was toxic would be an understatement. Seeing his physical appearance jolted even more data: specifics in his behavior were revealed and he apparently took pleasure in causing others distress - usually psychologically. I sensed quite strongly that he did not care about having a conscience, either; rather, he took pride and enjoyment in not having one. He thought of himself as being "better" or more powerful than others by being cunning and manipulative.

I was so overcome with this energy I came into contact with, I didn't realize I was staring at him. Noticing my shock, he muttered something derogatory. However, at that moment, I "mind-tapped" him and knew that he felt extremely vulnerable and defenseless, as he realized that someone else - perhaps the first time in a long while - saw him exactly for who he was. It was like his mask of sanity became invisible in that moment - something which made him feel very exposed and uncomfortable.

Fortunately, such distressing moments were few during this week-long period. Something else I noticed was the dreams I had written down during the weeks before, uniformly complex and off-the-wall, made perfect sense. I could interpret and decipher them completely along with dreams I had during this time.

Speaking and understanding foreign languages came much more easily as well. Prior to this experience, I was intermediately proficient in Spanish and Japanese. Now, whenever I heard either language, I knew exactly what was being said while it was being spoken. I would test myself, too - I would translate English sentences I had just read or spoken into either language with no difficulty.

And, prior to this experience, I had recently explored and dabbled in remote viewing.

Before, when I would practice, I would randomly select a picture from a stack of photographs about three inches thick. The photos were taken from a variety of scenes: graduation ceremonies, various vacations, weddings, parties, and more. Without looking at the photo selected (the "target"), I went into a receptive, meditative state of mind and jotted down any clues I had received with my psychic senses. After this experience, my ability to remote view was greatly enhanced as the "clues" I was receiving about the target were more pronounced and precise.

These are just some of the experiences I had during this week.

As mentioned before, after experiencing each of these phenomena, I unintentionally came across some reading material which would describe or explain it in detail. All of this helped to resolve the doubt or confusion I had about initial transcendental experience, yet the kicker came soon after. While I was web-surfing one day, I inadvertently came across a photo of the young man I had conversed with while in that altered state yet whom I had previously never seen. The image was a perfect match. Plus, the personality that emanated from the picture was identical to the personality I had met. I was stunned: "Holy shit! I was *channelling*!!??"

The most exhilarating post-experiential material I came across dealt with the actual experience itself. This, above all else, not only verified the experience, but it left me with the feeling of having an invisible teacher, one who allowed me (or introduced me?) to experience the lesson before it was taught. Before coming across this material, I would go into a sort of daydreaming state while I took may daily walks. For reasons unknown to me at the time, these alpha-wave mind-scapes always involved the image of a wheel - one that resembled a captain's wheel with eight spokes. I knew this was a Buddhist symbol yet thought this image specifically represented karma. But, after my curiosity was prompted by seeing this wheel over and over again, I began to research the meaning of this image online. Soon, I came across a webpage which referred to this symbol as the Wheel of Dharma, or "Dharmakara." Clicking on subsequent embedded links led me to the following information on Jhānas (or Dhyānas), which are successive stages of meditation. The first four stages, the rūpa jhānas, are known as "mediations of form" whereas the next four, the arūpa jhānas, are "formless meditations":

Description of the Four Rupa Jhanas

For each Jhāna are given a set of qualities which are "ferreted them out one after another" and "vanish":

1. First Jhāna — In the first jhana there are: "Directed thought, evaluation, rapture, pleasure, unification of mind, contact, feeling, perception, intention, consciousness, desire, decision, persistence, mindfulness, equanimity & attention"

2. Second Jhāna — In the second jhana there are: "internal assurance, rapture, pleasure, unification of mind, contact, feeling, perception, intention, consciousness, desire, decision, persistence, mindfulness, equanimity, & attention"

3. Third Jhāna — In the third jhana, there are: "equanimity-pleasure, unification of mind, contact, feeling, perception, intention, consciousness, desire, decision, persistence, mindfulness, equanimity & attention"

4. Fourth Jhāna — In the fourth jhana there are: "a feeling of equanimity, neither pleasure nor pain; an unconcern due to serenity of awareness; unification of mind, contact, feeling, perception, intention, consciousness, desire, decision, persistence, mindfulness, equanimity & attention".

Jhana Factors:

Jhānas are normally described according to the nature of the mental factors which are present in these states:

    1) Movement of the mind onto the object (*vitakka*; Sanskrit: *vitarka*)
    2) Retention of the mind on the object (*vicāra*)
    3) Joy (*pīti*; Sanskrit: *prīti*)
    4) Happiness (*sukha*)
    5) Equanimity (*upekkhā*; Sanskrit: *upekṣā*)
    6) One-pointedness (*ekaggatā*; Sanskrit: *ekāgratā*)

Factors per Jhana

The qualities that remain in each jhana are:

1. First *jhāna* (*vitakka, vicāra, pīti, sukha, ekaggatā*): The five hindrances [craving, aversion, sloth, agitation and doubt] have completely disappeared and intense unified bliss remains. Only the subtlest of mental movement remains, perceivable in its absence by those who have entered the second *jhāna*. The ability to form unwholesome intentions ceases.

2. Second *jhāna* (*pīti, sukha, ekaggatā*): All mental movement utterly ceases. There is only bliss. The ability to form wholesome intentions ceases as well.

3. Third *jhāna* (*sukha, ekaggatā*): One-half of bliss (joy) disappears.

4. Fourth *jhāna* (*upekkhā, ekaggatā*): The other half of bliss (happiness) disappears, leading to a state with neither pleasure nor pain, which the Buddha said is actually a subtle form of happiness (more sublime than *pīti* and *sukha*). The breath is said to cease temporarily in this state.

Psychic powers

Traditionally, the fourth *jhāna* is seen as the beginning of attaining psychic powers (*abhigna*).

The Arupa Jhānas

Beyond the four *jhānas* lie four attainments, referred to in the early texts as *aruppas*. These are also referred to in commentarial literature as immaterial/ the formless *jhānas* (*arūpajhānas*), also translated as The Formless Dimensions, in distinction from the first four *jhānas* (*rūpa jhānas*). In the Buddhist canonical texts, the word "*jhāna*" is never explicitly used to denote them, but they are always mentioned in sequence after the first four *jhānas*. The immaterial attainments have more to do with expanding, while the Jhanas (1-4) focus on concentration. The enlightenment of complete dwelling in emptiness is reached when the eighth *jhāna* is transcended.

The four formless jhanas are:

1. Dimension of Infinite Space — In the dimension of infinite space there are: "the perception of the dimension of the infinitude of space, unification of mind, contact, feeling, perception, intention, consciousness, desire, decision, persistence, mindfulness, equanimity, & attention"

2. Dimension of Infinite Consciousness — In the Dimension of infinite consciousness there are: "the perception of the dimension of the infinitude of consciousness, unification of mind, contact, feeling, perception, intention, consciousness, desire, decision, persistence, mindfulness, equanimity, & attention"

3. Dimension of Nothingness — In the dimension of nothingness, there are: "the perception of the dimension of nothingness, singleness of mind, contact, feeling, perception, intention, consciousness, desire, decision, persistence, mindfulness, equanimity, & attention"

4. Dimension of Neither Perception nor Non-Perception — About the role of this jhana it is said: "He emerged mindfully from that attainment. On emerging mindfully from that attainment, he regarded the past qualities that had ceased & changed: 'So this is how these qualities, not having been, come into play. Having been, they vanish.' He remained unattracted & unrepelled with regard to those qualities, independent, detached, released, dissociated, with an awareness rid of barriers. He discerned that 'There is a further escape,' and pursuing it there really was for him."

If I hadn't still been in a post-transcendental high, I would have fallen out of my chair upon reading this. Here, in ancient Buddhist teachings, was a thorough, detailed, and precise description of what I had experienced just days before. Not only was I blown away by the distinct descriptions of each stage, I was astounded that someone could provide such a thorough depiction of phenomena experienced in such an altered state of consciousness. I could not possibly describe these successive meditative stages better. Moreover, seeing that the fourth rupa jhāna correlated to psychic ability (referred to here as "abhigna"), I understood that channeling had actually occurred: it was not a fluke or a figment of my imagination.

Additional research described how this transcendental state of awareness is followed by a week-long phase of feeling connected and blissful, typically accompanied by heightened psychic senses and awareness.

I felt it was important to share this experience and information for a few reasons. First, it signifies that there is more to human perception and consciousness than is commonly accepted. With this comes a new, experiential existence as well as an unveiling of faculties and capabilities previously overridden, disregarded, or unnoticed. Through continued practice of meditation and mindfulness, dormant extra-sensory capabilities can be revealed.

Second, expanding on the metaphorical image of each human being a "drop of energy," I feel this experience speaks volumes regarding the nature of this energy. Our consciousness - or awareness - is not a sort of "imaginary ether" nor is it necessarily localized and housed in our physical bodies. Perhaps on a quantum level - or an energetic level more evasive - it is, in fact, plugged into some sort of "source", able to transmit and receive information on a sublime, etheric level. Like a drop in a lake, our energy retains its identity while merging with others to form a larger body. But what exactly is this larger body? And how big is it?

Third, what exactly is this energy that is our "drop" and what can be done with it? Is it mere consciousness or is it more? As illustrated in my experience, a heightened awareness, mindfulness, focus, and mental presence devoid of ego-attachment also expanded perception, which allowed various phenomena to be sensed. More still, the actual *state* of energy - that being of peace, joy, and love - seemed to catalyze or enhance the connection with this realm. Many credible mediums I have met since have spoken of the benefit of "raising one's vibration" in order to make this sort of contact. From my own channeling experience, this seems have validity. You may have personally noticed heighten synchronicity in your own life during periods of calm, presentness, and connectedness. What does this suggest about the frequency, resonance, or vibration of our own energetic "drops"? Also, what does this suggest about what might ensue when our energy is vibrating at a low frequency? Or a high one? And, what is to be expected synergistically when our energy merges with others?

Fourth, what does this suggest about meditation? Why is it that we feel connected, collected, calm, and renewed after a meditative practice? Is there a source we can connect to? If so, what is it?

What has become evident is that most of us are and have been stuck in a daily grind in which we begrudgingly go through the motions, often living hand-to-mouth, working to live and living to work, and strenuously so - usually in jobs that are personally and spiritually unfulfilling if not stressful, degrading, and draining. For various reasons, many of us have grown accustomed to living lives of anger, frustration, hopelessness, resignation, and despair. Hopefully, the first half of this book sufficiently illustrated where most of the population is currently vibrating and the causes behind it. One thing is clear: in order to change our given state of circumstances, we must either change these circumstances or ourselves. I suggest both.

✠

14

The Return of the Eagle

Rising from the Ashes

"The duty of youth is to challenge corruption."

- Kurt Cobain

Imagine living in a country where we could trust each other; where we could leave cars and homes unlocked without fear of anything being stolen. Imagine that people communicated with each other by _talking_ to them; where people met with each other face to face. Imagine that we cared about everyone and everyone cared about us. Imagine that people are honest with each other, both in word and emotion. Imagine that everyone was self-accountable and valued a clean conscience more than material goods. Imagine people treated each other the way they would want to be treated. Imagine more love going around. Imagine a citizenry united rather than fragmented. Imagine we valued human rights within others and ourselves, that we were valued and understood.

Imagine we played games rather than watch them. Imagine we craved personal company rather than that on a screen. Imagine we were all high on life rather than on a substance.

Imagine our food and water was as pure as only Nature could make it. Imagine that our homes were valued not for their size but for the love inside it. Imagine our schooling involving teaching our children to use their brains critically and creatively. Imagine our children grew up to love and respect others because that was how they were raised, so that they would love themselves, their elders, peers, and the generations that follow. Imagine that they played with each other in person rather than interact with each other virtually.

Imagine our armed forces were used to resolve conflict rather than start it. Imagine they were used only when needed.

Imagine a law enforcement comprised of guardians of mutual respect and safety, that they were of upmost honor and valor. Imagine that lawyers were representatives of wisdom, ethics, and protectors of one rule only - The Golden Rule - and that they represented reality rather than half-truths. Imagine judges who were only influenced by wisdom and moral integrity. Imagine our elected politicians sought their positions out of genuine desire to serve their constituents. Imagine the incentives for all were ones of personal, spiritual fulfillment rather than money and status. Imagine these public service professions were staffed due to ethical achievement. Better yet, imagine a country where none of these professions were needed.

Imagine our healthcare focused on healing our minds, bodies, and spirits.

Imagine our media spoke the truth, the whole truth, and nothing but the truth. Imagine they kept their opinions to themselves and didn't try to influence the public.

Imagine people didn't judge each other by their color or creed but by their character. Imagine that it didn't matter whom you loved so long that you did.

Imagine other countries noticed all this in ours. Imagine they were inspired by us rather than despise us. Imagine we started a trend.

This is all possible, but it all depends on how much it is *wanted*. As the first half of this book illustrated, the various pyramidal models which have caused an insurmountable degree of victimization and strife have thrived on manipulating mismanaged fear. This control over others has been enhanced by imposing additional fear in order to achieve a level of despotic control. And, as mentioned before, without this fear, these pyramids lose their foundations. This exploitation of mismanaged fear, imposition of additional fear, living in the ego, and violating the Golden Rule - all of which is a spiritual affliction at its core - is the bedrock upon which these institutions were founded. Without a source of willing victimhood, narcissistic supply, and enabling, these spiritually bankrupt manifestations could not have grown to the extent which they have.

Specifically, the remedy to this is to produce the polar opposite: by dissolving mismanaged fear through mindful awareness, staving off toxic tactics with the light of truth, realizing the authentic self through self-knowledge and self-love, and counteracting pervasive spiritual malignancy by regularly practicing the Golden Rule, the supply of energy which feeds these malignant entities is cut off. By tending to our own fears with love, we cleans ourselves of any internal toxicity. And once we hold ourselves and others to an ethical standard based on the Golden Rule with awareness and integrity, all of the afflictions rooted in spiritual malignancy we currently face dissolve. Shedding light on others' toxic behavior and spiritual malignancy not only preserves our own wellbeing and rights, it holds others accountable for their behavior. Doing so allows for the potential of penetrating other's egos as well as the issues behind their offense mechanisms, increasing the likelihood of their buried consciences to emerge as a result.

The more we intentionally treat others in a way in which we would want to be treated and hold others to the same standard, the more positive changes will take place. With a resurgence of empathy, conscience, and compassion emerges a greater and more prosperous sense of community in ways which are cultural, social, economic, and political. And, this transition from what is best for "me" to what is best for "us" will also foster a greater of unity and cohesion. The motto "united we stand; divided we fall" contains inherent value in this regard.

Before anything else, it is essential to start with ourselves. We will not be equipped to transmute the fear within the outside world - responsible for the many cultural, social, economic, and political afflictions we currently endure - until we dissolve the fear we personally harbor. Before we can authentically apply the Golden Rule to others, we must first apply it to ourselves, which involves tending to these fears with love. Only after transmuting our own internalized fears will we dissolve the defense or offense mechanisms that reinforce them. And, by honoring our own freedom and wellbeing, recognizing our own rights and acknowledging rules, and respecting ourselves first, doing so for others comes naturally. Applying the Golden Rule to ourselves first makes applying it to others second-nature.

As we increase our own self-knowledge, self-awareness, and self-love, we become more functional, social, and respectful. Simultaneously, we increase the propensity of countering the spiritually malignant goals of creating a willing victim, establishing narcissism, and reinforcing entitlement by becoming more vocal when we have been dominated or mistreated, cutting off narcissistic supply, and refusing to enable others, respectfully. Since we have addressed the fears behind our own toxicity and/or dysfunction, we will no longer play into such dynamics with others.

If we have been raised in toxic or dysfunctional families, many of us will start there, since functional persons affect their family members in a functional manner. If codependency exists, a functional family member will counteract and weaken the dysfunctional dynamics by refusing to enable. If emotional manipulation in the form of guilt trips, favoritism, playing the victim, exoneration, or another toxic tactic is commonplace, a spiritually wealthy family member will no longer respond to or condone such behavior and can alter the dysfunctional family pattern with truth mechanisms.

The more functional a family member becomes, the more authentic they will be. The more they realize their authentic self, the more they will break out of the dysfunctional family role they had been pigeonholed in. A Little Parent will, once and for all, do the job of parenting themselves and no longer bear the burden of abdicating their own needs out of supporting others. A Hero will no longer feel pressured to compensate for their family's inadequacy, and nor will they base their own self-worth on others' expectations and conventions. They will realize that being true to themselves is what makes them a winner, not kowtowing to losers, and learn that they are responsible for their own worth, not others'. A Scapegoat can understand that they were never a "problem" to begin with; the only problem was the dysfunction within the family unit for which they should have never been held accountable. They will realize that "ne'er do well" applies to their family's dynamics, not them. A Lost Child will learn it is not they who are invisible: their family's "love" is. If asserting their emotional and physical existence proves futile, they may learn that families who disregard their children are not worth much consideration. A Mascot will realize that there is nothing funny about dysfunctional and toxic behavior and that if anything is silly, it is catering to others who would prefer to believe otherwise. By refusing to diffuse the dysfunction with humor while shedding light on others' malignancy, the parody that is their toxic family members takes center stage. A Little Tyrant can learn a little respect, humility, and self-limitation. Whatever the case, the breakdown of a dysfunctional role within a family throws a monkey wrench in the dysfunctional operation of the entire family.

The more spiritually wealthy behavior is practiced and embraced and thus amassed by one or more family members, the more its influence brings the family closer to being healthy and functional. In time, a family can emerge in which all of its members have the same rights, all abide by the same rules, and the Golden Rule is upheld as it is practiced by example. Everyone is heard, no favoritism occurs, self-accountability exists, enabling vanishes, problems and feelings are openly discussed and acknowledged, communication is personal and thorough, respect is internalized and externalized, needs are acknowledged and met across the board, and no one is held accountable for anything outside their realm of duty. There is no ideological fascism or imposed dogma as each member creates their lives and beliefs authentically. Most importantly, everyone treats and is treated in ways in which they would want to be treated.

The more dysfunctional families convert from being dysfunctional to functional, the more the civilization they comprise will as well. As we learn to hold ourselves and others accountable, to give and receive respect, and to personally and mutually honor freedom within the family, our healthy conditioning will affect the interactions we have with others outside the family. Soon, members of dysfunctional families within the civilization will be influenced by members of other families which are functional. With enough influence, the dysfunctional and toxic dynamics of criminal/victim, narcissist/narcissistic supplier, and entitlement/enabling erode - the reverse of the "zombie effect" described in the first half of this book.

As these unhealthy dynamics vanish, so too will their prevalence in larger social structures. These structures - dependent on such unhealthy dynamics to exist - will themselves diminish as a result. As more of us cultivate our own self-knowledge and self-awareness, we grow to be more self-loving and accepting. In doing so, we develop a sense of peace and acceptance with who we are and what we have in life. Thus, the wall built with feelings of shame and unworthiness out of not having a wonderful career, fantastic relationship, an overly vibrant social life, perfect physical appearance, financial health, etc. that has separated many of us from more open, intimate, and interpersonal relationships crumbles. The need to masquerade our true selves behind an online "social networking" profile and limit their social interaction accordingly feels superficial, vestigial, and personally unfulfilling. The newfound comfortability and intimacy we have with ourselves gives way to a craving to have such relationships with others, as the compassion, understanding, and awareness we have for ourselves we can now impart to others. Instead of sending a text or an e-mail, making a phone call or playing a board game with others becomes more appealing. We also come to understand that any judgement we face for being "substandard" is no longer a reflection upon us; on the contrary, it is a reflection of those who are judging.

The shift in the preference of social interaction from virtual to interpersonal provides less prey for those who act malignantly online. Scammers, phishers, trolls, and other manipulating and toxic personalities will have less potential victims to project their fears of mistrust, vulnerability, unlovability and more upon. Having have less of an outlet, they will be alone to be with their issues, since their offense mechanisms will no longer be indulged. Hopefully, such emotional isolation will lead to some introspection and subsequent healing.

Perhaps with less time in front of a computer, free time will be used to go outside or go within. By mindfully interacting with others in person and/or meditating, any negative feelings which arise can shed light on unattended schemas. Provided these schemas are recognized and healed, self-knowledge and self-love will emerge.

In doing so, we come out of the zombie-like stupor and really begin to *live*. Those of us who had issues of unlovability will understand our true, genuine, and intrinsic self-worth and no longer welcome being made to feel less than. We will love others with equal authenticity. Those with deprivation schemas will embrace and tend to their needs and be mindful to those of others. Those of us who have unresolved issues of abandonment will find reliable, interpersonal support systems for company and comfort and will be emotionally available to others without ignoring our own needs. We will eschew those who are emotionally unavailable. Those who bore subjugation schemas will assert their will in a respectful manner while honoring others'. Those with inner fears of mistrust will trust again, yet with some discrimination, while valuing the trust others placed in them. Those of us with issues of vulnerability will have a more realistic assessment of personal safety and security while being mindful of the wellbeing of others. And those with exclusion schemas won't live in isolation, dread social situations, or live in fear of not being accepted. Those of us with perfectionism or failure schemas will, respectively, lower and raise the bar of achievement from an unreasonable level as we dissolve the fears behind them. And those of us with entitlement schemas will abide by rules and be comfortable when we do not get their way.

And none of us will compensate for our issues by creating an alternate reality or projecting the inner pain that we're too afraid to address onto others.

With our inner fears dissolved, we will be less susceptible to the propaganda of consumerism that exploits them, saving money as a result. We will realize the irony of "retail therapy" and that, despite living in a material world, not all of the cures reside there. Instead of "keeping up with the Joneses", we will have compassion for them, understanding that status symbols make up for emotional wounds.

For most of us this immunity to consumeristic propaganda is likely to increase our financial reserves, as more of us will spend within our means and on what is necessary, avoiding debt and wreaking havoc on credit and loan systems. Perhaps the money saved will allow for greater ability to choose which businesses we patronize, as we understand that our purchasing power can act to sponsor and support establishments which are ethical. In both cases, the transfer of public wealth into the hands of a few and currency production would diminish, which would lead to less inflation, which would impede the entire cycle.

With increased knowledge regarding our own truth and our own nature, we'll become increasingly aware that not only is Reality TV infused with fantasy, but other television programs as well. It will become more apparent that the press is endangered of being free and has, like much other programming, morphed into a megaphone for a corporate/ government hybrid entity that abstains from any broadcast which might incriminate it. As more of us employ critical thinking, more questions will be formulated which penetrate the spin, half-truths, and lies of omission broadcasted by the corporate media used to manipulate the general public. As we pursue answers, more of us will discover many sources of truthful, alternative media that have been desperate to be heard. With increased knowledge of our own nature and behavior, we will comprehend others with more depth as well, and more of us will gain better insight into what is actually occurring in current events both domestically and abroad and to see truth behind the smoke and mirrors. Maybe more of us will even grow to acknowledge and trust our intuition, understanding that it is more reliable than most corporate news sources.

The more we cultivate self-love, the more we'll understand precisely how self-evident our basic human rights truly are and the degree to which they have been blatantly violated by the federal government. Instead of protecting and serving the general public, our government as well as many abroad will be exposed as institutions that siphon rights and finances through manipulation and dominance, acting as a spiritually bankrupt parasites as opposed to public servants. With enough self-love, many will join the voices of others to counteract such corruption with truth mechanisms. The foundation of lies, manipulations, dominance, narcissism, and entitlement supporting such malignancy cannot withstand a crescendo of intolerance as more and more refuse to enable, adulate, and succumb to malignant, pathological liars. The louder this collective voice of truth, the sooner our government will be restored as it was intended: for the people, by the people.

Perhaps more of us will do the same with the morally corrupt corporations that bypass anything resembling ethical standards and obligations. The more of us who call out the harmful effects their products and services have on the environment and the human population at large, the more we will raise awareness to the physical and spiritual toxicity of such companies. This awareness will affect consumer activity, as customers change their purchasing habits to benefit other business which include ethics in their practices.

With cultivated self-love and self-worth, more of us will be compelled to call out spiritual malignancy in the workplace. We will have less reservations against holding others accountable to the same ethical standard - one rooted in self-love and based on mutual respect - we hold ourselves to. We will grow less and less tolerant of incompetent "superiors" and "supervisors" who motivate through fear rather than lead by example. We will realize that self-worth is the best motivator, and that those unwilling to personify this truth with positive reinforcement and empathy are not qualified to hold supervisory positions. We will grow intolerant of entitled superiors who get paid substantially more to do substantially less work.

With increased self-love and adherence to the Golden Rule, we will understand that our employment is an agreement based on give-and-take, and that any demands to perform duties outside of our job description or any attempts to reward a job well done with more work is indicative of an employer's entitlement, narcissism, and control. Since our fears of subjugation, vulnerability, and unlovability have been dissolved, this will not be tolerated.

Many of us may even come to realize that slavery has never ended, rather it has been reinvented to insidiously give the impression that those who are enslaved have some semblance of freedom. Whereas the slavery of the past provided food, shelter, and clothing directly, it may become clear that modern slaves are simply given a stipend to obtain such amenities on their own. Those of us enduring this treatment will be lucky if this stipend, with the rising cost of living, subsidizes all three necessities without going into debt. Hopefully with this realization, disenfranchised laborers working to live and living to work will realize that, not only are they not alone, but there is strength in numbers. With this cohesive strength, they can assert their own rights and challenge the abuses against them by going on strike. If they're ambitious and willful enough, they can band together, secede from the company, and start their own profit-share business and - perhaps for once - realize their own self-determination.

With less patronage to corrupt businesses, immunity to advertising propaganda, and outspokenness against worker exploitation, spiritually bankrupt corporations will reap less and less profit. Declining profit diminishes the ability to lobby, and less lobbying means less influence on policy making. With less corporate influence on policy, the more legislature will reflect the will of the people and not that of the corporate world. Perhaps with growing intolerance for such entities, those corporations which emulate spiritually malignant behavior will change their tune or disappear completely.

Many of us will realize that the attention, trust, and money we give to the spiritually bankrupt institutions of central banks, investment and retail banks, various corporations, the many politicians who comprise the government, the corporate media, advertising, entertainment, and electronic communication is what keeps them afloat. More of us will become aware that withdrawing this attention, trust, and money weakens them.

We will understand that these spiritually bankrupt institutions require a multitude of toxic tactics that manipulate, control, and exonerate themselves from abiding by the Golden Rule in order to survive. And, above all, we will understand that not tolerating such behavior and abiding by the Golden Rule causes spiritual malignancy and its manifestations to disappear.

Appealing to a Higher Power

"Watch your thoughts, for they become words.
Watch your words, for they become actions.

Watch your actions, for they become habits.
Watch your habits, for they become character.
Watch your character, for it becomes your destiny."

- Unknown

The bad news is, there is much room for improvement; the good news is, it has already started. Many of us have become organized and active against various forms of corruption both personally and in movements. Whether the spiritual malignancy is political, financial, economic, ecological, cultural, or sociological in nature, many of us have raised our voices, raised awareness, broadcasted truth, withdrawn our support, changed our personal consuming activity, or have become active in some other fashion. Those of us who have need to understand this: *none of your actions were or will be in vain.*

And I have some good news for you: you can take it further - easily.

It was mentioned earlier that overcoming a source of malignant authority or power can be accomplished in one of three ways, the first being avoidance. This option, though still viable in certain cases, has become less and less of a possibility as more and more control has been imposed, leaving nowhere else to go. For instance, there is not much one can do nowadays against protecting one's privacy since virtually every activity and method of communication is being surveilled. One can meet others in person or communicate via post but, outside of that, no other options exist. One could relocate to another developed country, but the same invasive activity is likely to exist there, too. The same circumstances apply to diet as well. We can choose to avoid foods made from GMOs but...what's left? Not much, really, and starvation isn't an option. And, since labeling food products made with GMOs has been blocked, how can one tell? Corporate interests are bound and determined to ensure that you cannot. Sure, we still have the ability to choose which banks we deposit our finances in, which companies we give our businesses to, and which television programs (and their corporate sponsors) we endorse through viewership but, with expanding corporate monopoly and influence, the ability to counteract malignant power through avoidance is waning.

The second option - to confront the malignant authority - has, in many cases, proved ineffective. Since the power many spiritually malignant entities wield is vast, challenging it would require a resistance greater or at least equal to its power. Throwing large rocks at a renegade armored vehicle might slow it down but, chances are, it isn't going to stop it; a concrete wall would, for sure. But, in order to build that wall of resistance, there needs to be enough cinder blocks. Many of us have realized this and have attempted to convert "sheeple" into blocks, oftentimes to no avail. While it is beneficial to attempt to raise others' awareness to corruption, we live in a free will environment and cannot force anyone to accept reality let alone do something about it. Many sheeple "cope" with impending danger by denying its existence. Others will "wake up", but feel they're powerless to stop it (even with help from others) and remain docile; to them, it's better to stay on the sidelines than get hit. Some of them figure that, if they lay low, it will eventually work itself out or they'll be spared. It won't, and neither will they, foolish as it may seem.

Whatever the case, those of you who have tried to "wake up" others with no success, consider this: those who are "asleep" are asleep for a reason. Outside of a willful ignorance or an unwillingness to engage in an internal dialogue involving critical, independent thinking, the causality behind their denial or strong-mindedness is fear (and this probably something you may have noticed already.) You may have also noticed that their fears have caused some of them to become toxic as well, as this fear takes the form of arrogance (or narcissism.) If so, understand that their toxicity makes it even more difficult for them to acknowledge spiritually malignant traits in others. Since they embody them, they won't be capable of making a distinction with respect to others who are also toxic: to them, they're kindred or "normal." If you want to convert them, you would need to convert their fears first and, frankly, that is not up to you. The best you can do is gently work with them in confronting their fears and lead by example by living a life which converts fear into love.

And let's face it: confronting spiritual malignancy, whether it is a personality, an authority, or an entity, isn't fun. A backlash of retaliation fused with emotional, psychological, and even physical distress can be counted on. Especially if they are in a position of power, going head-to-head with toxic personalities requires a good deal of inner strength, psychological wherewithal, selflessness, tenacity, and courage. Only well-equipped individuals will prove formidable in overcoming the denial, projection, manipulation, retaliation, and exoneration that comes with such an ego-centric mentality.

This is not to suggest that avoiding or confronting malignant authority was, is, or will be futile. In fact, those of us who have partaken in both should not feel powerless, defeated, or disheartened, nor should we feel nothing has come from it. The purpose of both avoiding and confronting malignant authority is to weaken if not end its tyrannical, narcissistic, and entitled character that dominates and harms others. Just because it is still evident does not indicate that it hasn't been lessened. It's hard - if not impossible - to gauge how much has been accomplished when the benchmark is based on the *absence* of such behavior. Again, you're efforts have not been in vain - I assure you.

However, ask any whistleblower who has gone through the chain of command to report any corrupt, criminal, or unethical behavior if, in retrospect, they would have done anything differently. I guarantee you they would say this: "I would had gone straight to the top instead." As someone who has blown a whistle several times in various work environments, I can say from experience that *appealing to the highest and most benevolent power possible is the most efficient, effective, and psychologically/spiritually sparing way to counteract malignant authority.* The cases which involved confronting the malignant authority directly sometimes worked in my favor, but other times resulted in termination of employment or a prolonged, arduous battle. In every case, a harassing, retaliatory quagmire ensued which resulted in much anxiety and sleepless nights. The instances in which I approached their direct superior often had the same results. But when I had the ear of a benevolent person in a very high place, justice always came swiftly. Appealing to the highest power possible bypasses the toxic rigamarole encountered in bureaucratic or hierarchal structures and is far more reliable.

Those of us who have tried to "wake up" others by spreading the truth and raising awareness through organized movements may wish to consider the following metaphor. Consider your predicament as being like a pan of stovetop popcorn placed on top of an ignited range. When exposed to heat, some of the kernels will "wake up" and pop relatively quickly. Some will take longer, but eventually pop as well. Still others, regardless of how long they sit on top of the heat, do not and will not pop, regardless of the fact that they've been on top of the heat source and around other popped kernels for a good deal of time. If too much time is spent waiting for the remaining kernels to pop, those which have popped will start to burn. It's time to take the pan off the stove and offer the popcorn to someone who will appreciate it while it's still edible. It will appreciate the kernels which popped and disregard those which did not.

So, those of you who have been involved in activism aimed at exposing corporate corruption, fraud within the finance sector, secrecy and high crimes within the government, or any other example of spiritual bankruptcy may wish to consider the third option: appeal to a higher power. I am not referring to some world court or an international judiciary body.

This higher power I am referring to is the highest power of all: God. Whether you believe in some sort of intelligent design, "the Universe", Nature, a Unified Field, "Spirit", God, or some sort of universal energy, I recommend taking the time to establish a relationship and put out requests for assistance. Again, we live in a free will environment, and God (or whatever you believe in) will not intervene unless it is *wanted*.

For some of you, this may take the form of prayer. Not the kind of prayer that involves the mindless internal rambling of words someone else had written, but sentiments or requests that that are both genuine and heartfelt. Like the telepathic form of communication which occurs during channeling, the messages you transmit during prayer are in the form of concepts and questions along with their emotional components. More often than not, we do not "think" in sentences. When we plan to go to the grocery store, not many of us take the time to mentally state to ourselves, "I need to go to the supermarket." Rather, many of us have the concept in our minds the we need to go to a certain location to buy food. More often, the thought processes which occur in most of us are visual, conceptual, or involve associating some sort of feeling. We may think about the store itself, the fact that we are running low on certain food items we need to replenish, visualize in our minds what it looks like, what we need to buy, what we need to buy looks like, how far the store is, how it feels to be in the supermarket, the way we need to go to get there, and so on.

Prayer works the same way. If we pray in mental verbiage, it is imperative that the words have some substance attached to them. Otherwise, if the prayer is "said" in a meaningless and droning manner, consider it a dud. Growing up Catholic, I remember being in church as a kid and hearing the Hail Mary during mass. More often that not, it was recited rather than considered. From the start, it sounded like a facacta trumpet from a Peanuts cartoon: "Hail Mary, full of grace, wah wah wahwah wah..." The words being uttered by the large roomful of people had no feeling or intention whatsoever as they were just saying words and nothing more. I can't imagine anyone named Mary who would indulge being spoken to that way. Would you appreciate being spoken to with words lacking in any meaning and without personal acknowledgement? Well, neither do those in spirit. In fact, they can't because there is little to no meaning attached since the energy behind it is bland at best. The most important ingredient behind prayer is the *energy* behind it. (And, if the prayer is addressed to someone or something in particular, it's best to address them as well.) Whether prayer is mentally verbalized, conceptualized, sensationalized, or visualized (similar to creative visualization), there must be some energy behind it to be effective. What you pray for is what you energetically transmit. Many of us do not realize that we actually do this all the time, but on autopilot; and this is karma. Prayer, basically, is intentional karma. So, it's not just our thoughts which influence our reality, it's the energy we send out.

Most of us who have been raised in religious or spiritual backgrounds have been taught to pray. That is, we have been introduced to an energetic means of sending out requests for insight, guidance, or some kind of manifestation from a higher source or power. However, although we have been taught to communicate *to* this higher power, few of us have actually learned or have been taught to listen to responses. If we go throughout our life unconsciously or always being bogged down by a left-brained lifestyle, chance are we won't.

This is where meditation comes in. When we quiet our left-brain or egoic mind through mindfulness and meditation, we allow for ourselves to be receptive to responses. Whereas prayer is "talking," *meditation is listening*. Since our prayers (and all of our karma, for that matter) are transmitted energetically, their responses are received energetically as well.

Since energy is transmitted conceptually, visually, emotionally, and verbally with "soul speak" during prayer (and with karma as well), this would account for the responses being psychically received claircognizantly, clairvoyantly, clairsentiently, and clairaudiently, respectively. At a psychic level, *energy is received the same way it went out. Thus, prayer and meditation make communication with the spiritual plane a two-way street.* This is the same principle behind remote viewing: the subconscious is given a task, then the conscious mind observes it to extrapolate and interpret the answer.

Meditation and remote viewing are not the only ways to allow our subconsciousness to receive this etheric input. When many of us are faced with a dilemma, conundrum, or life decision, we'll "sleep on it" before deciding on a plan of action. Prior to going to bed, we acknowledge what it is we're dealing with, let it go, and let it be as we slip into that unconscious state. Usually, we wake up the next morning with a refreshed perspective and greater clarity with regard to our situation. Or, we may even have a symbolic dream that provides some insight. Like meditation, the messages received during the dream state are claircognizant, clairvoyant, clairaudient, and clairsentient. Keeping a dream log can be especially helpful in understanding the "language" of our subconsciousness. Sometimes dreams can relay information quite literally; other times, the content may be rather cryptic and symbolic. By journaling our dreams while being aware of our circumstances during our wakefulness, we establishing correlations between our consciousness and subconsciousness, thus making this sort of "dialogue" more comprehensive. If we have dreams that are surreal or convoluted, observing them with a receptive open-mindedness while embracing our creative and intuitive side (or "right-brain") can help us make sense out of them.

Is prayer necessary to receive these sorts of messages? Not at all. Just as one can choose to talk more than listen, one can choose to listen more than talk. By choosing to listen, various unresolved issues, guidance, and insights may be provided. This may account for the reason that many of us experience a spontaneous recall of repressed memories - traumatic, pleasant, or neutral - during meditation which had previously been long forgotten. There is often an underlying purpose for such recollections, usually for our growth and healing. But, if we want specific guidance, clarity, or direction, we must make that request: "ask and you shall receive."

The responses to the energetic output of our prayers and karma are not excluded to messages received during meditation, mindfulness, or a dream state. Here, it is vital to understand that *everything is energy: including our prayers and our karma.* All physical matter is composed of molecules, which are composed of atoms, which are composed of protons, neutrons, and electrons, which are composed of subatomic particles, and so forth. When you break it down, all physical matter is comprised of energy as well. Therefore, the energy we send out psychically in the form of prayer or karma can (and often times will) influence the energy comprising matter in the physical plane. Thus, the more we send out energy - through prayer, karma, creative visualization, or by *wanting* - the more it is likely to manifest itself in our emotional, psychological, and physical reality.

This is of vital importance for those of us who are aware of the many injustices that exist today. First, give yourselves a good deal of credit: taking the red pill of truth requires logic, intellectual and emotional intelligence, integrity, self-awareness, critical thinking, understanding of human nature, courage, and most of all, a love of freedom, your country, and your fellow man. You chose to be this way yourself.

The energy you send out is influential and yours to use wisely. However, some of us who are aware of the many crimes committed by those in positions of power as well as their malevolent agenda have been living in fear, despair, anger, even paranoia. Being scared is understandable, *but comprehend the effects of the energy you carry, the energy you put out, and your directed intention.* If you are reacting to what has already occurred and what is impending with fear and panic, this reactionary energy will (or, most likely, has) affected you negatively in some way. If you can relate to this, take a moment of introspection and consider your thoughts and feelings surrounding this. Notice how your external reality has been affected by your fearful thoughts and feelings.

Now, face your fears. Really face them. What are they? What are you telling yourself? How are they holding you down? How have they affected your life? How do you *feel?* Now, consider how can you react differently that would affect both yourself and your circumstances in a more productive manner.

Know that your ability to co-create with your energy is the key to your freedom. Those in power can monitor your purchasing habits, intercept your e-mails and phone calls, enforce incessant taxation, exonerate themselves and others from abiding by laws, and manipulate financial markets, but they cannot regulate, monitor, or prohibit what you do with your spiritual energy and your extrasensory perception. And they never will.

And, perhaps the most important thing I can share with you is this: the energy behind every planet, every mountain, every person, every plant, every animal, every molecule, every atom, every sub-atomic particle, every photon, every Higgs Boson, and everything that is seen and unseen, I sincerely believe is God, or Infinite Intelligence. And this energy is unconditional love and uncensored truth. God is at the core of everything.

And, whether you believe in God or not, each of us is endowed with free will. This ought to be apparent to everyone regardless of your belief system.

This free will, to me, is unconditional love. Many people question, "Well, if there is a God, why doesn't God intervene with everything that's wrong in the world?" If God were to intervene, that would imply that we could do "wrong" in God's eyes. If someone were to love another person with unconditional love, no degree of harm, corruption, malfeasance, deception, or destruction they have imposed on themselves or someone else would ever cause them to be unloved. God gives us the ability to choose so we can learn from everything we do right and everything we do wrong (which, really, amounts to works and what does not.) The energy we have been given is thus for us to decide what to do with. *You* direct it, and your freedom to direct it is God's will. In other words, God wants what you want - and God wanting what you want is unconditional love. Ultimately, it is not God who assesses our selves and our choices - it is us. The reason for this is for everyone to learn and to enhance our comprehension - *from direct experience* - as to what love is which, inevitably, is God.

I see God as an unconditionally loving and wise parent who allows Its children to make mistakes. If God were to intervene, God would be interfering with the learning process. Without allowing children to experience the consequences of their "mistakes," they don't learn. This is the reason children of overbearing and overprotective parents who insist on making all the choices while "doing everything for their kids" turn out unsure, incompetent, and unable to take care of themselves.

And I do believe that God does take measures to protect and guide Its children, but it is subtle and not always readily noticeable, especially by referring only to the five physical senses. Plus, I feel that this influence is enhanced if a bond or relationship is forged.

So, if you want world peace, visualize it. If you want justice, will it. If you want more people to wake up, pray for them. Whatever the case, *you have to mean it*. And, whatever the case, *you're responsible for it and you will, at some point, hold yourself accountable for it.* If you don't know what to do or what to pray for or how to go about things, ask for the highest guidance that can be given to you. But *answers are only given in response to questions*. And, *answers cannot be heard if they are not listened to.*

If it does not appear that your prayer have been answered, it could be because it is still manifesting. Or, it could be because it is so subversive, it isn't readily noticeable or popping right up in front of your face: God isn't McDonalds. But, more often than not, it is due to the contradictory karma your autopilot is sending out. For example, say you're praying for (or visualizing) a wonderful and successful career to manifest in your life. If you are subconsciously harboring a failure or unlovability schema and its respective energy in the form of "I m not good enough" or "I don't deserve it," the energy of your prayers will be nullified. This is precisely the reason it is essential to address and dissolve our fears and replace them with love. Once that counterproductive energy is converted from fear to love, the changes that will suit our highest self and best interests (and those of others) will emerge. After "I don't deserve it" is acknowledged, tended with love, and replaced with "I do deserve it," the obstacle is removed. So, if something you wish to manifest is not coming about, either look for or ask about the energetic force which is blocking it.

Converting this negative energy can be hard work, especially if we are accustomed to a manic lifestyle in which we are always "on the go" or if we tend to engage in activity that "takes our minds off things." In doing so, we are basically enabling the negative energy by running away from it or telling ourselves, "I don't care to remove the energetic obstacles which are getting in my way." Here, it is important to understand that apathy and avoidance are choices. Plus, it becomes exponentially more difficult to observe the activity of our inner autopilot if our minds are in a million of other different places at once.

Conversely, this would explain why "what goes around, comes around" doesn't always happen. I can think of plenty of people who have lied, manipulated, swindled, controlled, subjugated, harmed, disregarded, intimidated, blackmailed, smeared, even disappeared others in order to get what they want (usually some sort of power, gratification, or ethical exemption) without experiencing the same transgressions being subsequently inflicted upon them. I'm sure all cf us can think of an example. If their core belief is that they can get away with anything without any repercussions, they will. This strong sense of entitlement that comes from divorcing the conscience is the secret behind successful, unscathed psychopaths and those who are spiritually bankrupt. But, as will be discussed later, this only goes so far. For now, it is worth mentioning that the greatest favor you can do for these types is to take measures to reacquaint them with their consciences. *You can pray for this, too.*

In light of this, we must also take into consideration another reason behind our manifestations being blocked, and that is the will of others. If it is possible for a certain outcome to be influenced by the will of someone else or a group of others, a conflict of intentions can arise. Take, for instance, someone who intends to arrive at work on time. They envision themselves getting to their destination by the time they are to start their shift or with some time to spare. They give themselves ample time to drive to work so that they do not have to rush and go over the speed limit, with some slack just in case any unforeseen obstacles impede their commute. While on the way to work, another car pulls out in front of them and its driver decides to take their time and do less than half the speed limit. Being on a two-lane road where passing is prohibited, the commuter must now drive behind the other car at twenty miles-per-hour in a forty-five miles per hour zone, causing them to be late for work. As we can see from this example, the will of the second driver countered the will of the first.

So it is important to realize that, although our thoughts and energy affect our reality, they may not be the only influence at play. Most often, we are not the only co-creators of the environment we experience. Anyone who has worked in a toxic environment can relate to this. Those of us who have can think of a time when we went into work with an upbeat mood and found it difficult to maintain it while being surrounded by miserable or nasty co-workers. If the synergistic karma of the larger whole is poor, those of us with good karma will have our own good energy challenged. Conversely, if we are in a bad mood, being it the presence of others who are compassionate, uplifting, and upbeat will alleviate it. This ties into the whole "water drops in a lake" analogy described earlier.

It is also important to realize that the principle behind prayer, visualization, and directed energy is *the intended influence on the physical plane by deliberate, energetic means.* This being the case, it makes sense that things we pray for or visualize usually do not physical manifest instantaneously. Wishing for a new car will most likely not result in it appearing in front of your home the next day. Instead, you may get a spark of inspiration about how to generate more cash flow in order to purchase a new car. When you intuitively get an idea or that spark of inspiration, that is the return phone call to the voice mail you left - *and you have to act on it in order to manifest your request in order to realize it as soon as possible*. We live in a material world, so change on the physical plane is most efficiently brought about by physical impetus. Sure, you could continue to want, pray for, or visualize in order to manifest your request - and that energy will eventually make it happen, depending on the strength of your will - but it will take longer than taking some physical action. And, with prayer, creative visualization, or any form of directed energy, you get what you give. The more you give out, the more likely it is to manifest.

Otherwise, if your energetic output is requesting *energetic* feedback - such as higher guidance, direction, ideas, suggestions, or advice - you can expect it much more readily. *But you have to be receptive to it; you have to listen by putting your ego aside and getting out of your own way*. When I get stuck writing this book, this is precisely what I do: I ask, I let go, I receive and, hopefully, I remember to say "thank you". And this is the same principle behind mediumship, which is essentially a psychic, energetic exchange between the energy of a soul on the earth plane and a soul in the spirit plane.

Again, if you do not believe in God or a higher power, it is not my intention to convince you one way or the other. It is my belief that there is some sort of Universal Intelligence, yet I understand that this is a belief which cannot be proven. Nor can it be disproven. Yet it is also my belief that, for all intents and purposes, a belief in a higher power is not necessary to live a moral life or a spiritual one, for that matter. Nor is it required to expand perception beyond the five physical senses.

However, just because something can't be proven does not mean it doesn't exist. And just because something can't be proven doesn't mean it can't be experienced or observed. For millennia, humans could observe inherited physical traits expressed in the progeny of many species. We could observe and predict trends in the traits of physical inheritance without exactly knowing how it worked. It was not until the middle of the last century that DNA was understood and proven to be the physical material behind genetic inheritance. We could observe light for years and years as well, but only recently have we learned it is composed of particles and has a speed.

One thing religion and science have in common is that they both delve into explaining that which is perceivable but not fully understood. Whereas religion has historically assigned a divine attribute behind unexplainable phenomena (and has been off course, in some cases), science derives verifiable data based on the five physical senses and subjects its hypotheses and theories to rigorous testing, not drawing conclusions until every variable has been accounted for and results are found reliable, replicable, and conclusive. Science is meticulously rational in posing questions and challenging what it does not know and, often, what it believes to be true. Without a solid grasp on what it knows and knowing what it does not know, science would be ineffective. Our technological advancement would not be where it is today otherwise and there would be mishaps left and right. Drawing conclusions without scrutiny based on observation or acknowledging alternative potentials makes for spectacular dogma, but horrible science.

Therefore, to be effective, science must distinguish between the role of a healthy skeptic which entertains pertinent questions based on observation and that of a perennial doubter which adheres to "conclusions" while refusing any scrutiny. The latter has an air of fearfulness and arrogance, neither of which is productive, rational, or even valid.

And let's face it: we don't know everything. It's likely that there is more that we do not know than what we actually do. It is one thing to be assured of what it is we know, but a closed mind has never proved advantageous. In fact, it closes the door to understanding, knowledge, and truth as we can perceive it. Rather, it keeps people ignorant and, at times, arrogant.

Although statistical data *highly suggests* the existence of a certain phenomenon (and, to me, is so statistically probable, it proves its existence beyond reasonable doubt), science has not *proven* one way or another the existence of God. As long as science is based on the five physical senses, it may never be able to do so, unless it is willing to expand its observational criteria. For this reason, I do not and will not force my beliefs upon anyone.

If you do not believe in God, all I ask is a willingness to be an open-minded, healthy skeptic willing to draw and test beliefs based on expanded perception and experience. I ask that you be willing to attempt to see light without needing to explain it. And, in truth, I'm not asking you to believe in God - only the potential that there is something *more* than what we have been accustomed to perceive with the physical senses and to get acquainted with it. If you're not willing to experience, you're not willing to learn. If you're not willing to learn, you're not willing to pursue truth.

Regardless of what your beliefs are, it is becoming more apparent that there is some "source" of energy on a sublime plane *from which* we are able to receive and *to which* we are able to impart emotional and intellectual intelligence that interacts with our subconsciousness and influences our consciousness and physical reality. Understanding this phenomenon, be it some kind of Infinite Intelligence or something else, provides key insight into how this energy has inadvertently affected the current state of affairs on our planet and how it can be used to heal it - and our planet herself.

If such phenomena alludes to the existence of some kind of higher source or power, it's time we appealed to it. And if there was ever a time to develop our spirituality, it is now.

C

15

The Wheat from the Chaff

The Great Divide

"When the power or authority comes in the hands of unfit persons, then wait for the Hour."
"Near the establishment of the Hour, good deeds will decrease."
"Ignorance and tribulations will prevail."
"Miserliness will be thrown into the hearts of people."
"Honesty will be lost in the end times."
"A time will come when a man will not care about how he gets things, whether lawful or unlawful." -
Imam Bukhari

"When the old have no compassion for the young, when the young show no respect to the old." - Caliph
Omar

"Bribes will be called gifts, and will be considered lawful." - Amal al-din al-Qazwini,Mufid al-'ulum wa-
mubid al-humum

"Gains will be shared out only among the rich, with no benefit to the poor."
"Female singers and musical instruments will become popular." - at-Tirmidhi

"There will be an abundance of critics, tale-carriers, backbiters, and taunters in society."
- Al-Muttaqi Al-hindi, Muntakhab Kanzul Ummaal

"Time will pass rapidly."
"Wealth will increase so much so that if a man were given 10,000, he would not be content with it." -
Ahmad and Bukhari

"In the Last Days, there will be such people, who, when they meet, curse and abuse each other instead of
greeting." - Allama Jalaluddin Suyuti, Durre-Mansoor

"Meanness and greed will multiply." - Ibn Majah

Dishonesty will be the way of life.
Falsehood will become a virtue.
Imbeciles will rule over the wise.
Pride will be taken on acts of oppression.
Blood of innocents will be shed.
Usury and bribery will become legitimate. - attributed to Imam Ali

"Leaders of people will be oppressors." Al-Haythami

"Years of deceit in which the truthful person will not be believed and the liar will be believed."
"False testimony and concealing evidence will appear."
"At that time, people will sell their religion for a small amount of worldly goods."
"There will be a special greeting for the people of distinction." - Imam Ahmad

"Children of fornication will become widespread or prevalent."
"The children will be filled with rage."
"Children will be foul." - at-Tabarani, al-Hakim

- Signs before Yawm al-Qiyamah, or the Last Judgement, in Islamic Tradition

As mentioned in the previous chapter, many of us have become awake in many ways. It has become apparent to many of us that our Republic based on God-given rights and the goals of life, liberty, and the pursuit of happiness has been jeopardized by many of our "democratically elected" public servants. It is clear that such "elected officials" no longer represent the interests of their country, but rather corporate and foreign entities (usually merged) whose interests increasingly contradict the wellbeing of our country's populace.

And, it has become apparent that many of those who gravitate to political and legal professions do not do so out of a desire to serve or represent their countrymen, their Constitution, or rule of law. Rather, they seek to serve themselves, as they derive status, power, and wealth supplied by the bribery and seduction of corporations, a parasitic central bank, and our tax dollars. Many now see that the faces behind the masks of sanity aren't human: they reflect a group of souls devoid of compassion, empathy, remorse, and conscience. "Yes we can!" is no longer a motto applicable to the resilience of a once great nation, but to the entitlement of a group of spiritually bankrupt politicians and their benefactors.

It has become clear to many of us that this supposed "two-party" system is a facade, rendering Washington as one of the most elaborate reality shows on Earth. As each "side" takes turns being the "good guy," nothing "good" comes out of legislature as constitutional rights are whittled away, more wars are waged, quality of life is diminished, cost of living rises, national debt soars, and tyranny replaces liberty. Each side blames the other, but neither holds itself accountable. Who is then? More and more of us are finding out.

Many of us are now aware that Washington has served as a decoy for the true ruling center of our country - Wall Street - which has decided its country's life, liberty, and pursuit of happiness should be replaced by its own narcissism, entitlement, and control. To realize this, profitability and control have taken precedence over human rights, loyalty, health, dignity, and self-determination - at all costs. Many now realize that most of the "jobs" created by many of these corporations do not provide sustenance. Rather, they offer indebtedness, stress, and lifestyle immobility, if not an early grave. And more of us are becoming aware of the exact toll this insatiable quest for profit has taken on environmental and human wellbeing - physically and spiritually.

More and more of us are noticing that the bogus dualism portrayed in Washington is reflected in much of the corporate sponsored media, acting to manipulate rather than educate. More of us are seeing that true journalism is being threatened while cronyism is being rewarded.

Those of us who are not politically savvy or fully aware of the current political and economic corruption have noticed significant socio-cultural deterioration in recent years. Many of us have seen a growing disconnect in interpersonal relationships, an increase in egocentric self-involvement, a gravitation toward greed, an escalation in nastiness, a rise in ignorance, a general lack of accountability toward self and others. We now comprehend the extent to which "Western Civilization" has become an oxymoron.

Regardless of our level of awareness, many of us who have woken up are taking counteraction.

Still, others of us within the general population have remained asleep. Ignorance being bliss, they hold steadfast to the false "reality" consisting of heroic, benevolent political figures who care about public servitude and sought their positions as a result. Despite the overwhelming evidence indicating that such figures' primary allegiance is to corporate, financial, and foreign interests and not to them, they cheer and endorse them.

Despite blatant contradictions between word and deed, they do not ask questions. Rather, their worldview is based on political soundbites and media propaganda, which create a more pleasant reality, however counterfeit, incomplete, and illogical. Instead of basing their endorsements on a candidate's prior voting history, experience, outside connections, and historical character, they back their political candidates based on image, their "brand," and their "word," regardless of whether or not they plan to see if it is kept after being elected. Even when their elected officials fail *to attempt* to fulfill their campaign promises only to endorse contrary legislature after being elected with no explanation, their heads are kept in the sand. They do not bother to monitor their candidate's performance to see if it reflects their campaign rhetoric. They're simply happy enough that "their guy" won, and its back to living a routine life in ignorance or, perhaps more appropriately, disregarded fear.

Their heads are kept below the surface even as "their guys" violate the very Constitution that safeguards their country's freedom. The reasons for such violations, despite being questionable at best, are not explored. Whether its provisions that strip human rights such as Habeas Corpus and freedom of assembly or unconstitutional declarations of war (or even those with Congressional consent) based on questionable circumstances, they are accepted as being necessary for their protection. This acceptance of a repeal of liberty and human rights as a means of security could not be more ironic and nonsensical, but they do not care to address this either. They do not consider what might happen to them without such rights intact. As long as everything is fine in "their world" for now, that's enough for them.

Sadly, this willingness to succumb to falsehoods is often a result of wanting to "fit in," be seen as "patriotic," or adopt what is trendy. Other times, when their inaccurate worldview is challenged, they bristle or shut down - even when presented with irrefutable, contrary evidence. They adhere to their fantasy out of fear or a stubborn arrogance in admitting they might be wrong.

Others simply do not care about the dire straights their country - and the world - is facing, despite the extent to which the economic, political, and cultural turmoil cannot be unnoticed. Worse are those who attempt to conceal the truth by lying, manipulating, debasing, chastising, and intimidating the sources which promote it.

Unfortunately, this willful ignorance and its protection expands outside politics to include corporate, financial, and cultural corruption as well.

Moreover, many of these individuals have adopted a cavalier, superficial, shallow, banal, antisocial and/or toxic character reflective of their political, economic, cultural, and personal perspectives. In their social interactions, they tend to be impersonal, distant, aloof, indifferent, unfeeling, dispassionate, and removed, if not manipulative and toxic. They tend to be self-involved without much, if any, concern for others. At their worst, they work against any concern for others to further their own agenda.

Rather than ask questions and seek answers, they gravitate to insipid television programming, tabloid marketing, or a corporatized pop culture. Despite their lack of research and investigation, they believe they know everything.

What has been noticeable in recent years - the past decade, in particular - is a growing polarization within the general population. At one pole, there is a collective of those who continue to go through the motions as they follow a manipulated culture; one which has conditioned them to be ignorant and docile as they are systematically victimized politically, economically, and vocationally. This "culture" has also coerced many them to increasingly disregard the Golden Rule. As they gradually resemble malignant powers more and more, they enable and/or adopt the spiritually malignant traits of self-involvement, self-importance, arrogance, entitlement, narcissism, and control. Uniformly, they remain unaware of their inner fears which served as a foundation for their low self-esteem, diversionary activity, inflated sense of self, and tendency to project their negativity. Without transmuting these fears, they increase their likelihood of becoming toxic.

At the other pole, there are those of us who foresee the destination of the path we've been coerced to follow, and it is unkind. Seeing that the path leads to anti-socialization, oppression, criminality, malignancy, and poverty, we've made a u-turn. If this were the classic movie *It's a Wonderful Life*, we've headed away from Pottersville and back toward Bedford Falls. We want to live in a world where people are trustworthy, open, personal, social, friendly, self-accountable, self-reliant, self-determining, kind, and care about others.

We don't want a world of "have" and "have nots." Wealth earned by an honest living is one thing, but doing so malignantly is another. We want to live in a world of cooperation and compassion, where people do not have extraneously more than they need out of manipulating, exploiting, or controlling others while others toil excessively with nothing to show for it. Nor do we want a world where people expect things to be given to them without contribution, effort, respecting rules, or anything in return, even gratitude.

Especially those of us in the middle class, we see that others - at "the top" and "the bottom" - have acted parasitically on our self-reliance, self-accountability, and self-determination: the precise and now endangered reasons this country had been a success for so long. To get back there, we know we need to follow the Golden Road.

In short, what we have is an increasingly divided nation. Part of the population, to whatever degree of awareness, is pursuing, endorsing, *or enabling* falsehoods, fear, and criminality whereas the other advocates the polar opposite: truth, love, and justice. One side upholds the Golden Rule, the other disregards it. As the divide becomes more sharply defined, many of us are seeing that if there was ever a time of conflict between "good" versus "evil," it is now.

Many of us are realizing that apathy, unawareness, and inaction toward violations of the Golden Rule enable destruction. Many of us, aware of the severity of the situation, realize that we must partake in spiritual activism now more than ever.

As more of us join others in spiritual activism, some of us will gravitate to spreading truth. Others of us will cultivate and spread love, within ourselves through self-knowledge and toward others by being mindful of the Golden Rule. Others among us will pursue and deepen our understanding of justice which, really, is fairness or "brotherhood." Some of us will do any combination or all three.

Deepening our understanding of any of the three will lead us to the other two and, as we will find, at their basal level, they converge. *Those of us who do this will understand that the mergence of the energies of truth, love, and brotherhood is the energy of Liberty, the energy of compassion, and the energy of the of Infinite Intelligence - and that this truth, love, and brotherhood is the Blessed Trinity.*

Many of us who have started are realizing that not only is God on our side, God IS our side.

Those of us who have are deepening our connection to this Infinite Intelligence. We are understanding the Universal Laws of dharma, karma, attraction, and intention by application. In doing so, we *get* the Golden Rule; we see *why* it holds tremendous value.

And, remarkably, there appears to be an increasing number of us who are realizing that there is more to human perception than the physical senses of sight, sound, touch, taste, and smell we were told were "rational." As those of us who are exploring our extra-sensory abilities and capabilities, we are encountering amazing experiences and a new, vibrant reality.

Now, the more of us who are politically awake become spiritual aware and the more of us who are spiritually awake become politically aware, the Love Revolution cracks wide open. *And this Revolution is one of Compassion.* More will be discussed on this in the next and final chapter, but first:

An Open Letter to the Elite

"We affirm that the doorway to reformation is never closed against any soul here or hereafter."

- Eighth declaration in the Spiritualist Declaration of Principles

To whom it concerns:

You know who you are, and you know you're history. Before proceeding, I want to make it very clear that I do not judge you. I want you to know that God loves and forgives you. I forgive you and know that it is not my place to judge you. Whether or not you will forgive yourselves is a different story entirely.

We've all done things which have gone against our conscience. I certainly have and so has everyone else. There are many things which I have regretted, have been deeply ashamed of, and wish I could do differently. I don't judge you for what you have done because I know, as regrettable as I have felt, that it is in no way appropriate for anyone to judge me. To justly do so, they would need to understand every fear, every situation, every piece of my history - every logistical, circumstantial, emotional, psychological, and spiritual piece of evidence surrounding the choices behind my actions. I truly feel that, without such knowledge, it would be unfair for anyone to judge me. Because I respect the Golden Rule, I know it would be unfair for me to judge you for the same reasons. I sincerely do not, and it is because of this that I have not named a single one of you in this book.

However, I've come to understand that we learn from our light as well as our dark, and that this is entirely our decision while we are here on Earth. Whether or not we learn the lessons behind that by which we inflict emotional, physical, psychological, and spiritual pain on ourselves and others is, like the actions themselves, a choice given to us by God. In this, we are perfectly imperfect: that which we do "right" and "wrong" is more appropriate assessed as "what works" and "what does not." No matter what our choices are, we have the choice to learn from them.

But, in order to learn from both our light and our dark, we must be connected to our conscience. Our conscience functions out of the ability to empathize: the ability to imagine the physical, emotional, psychological, and spiritual condition our actions placed others in. This ability to empathize is reinforced by our own positive and negative experiences we've had in interacting with others and being emotionally honest with ourselves as recipients of others' actions.

Our conscience enables us to acknowledge, "I know what I did and how it hurt you. I imagined myself in your position, and I understand what it felt like. I don't like the way I treated you, and I'm sorry." Our conscience directs our awareness to its own infliction - remorse - and to the pain we've caused others. Tending to both absolves and heals both our hearts and those we have hurt.

Learning from our dark requires we acknowledge the truth. Disregarding the hurt we've caused others by ignoring or justifying the misdeed or reinventing history causes our conscience to remain tainted as we dismiss the lesson completely. Also, those we have hurt are now responsible for the repercussions of our actions and must heal themselves. And, since the lesson has been discarded, the inner pain which spurned the misdeed goes unacknowledged, history is bound to repeat itself, and we deprive ourselves and others from being loved and healed as well. We are likely to worsen as a result.

Our conscience is the part of us which connects us to God - that is, Unconditional Love, for ourselves and for others. By turning our focus away from our conscience, we turn away from knowing God.

So, why do people turn from their conscience? One reason is selfish cowardice: they are afraid to feel the pain they've caused others and do not care about the fact that others are feeling it, despite the fact that they've "benefitted" from the transgression in some way. Another is pride: they cannot face the fact that they are imperfect, so their egos override their inherent imperfection by ignoring remorse and accountability. The stronger the remorse, the more the ego is needed to create a polar opposite "reality" and thus destroy the truth.

At the core of both selfish cowardice and pride is the ego at its worst: arrogance. It is arrogant to think that one is above the very God who created us and to whom the conscience is connected and it is very arrogant to think we are perfection. Arrogance is behind all entitled, narcissistic, and dominating behavior.

Arrogant is the worst thing to be. It keeps us from growing, it keeps us from loving our highest Self, and it keeps us from God.

Let's consider your behavior, out of truth and not for me to judge.

A portion of you have made enormous amounts of money by controlling its production. Outside of the money you simply made for yourselves, you made more by charging interest. This interest, the general public being required to pay for, has not only increased your quality of life, it has increased the cost of living. In many cases, it has jeopardized others' self-determination and survival. Such tribulations have been enhanced with the inflation due to increased currency production and the manipulation of financial markets. You have taken more money from those who are struggling by means of toxic assets, predatory lending, and requiring those already struggling to adopt your accountability and financially bail out your behavior.

With this money, you and like-minded others established corporations which, like your central banks, generate money and power by subjugating, dominating, and disempowering the masses of people under their control. You made much money by exploiting their energy. The profits you made financed your plans to derail (if not obliterate) any business opposition which observed human dignity to the point where your will, as unconscientious as it was, would become unchallenged through monopoly. Your accountability was evaded when you endowed these destructive entities with human rights.

Your ability to continue doing so was safeguarded as your profits allowed you to buy politicians, if not become ones yourselves. This allowed you to create policy which reinforced, enhanced, and shielded your malignant endeavors and made you more money. Now, the existence of a government which originated for and by the people to protect life, liberty, and the pursuit of happiness was under threat by your own goals - which were opposing. But, this additional form of power and income, along with taxpayer dollars, afforded you control of military and intelligence agencies. Other than the ones you created, many of these agencies were gradually converted from serving the public's safety to a means of investment in order to keep your money coming in - even if it contradicted the public's best interest. Some of these agencies procured prospective sycophants as they were "hired from within" and promoted to do your bidding.

To maintain this façade that a government "for the people, by the people" still was still intact, your money was used to manipulate "the people" into an alternate reality. You accomplished this by purchasing corporate media, and some of you even made a profit in the process.

In order to extract even more money from the public, more propaganda was purchased in the form of advertisement, entertainment, and religious ideology. Now, with media, advertisement, entertainment, and religious beliefs under your control, you dictated culture. Much of the public could now be emotionally, intellectually, financially, and culturally manipulated into spending in a way which made you more powerful and behaving in a way that made your narcissistic, entitled, and controlling behavior appear "normal." You coerced many them to mimic your toxic traits and you taught them to become arrogant. And the many material and technological distractions which you produced diverted the much of the public's awareness of it. Some of you aren't even citizens of this country whose policy, economy, and culture you manipulated and exploited. Others of you are dual-citizens whose allegiance is clearly not to the United States or any other country for that matter - it's to yourselves.

As postulated previously, perhaps all this was done to avoid experiencing the negative feelings linked to your fears of unlovability, abandonment, deprivation, mistrust, exclusion, vulnerability, failure, perfectionism, and entitlement.

Or - and I'm speculating here - maybe it's because generations and generations before you in your bloodlines have gone through great and, perhaps, unconscionable measures to ensure that you never feel anything resembling fear or its resulting emotional strife.

Maybe everything was provided to you so that you never had to experience deprivation. Maybe a nanny was hired so you never felt alone. Maybe they bribed people to tell you how wonderful you were just so you never felt unlovable. Maybe they bought your "friends" for you so you always felt included. Maybe they made sure you got into a prestigious university and pulled strings to land your illustrious career just so you would never feel like a failure. Maybe they also purchased your good grades for the same reason. Maybe they ignored your shortcomings so you always felt perfect. Maybe the home(s) you were raised in was so protected you never felt unsafe. Maybe your health was endowed with the best care so that you would never feel your own mortality. Maybe you were just raised as little tyrants who grew up to be big ones. Maybe you were brought up to believe you and your families were "special." Maybe you never had much, if any, reason to experience emotional, psychological, or physical discomfort - or any sort of suffering which is part of the character-building learning process of the human experience. If so, it must have been hard to endure such an upbringing. I mean that sincerely: it must have been hard to have been denied the opportunity to make it on your own by the very parents who brought you into this life. I can't imagine how you perceive yourselves as a result.

If any of this is accurate, it would be part of the reason I don't judge you: *maybe you can't relate to any of the suffering you've caused others because you've been denied the experience of emotional strife that is necessary to build empathy, which is a requirement in order to have a conscience.*

But that can't be entirely true, can it? Why else would you go to great lengths to lie about, conceal, and manipulate others concerning your behavior? Anyone who caused another pain without having an idea what it was like would have no reason to disavow it; it would just be understood that you didn't know any better. But, *you do*, due to your God-given conscience, whether you acknowledge its existence or not.

Whatever the case, your activity is staggering and your life of luxury has left you spiritually bankrupt. You have created an artificial, parasitic form of sustenance known as interest-based currency. You have overrode the will of others through cunning, manipulation, and intimidation. You have determined which persons govern a populace and which economies thrive and fail. You've subjugated nature. You've taken an absurd amount of innocent life (and, at times, blamed it on other people or circumstances.) In summary, it is evident that you have took it upon yourselves to act as though you are God.

Don't expect an award, because your performance has been abysmal. Whereas God provides, you deprive. Whereas God is open, you are concealed. God is truth, you are false. God gives us freedom, you oppress. God honors free will, you manipulate it. God gives us opportunity to heal our inner anxieties, insecurities, and fears; you exploit them and create more to exploit. God loves us for our strengths and weaknesses and our ability to choose actions based out of love or fear: you've detest those whom you've governed through fear. Most of all, whereas God teaches us to love ourselves unconditionally, you've taught and capitalized on teaching unconditional fear.

You have been very arrogant.

Your egos have destroyed *truth*, for yourself and for others. Your egos have destroyed *love*, for yourself and for others. And your egos have destroyed *fairness*, for yourself and for others. Considering all three:

Your egos have worked to destroy God, both within you and outside of you.

The ego can be used to distance ourselves from our consciences but, as hard as some of us may and will try, it cannot and never will completely separate us from them. For that, we have the subconscious - the constant reminder for us to choose to try to ignore.

My question for you is this: *Who do you think you are and what do you think is going to become of your energy once it separates from your body?* I ask this because I have some news for you. From my out-of-body experience a decade ago as well as many accounts of near-death experiences, when the soul leaves they body, the conscious merges with the subconscious as the ego no longer serves as a barrier between them. This means we will all be exposed to our fears *as well as* the extent to which we have adhered to or violated our conscience or, more appropriately, how close or far we are from God. *Without reacquainting yourself with the conscience you divorced, this will be your hell. God doesn't judge us: We judge ourselves as measured by the relationship we have with our conscience.* Although I forgive you, I hope you're able to forgive yourselves. I can't comprehend how you could but, admittedly, that isn't my job.

You have so much ability to atone and make this world a better, more peaceful place, it's unbelievable. You *could* go about things much more differently. Otherwise, go right ahead: keep manipulating, ignoring, humiliating, slandering, silencing, disempowering, interrogating, intimidating, imprisoning, torturing, and disappearing those who personify your conscience. They're trying to do you a favor. Keep it up and see where it gets you. It won't help you get rid of your conscience.

Some of you - thank God - are realizing this and changing your tune, and this is causing discord among you. The rest of you will be bound and determined to continue to carry out more malignant activity which you will use your egos to rationalize and justify. Know that it is this very mental state which will be your undoing, as your egos continue to battle those of your partners in fear as you try to dominate each other. Don't say no one warned you.

Again, I forgive you and would wish you no harm were you to experience true remorse for your behavior. Although I forgive you, I've questioned many times whether or not I could possibly feel any love toward you. It's a tough call, but I guess I must if I expended the energy to write this open letter to you without addressing you specifically. The one thing I am sure of: I feel very sorry for you.

In closing, please grow *Up*. You'll only destroy your selves otherwise. But know that God will still love you if you do. Will you?

✝

16

A New America, A New Earth

Antipathy for the Devil

_"The greatest trick the devil ever played
was convincing the world that he did not exist."_

- Charles Baudelaire

Once we comprehend the extent to which our unattended, unmitigated, and unresolved fears enabled, supported, and strengthened the many malignant hierarchal pyramid conglomerates thriving on dominating, depriving, exploiting, manipulating, and victimizing others, we comprehend the true power we hold both collectively and individually. When we transmute our fears into love, not only does the foundation of these malignant conglomerates weaken, but we transcend to achieve our individual and collective Highest Self. The more of us who do so, the more we change the course of human history.

For years, if not centuries and millennia, Western Civilization has travelled down an egocentric path consistently focused on _more_: more time, more speed, more convenience, more productivity, more profitability, more wealth, more power, more horsepower, more control, more efficiency, more strength, more knowledge, more technology, more output, more "brand new!," more "bang for your buck," more modern, more luxury - you get the idea. Behind a good part of this trend was a desire to preserve life and make it more convenient and enjoyable. However, in modern history, this drive for greater convenience has been exploited to be consolidated to a small fraction of the population - much to the detriment of the majority. As opposed to global betterment, the advancement of knowledge and technology has brought upon worldwide stress and strife as a self-declared select few have hoarded the conveniences such advancements have produced.

For many of us relying on such conveniences during this time, we allowed the technological advancements in goods and services to supplement our spiritual/psychological development and needs. In doing so, we have traded spiritual health for material goods, sometimes shedding our conscience, self-awareness, and socialization in the process. Instead of tending to spiritual and emotional afflictions with love, we disregarded them by pleasuring the ego through the five physical senses by purchasing products.

In essence, we have relied on knowledge and technology to appease the ego while suppressing the soul, and the price of this "convenience" has cost many of us our self-knowledge, conscience, and humanity.

Another problem with enabling the ego-centric "more" is that someone needs to compensate for it. That "someone," in recent years, has been a sizable portion of the general population. To produce more time, speed, profitability, and productivity, the "careers" which have been generated as a result demand an overly fast-paced, hyperactive, multitasking, time-constrained, highly distracted, and often frazzled "human resource." The side effect is a general population who, now adopting a hyper-egoic mentality, has tremendous difficulty slowing down their mental activity and employing the mindful introspection necessary in connecting with their core self, thus digressing their ability to assess and tend to their spiritual condition. If materialism hasn't manifested a massive spiritual disconnect, the demands of the material world have.

However, that "human resource" has increasingly become less and less a necessity as technological advancements replace it. Not only has job production been limited to vocational positions resembling manic robots, but these very jobs are endangered by technological replacements - all in the name of profitability. With a decreasing need for human labor, survival becomes an issue. Now, instead of technology easing life's burdens, it threatens life itself.

The grand fallacy of pursuing an ego-driven path is that it is insatiable to the point of implosion. The ego's unquenchable need for gratification demands more knowledge and more technology, both of which require more raw materials and energy derived from natural resources. Expecting a finite, material world to accommodate amassing spiritual debt is unwise at best.

Look at the demands we've placed upon the Earth to appease our psychological and spiritual issues. Since the Age of Industrialization, much pollution, a pillaging of natural resources, the endangerment and extinction of many species, the genetic alteration of various species, devastating deforestation, and tremendous waste have been byproducts despite famine, malnourishment, and disease still being widespread. This can only be accommodated for so long. Expecting our planet to uncontestedly enable and compensate for our issues is exhausting her ability to sustain life in general. Those behind the procurement of atomic, biological, and other weapons of mass destruction have endangered her ability to do so. Mankind has arrogantly demanded Mother Nature accommodate its ego to such an extent, she is saying, "I can't take it anymore" and is close to having a nervous breakdown.

And so are many of us. Even when conveniences such as internet connection speed or fast food are already expedited to begin with, the ego grows accustomed to it or wants it faster. When the quest for goods and services fails to immediately gratify the ego, the person who has grown reliant on such expediency experiences the frustration, anxiety, anger, fear, or any fear-based derivative these goods and services have been used to anesthetize. Eventually, the stockpile of previously hindered schemas begins to surface, the ego fails to keep them in check, and a meltdown ensues as the core issues make themselves known. More often than not, another means to gratify the ego is sought as a supplement.

Then there are those of us who, like Mother Earth, have born the brunt of enabling others' egos and find ourselves "on the verge." Like her, our physical and inner resources have been sapped to accommodate the gratification of others. As the insatiable conditions of our jobs demand more than is humanly possible, our circuits are fried as we scramble about, run around ragged, unrelentingly play "beat the clock," and pray for the workday to end to get a moment's peace. Even then, the demands of the outside world can be unyielding. After the workday, many of us face arduous commutes, struggle to keep up with mortgage and rental payments, fret about paying rising bill costs, manage a household, and try to keep our heads financially above water. Our physical, emotional, and spiritual bodies will be fortunate enough to experience enough "down time" to recuperate at the end of the day.

Those of us in this category are experiencing increased burnout, difficulty in focusing and concentrating, excessive worrying and guilt, an inability to "think straight," emotional outbursts and irritability, absentmindedness and being sidetracked, feelings of resignation, exhaustion and lethargy, difficulty falling or staying asleep, a loss of enjoyment in life, depression, paranoia, social withdrawal, panic attacks, pain and stiffness in muscles and joints, clammy palms and excessive sweating, depleted sexual libido, trembling, weight gain, and digestive issues. These are all symptoms experienced by a living being reacting as though it were in survival mode. In truth, this is accurate, and it is not healthy. Sadly, many in this group are here because they were unwilling to compromise their morals. But, like Mother Earth, our systems simply cannot take it anymore, and we're expected to believe taking a pill will cure them. *It won't.* Those in this category are, for now, living, breathing proof that an ego-driven civilization is not sustainable.

We have been headed toward a collective nervous breakdown all because we have been willing to put up with enabling the egos of a "privileged" and powerful minority who are not experiencing any of the spiritual, psychological, or physical strife asymptomatic of a nervous breakdown. Since their egos are forcefully accommodated, the masses who support them take these symptoms on.

In the last chapter, it was described how the energy behind Infinite Intelligence is that of Liberty, consisting of the energies of truth, love, and justice. Naturally, and provided these energies were honored, this would produce peace, prosperity, and equality worldwide.

However, this has not been the case in recent history. In fact, it has been the opposite. Instead of abiding by truth, love, and justice, the opposing energies of lies, projected fear, and injustice have prevailed, due to the collective ego of a government/corporate conglomerate. This entity embodying the counter-energies of Infinite Intelligence is aptly referred to by Michael J. Murphy, creator of geo-engineering documentaries such as "What In the World Are They Spraying," as "the Beast." [18]

And "the Beast" - not necessarily an entity, per se, but an *energy* - has become powerful. Instead of peace, prosperity, and equality, "the Beast" has produced havoc, scarcity, and oppression worldwide. This is apparent in the growing number of wars, decimated economies, impoverished civilizations, oppressed peoples, tyrannical regimes, and disaster capitalistic endeavors. Those in support of all this have gravitated to positions of power: "the Beast" has given them something in return for worshipping "him" - "elite" status. It is therefore no surprise that the more those within the population were willing to appease the Beast's goal of ultimate power by spreading lies, fear, and injustice, the more they have climbed up the hierarchal tiers the Beast created.

How did this come to be? First, the means of spreading lies, fear, and injustice by which "the Beast" grew in power went largely uncontested. Had more of us countered these means by promoting and pursuing truth, love, and justice, the Beast wouldn't be as powerful as it is today.

Second, a good number of us were supposedly impervious or unaware to the Beast's activity. As the saying goes, *the greatest trick the Devil ever pulled was convincing the world he didn't exist.* In other words, the Beast had covered up its own existence. This was accomplished through extensive lies, manipulation, and propaganda. So many of us bought into such lies.

But were we so impervious to "the Beast's" activity that we were "blind" to it? Many of us have known about things like workers in sweatshops, casualties of war, and coups sponsored by the military-industrial complex and did nothing to shed truth, love, or justice on it. Some of us even took advantage of it. Others of us have simply denied its existence by choosing to remain ignorant or look the other way. We sat down on a couch, cracked open a beer, and watched the game. Our apathy and denial, inevitably, has fed the power of "the Beast."

Look at where our apathy, denial, and capitulation has gotten us: a place where lies, fear, and injustice reign.

Needless to say, mankind is at a pivotal point in its history. We are witnessing sharper definition between the two opposite energies of Infinite Intelligence and the Beast. We are seeing a more distinct dichotomy of truth versus lies. And justice versus injustice. Charity versus crime. Knowledge versus ignorance. Action versus apathy. Awareness versus unawareness. Peace versus war. Prosperity versus strife. Nutrition versus famine. Generosity versus greed. Common courtesy versus self-absorption. Intimacy versus disconnectedness. Compassion versus cruelty. Passion versus indifference. Accountability versus exoneration. Respect for rules versus entitlement. Self-love versus narcissism. Freedom versus control. Conscience versus ego. Liberty versus tyranny. Life versus death. True versus false. And, *good versus evil.*

Overall, it is apparent that there is a conflict between the power of Unconditional Love and that of unconditional fear.

Not only is there time to reverse it, there's time to stop it. But, it is our choice whether or not we to continue to our collective breakdown - which may manifest itself economically, financially, geopolitically, environmentally, and/or socio-culturally - or we make a nervous breakthrough.

We must decide either to embrace the energy of truth, love, and justice and align ourselves with Infinite Intelligence or continue to cater to the energy of falsehoods, fear, and injustice and succumb to "the Beast."

If we choose Infinite Intelligence, it is vital to first dissolve the part of the Beast which lives inside us. We must own up to the lies we tell ourselves and others and dissolve our own denial so we can recognize truth both internally and externally. We much accept that close-mindedness leads to small-mindedness. We need to face our fears, insecurities, and low self-worth and tend them with compassion and love. We need to understand the casualty behind our own toxic behavior in causing others to feel the pain we have neglected. We must honor justice for ourselves and others by being mindful of accountability and God-given rights as they pertain to the Golden Rule. We also must learn to forgive.

And it is paramount that we grasp how unconditional fear is responsible for the current hell on Earth, and that challenging this unconditional fear with unconditional love is *essential* for overcoming it. In this, a revolution must involve a spiritual component; it has to. Taking measures to protect ourselves economically, politically, financially, physically, and culturally are beneficial, yet "The Beast" now has more weapons, more money, more elected officials doing its bidding, more widespread cultural influence, more technology, and more structure. This is not to suggest that such measures should be abandoned - in fact, any physical means to manifest truth, love, and justice have been and will continue to be helpful. But, let's face it: unless more wake up and take action, they haven't been enough on their own.

The good news is, they don't have to be. The best news is, we have access to a Power which, unlike "the Beast," is both infinite and more powerful.

The more we spread truth, love, and justice, the more we will be in tune with Nature. The more we are in tune with Nature, the more we bring about an atmosphere of creativity and peace. The more creativity and peace, the more we connect with our own spirituality. The more spiritual we are, the more we will connect to this unconditionally loving Higher Power. The more we do this, the sooner it we will witness...

The Resurgence of the Ankh

"We affirm the moral responsibility of individuals
and that we make our own happiness or unhappiness
as we obey or disobey Nature's physical and spiritual laws."

- Seventh principle of the Spiritualist Declaration of Principles

Just like the ego-driven culture, the ego itself cannot sustain the system to which it belongs. The ego, or the "left-brain," serves to prevent and protect against emotional strife but it cannot resolve or heal it. After being solely dependent on the ego for self-preservation for so long, it becomes counterproductive. Where the ego had served to protect the system from emotional pain through mental force, intellectualization, and response, if it relied upon for too long, it will realize it can no longer protect and seek to destroy. In short, if it is unable to protect us from our inner and outer "demons," it will seek to kill them as a means of protection.

Here, the ego becomes destructive. If issues are internalized, the person who has grown dependent on the ego as protection from emotional distress will manifest a low self-concept or take direction to anesthetize the pain through material substance or activity. If gone on for too long, the ego will cause this person to self-destruct by means of a mental breakdown, overdose, overindulgence, or suicide. Inevitably, the ego accomplishes its purpose: it protects its host from pain even if avoidance of the pain amounts to self-destruction.

The degree of destruction is worsened if the emotional pain is externalized. In completely shielding its host by denying the existence of emotional pain, the ego causes the person to develop overcompensation and projection as a means of protection. Here, the ego is used to convince its host that their pain is absent or exists outside of them. When the host's inner pain worsens as a result of being denied or projected, the ego will seek to control its external manifestations through outwardly toxic means of entitlement, narcissism, and domination. When this fails, the ego "kills" the inner pain by attacking - even killing - the scapegoat who served as the outlet for this pain. Tragically, the root cause for the pain still exists in the heart of the perpetrator and the toxic activity will continue.

This is not to suggest that the ego is a "bad thing" - far from it. The left-brain is responsible for the mental faculties of our conscious mind states, such as analytical capabilities, rationale, strategy, discipline, a sense of self, an understanding of linear time, a relationship to space, and connection to the five physical senses - all of which are essential for our protection, survival, and establishment in the physical world. To abandon the ego completely would likely lead to vulnerability to the point of being fatal.

Civilizations which tend to be left-brained are known as "patriarchal." They tend to realize great material comfort by realizing advancements in technology and science. With a focus on strategy and defense, they tend to be well-protected. And, through discipline, religious and cultural ideologies tend to be well defined.

However, when the egocentric nature of the patriarchal civilization uses its left-brained mentality to override its collective spiritual or right-brained needs, it grows to be toxic - just like the person reliant on their ego in managing their schemas. As mass spiritual pain grows and goes unattended, the collective ego eventually becomes overactive and even seeks to kill what it perceives to be the source of strife, and this imbalance of consciousness leads to much damage both within the patriarchal structure as well as outside of it. The material comfort once provided now morphs into materialism, greed, and theft. A focus on self-identity gives way to pervasive malignant narcissism. Goodwill is replaced by self-centeredness. Law no longer reflects justice based on emotional intelligence, but a system that permits immorality through loopholes and manipulative, intellectual justification. A law-enforcement system which once served to defend and protect the public's rights now subjugates and violates them. A political system sworn to serve the Constitution begins to shred it. Religious institutions replace their spiritual foundations with dogma that justifies condemnation and hate. Wars of protection are replaced with wars of aggression.

And, the Golden Rule loses it luster. Instead, the toxic patriarchal system seeks to avoid accountability, low self-worth, and a lack of control by turning to entitlement, narcissism, and domination. As a result, lies, fears, and injustices abound.

As such, wholly ego-centric, left-brained civilizations will invariably meet the same fate as ego-centric persons: they will embrace the destruction of self or others as a means of avoiding pain. This has been the road the United States has been on, and it is close to reaching a dead end.

While the ego is essential for self-preservation, *it cannot heal that which it served to protect*. Since the wounds it shielded are spiritual, we cannot expect a cognitive function to cure that which is spiritual in nature. Just as physical wounds are most effectively tended to with physical remedies, spiritual wounds need spiritual remedies.

For spiritual care to take place, the ego needs to literally drop its guard. It cannot be forced out of the way; it needs to relax in a safe place free from threats for it to wind down and feel at ease enough to step aside. Right now, our country - if not, our planet - is facing a spiritual crisis. To do our part in fixing it, we must tend to the collective ego as well as our own in the same way. We must give our egos a peaceful, nonjudgemental sanctuary where they are allowed to relax *on their own*; all we need to do is be mindful as they do so. Once they do, whatever wounds they were protecting will be noticeable, and we will be in a good frame of mind to heal them - with truth, love, and fairness, or compassion.

For this very reason, it is imperative that more and more of us build up our own spiritual wealth and become spiritual activists. We need more of us to compassionately shed truth on lies, love on fear, and justice on transgressions both internally and externally.

Honoring our right-brain through mindfulness and meditation is crucial for this revolution, as it sheds truth, love, and justice with compassion and peace within ourselves. We cannot tend to the lies, fear, and injustice in the outside world in a compassionate, peaceful manner until we heal our inner wounds with truth and love and reconcile with our own consciences in the same way. Most of all, we need to treat ourselves with compassion before it can permeate into the world around us. This is all dependent on whether or not we honor a new consciousness, which is that of being mindful and embracing our spiritual side.

The more of us who do so, the sooner a brighter, more peaceful and balanced civilization will emerge as the right-brain joins the left and the ego is accompanied by mindful awareness. What comes with this new awareness is the birth of a healthy matriarchal society, where the left-brain provides protection but *the right-brain is the foundation.* The "feminine" right-brain, in a sense, *is* us: it is the spiritual part of us that experiences existence and perception in the form of emotional and intuitive sensing. The "masculine" left-brain exists to protect and mobilize this existence through cognitive, rational functioning based on the five physical senses and how they relate to both the physical world and our spiritual center. Considering both the subconsciousness of the right-brain and its egoic protecter that is the left-brain, this relationship renders each and every one of us to be emotional beings who think, not thinking beings who are emotional. This prioritization is the premise behind the matriarchal civilization.

Many of us have started down this path by reassessing how we perceive and process information. Living a left-brained life dictated by rationalizing and intellectualizing has caused many of us to dismiss any data which was received intuitively by the right-brain, much to our chagrin later on. We've taken heed of this and stopped second guessing it. Now, we pay attention to the gut-feelings, premonitions, or any extrasensory input we receive - and soon find ourselves glad that we did.

Many of us are realizing that too much left-brained control stifles creativity, which is imperative for productivity, advancement, and growth - thus, optimization. In fact, we've learned that complete reliance on the ego to manage affairs proves counterproductive, if not destructive. We see that planning which is self-referential with relaxed expectations, less rigidity, and buffered with intuition is both de-stressing as well as the most fruitful. We thus allow our strategy to be guided by chance, inspiration, and creativity. We give room for things not always "going our way," putting our egos aside in realizing that rigidly enforcing "our way" may not always produce the best results. We know that controlling others stifles their growth as well as our own.

Many of us see this reflected in our educational systems. We see the current system of dispensing and memorizing information as inherently inefficient and flawed. We're finding that forcing children to cram and digest vast amounts of dictated data only to regurgitate it on paper teaches them how to jump through hoops, not learn. As a result, little of this information is retained or used later in their adult life, especially in work they will be fortunate enough to find fulfilling. The energy used in both inculcating and "learning" such unretained and impertinent information is, in truth, a waste.

We are also noticing the ill effects of an educational system which not only teaches in a left-brained manner, but focuses solely on left-brained subjects. As educational systems withdraw creative, abstract, and imaginative programs such as the arts from their curricula, we teach our kids such activity has no worth. This could not be more detrimental as our right-brain *is* our essence and honors our expressional worth, and many of us are noticing the effects this is having on our children. Many of them grow lacking in spirituality, humanity, empathy, social skills, emotional awareness, emotional expression, emotional intelligence, or worse - emotional restraint as their spiritual bodies rebel. When they are not having outbursts, they are mechanical as their personalities emulate the emotionally shallow, mundane, and robotic music and pop culture manufactured today. Their right-brain allows them to be aware, and ignoring it promotes not just a deficit in awareness, but attention-deficit. Instead of caring for our kids' right-brains, we have given them Ridalin.

We know that the learning process most effective, efficient, and spiritually fulfilling is one based on curiosity, expression, and experience by asking questions and finding answers. We learn and retain things much better when we do them on our own as opposed to being told how to do them, and we naturally absorb information in subjects we are curious about and interested in. Pursuing this also build self-esteem. This active learning process thus realizes that prioritizing intrinsic passion equals success and that this honors the expressions of our children's highest selves. As they organically gravitate to a vocation authentic to them, this enlivens the Greater good as well as their own. Further examination reveals that this sort of educational system is in alignment with the energies of truth, love, and fairness of Infinite Intelligence. In allowing kids to authentically honor their curiosity, their truth is respected. By giving them the freedom to pursue any course of interest without restriction, subjugation, or dictation that a certain path is "wrong," we love their choices unconditionally. And, by giving them the choice whether or not to ask questions and find answers, they have the choice to be as ignorant or knowledgable as they choose. By teaching them that they "get what they give," this honors justice.

Many of us noticing how this educational system based solely on a left-brain mentality leads to the spiritual dissatisfaction of being vocationally pigeonholed. In adopting a profession where our "career" is placed in a box with a one-word label, we've grown to realize that spending our entire adult lives spending at least forty hours a week performing the same task in the same field isn't just mundane, it is spiritually imprisoning. We see that the lack of vocational freedom is reinforced with the absurd costs of tuitions, as and it is obvious that more and more facilities of secondary education are businesses for profit, not schools of higher learning. Earning a degree now guarantees debt, which is only reinforced by the lack of opportunity.

Despite this, many of us are finding ways to honor our zest for life and our various passions by wearing more than one hat in our professional lives. We've decreased our full-time work load to allow more time and energy to be spent exploring other interests. As the waitress cuts back her shifts to include writing in her daily life, the scientist makes time to compose music, and the salesman uses the hours cut back to start his own business, they realize that more is learned from experience than a lecture hall.

Many of us making these gradual shifts in vocation are not only realizing our authentic passions, but we prosper financially, spiritually, and physically as a result. More and more of us are realizing that we must take charge of creating our own vocational paths as opposed to leaving it in the hands of big business. If we don't, we know that the will of a larger entity will usurp our own as we enable and empower it with extraneous, soul-draining labor. And, we see how toxic work environments and demanding jobs created by large companies and corporations are not only financially constricting and confining, they have affected our health spiritually and, in turn, physically.

Largely because of this, more of us of gravitating to and exploring means of holistic healing as an alternative to conventional medicine. It is becoming more clear to us that afflictions in the spiritual bodies are often the causality behind psychological and physiological dis-ease. We see that stressful and toxic conditions are the basis for illness and premature aging, and we seek new methods of healing and toxic conditions are the basis for illness and premature aging, and we seek new methods of healing which address the root cause. We recognize that physical and psychological healing is not excluded to medical advancements based on physical science, but holistic means based on the relationship between the somatic and the energetic bodies. Those of us partaking in such healing are witnessing beneficial side-effects of such treatments, unlike those of mass-marketed medications. We have awakened to the fact that the psychoactive drugs used to treat symptoms of spiritual afflictions (such as anxiety, stress, insomnia, and the like) have ill-effects and that such spiritual conditions are exploited by pharmaceutical companies. And we now see that medication production and health insurance companies exist as a means of profit, not healing.

For some of us, we have reevaluated the spiritual fulfillment of our conventional, "organized" religions. We admit our lack of fulfillment from these institutions as they strictly adhere to dogma and doctrine in order to protect moral codes. Having taken a left-brained stance, they served to protect the conscience which conveys spiritual morality from the right hemisphere to the left. We now understand that these organizations are useful in protecting spirituality, but do not prioritize connecting with it. We have also noticed that some modern-day versions of such religions have even taken on a fanatical, hysterical, and histrionic approach to religious ideology. As they condemn any questioning and independent thinking, impose strict and irrational dogma, and place fear on the pulpit, their followers are brainwashed and coerced into toxic belief systems and behavior as they react to a perturbing sort of divine panic. In doing so, these institutions reveal themselves to be spiritually corrosive cults rather than organizations concerned with spirituality. Worse, they now echo the same toxic pyramidal structures which dispense fear down their tiers in order to manipulate power toward the top.

Instead, many of us seek to forge an understanding of our inner and highest self through meditation and introspective practice, thereby aligning ourselves with our subconscious, emotional, and spiritual core. We seek a practice which explores spiritual existence and perception not only to connect with our souls, but other souls as well. We seek a religion where spirituality is both fundamentally *and* flexibly empirical and experiential. We see now that God is Unconditional Love, that we are all children created from a natural Intelligent Design, and God will be our parent if we honor that relationship - and that we all have the opportunity to be "Sons and Daughters of God." Those of us on this path who are realizing this are experiencing objectively verifiable information which proves this relationship beyond reasonable doubt.

Many of us who are meditating, expanding our awareness, and broadening our consciousness are beginning to perceive the cyclical aspect of time. In addition to its linear progression, we are noticing time's seasonal nature and, at its core, an eternal "now."

Just as with our perception of time, increased meditation and an expansion of awareness is rendering the waking consciousness associated with the left-brain - the only "reality" we've been persuaded to perceive or believe in - to be incomplete. Awareness is taking on new meaning as more of us experience altered states of consciousness. As we progress, this new awareness is allowing more and more of us to realize that we have more senses than just our five physical ones, opening us up to an entirely new world.

In general, many of us are making the shift from prioritizing ego gratification to spiritual care, as we understand that *not* doing so puts the cart before the horse and often leads to an accident. With this new mentality and the other growing trends just described, there are many indications that the transition from a now toxic patriarchal civilization to one which is holistically and spiritually matriarchal has already started.

Whereas the patriarchal society is guided by the ego or left-brain, the matriarchal society embraces both hemispheres yet with emphasizes the right. Many scholars and archeologists believe that the civilization of Ancient Egypt was, at least in part, matriarchal-based as symbolized by the ankh:

A hieroglyph which carried the meaning "life," the ankh has a shape which is thought to represent the union of the feminine and masculine energies. The phallic, upright base of this symbol is interpreted to represent the "male," while the oval above it (potentially indicating the "feminine" being prioritized) depicts the womb, or the "female." Together, they represent life.

And it is the energies of truth, love, and justice of Infinite Intelligence which support life itself and the reason behind the prosperity and harmony of those civilizations which honor it. If the ancient Egyptians were matriarchal, it would certainly account for their creatively rich and prosperous civilization. Their artistic alphabet alone contains an ethereal beauty about it.

Yet perhaps the most important component of a matriarchal society is that its citizens will consider their collective Self as opposed to just their individual ones, and that doing unto others *is* doing unto oneself: the Golden Rule becomes *Golden Law, it applies worldwide, and it is based on* **compassion.** More and more of us are getting on board with this as well.

As we shall see, the more of us who heartily commit to the Golden Rule and appeal to our spiritual and creative side, the sooner it will be:

On Earth as it is in Heaven

"Therefore all things whatsoever ye would that men should do to you, do ye even so to them: for this is the law and the prophets."
- Jesus Christ (Matthew 7:12, King James Version)

"What is hateful to you, do not do to your fellow. This is the law: all the rest is commentary"
- Hillel the Elder

"Hurt not others in ways that you yourself would find hurtful."
- Udana-Varga 5:18

"Tse-kung asked, Is there one word that can serve as a principle of conduct for life?'
Confucius replied, 'It is the word 'shu' - reciprocity. Do not impose on others what you yourself do not desire."
- Doctrine of the Mean 13.3

"None of you truly believes until he wishes for his brother what he wishes for himself."
- Number Thirteen of Imam Al-Nawawi's Forty Hadiths

"One should not behave towards others in a way which is disagreeable to oneself."

- Mencius VII.A.4

"Respect for all life is the foundation."
- The Great Law of Peace in Native American Spirituality

"Be charitable to all beings, love is the representative of God."
- Ko-ji-ki Hachiman Kasuga

"Compassion-mercy and religion are the support of the entire world."
- Japji Sahib

"We believe that the highest morality is contained in the Golden Rule:
'Do unto others as you would have them do unto you.'"
- Sixth principle in the Spiritualist Declaration of Principles

"First they ignore you, then they ridicule you, then they fight you, then you win."
- Mahatma Ghandi

Referring back to the "drops in a lake" metaphor and the ways our individual energies merge to form a larger energetic body, it is easy to see how unresolved, inner negative energy reinforces the dysfunctional relationships that collectively give rise to larger toxic organizations. These larger organizations evolved as collectives of the defense and offense mechanisms of the "drops" which comprised it, with various egos within these organizations adopting these mechanisms in order to "manage" their individual negative emotions. However, the dysfunctional dynamics within this mass collective of defense and offense mechanisms reinforce and promote each other, resulting in the strengthening of these organizations' spiritual malignancy which, eventually, snowballs toward spiritual bankruptcy and mass destruction.

From this metaphor, it is clear that dissolving these toxic, hierarchal organizations requires cleansing the drops which comprise them. If the fears behind the defense and offense mechanisms of its individual participants dissipate, so too will these larger manifestations.

By incorporating and promoting right-brained consciousness, matriarchal societies prevent this mass dysfunction (and subsequent destruction) since mass spiritual essence is prioritized. Instead of catering to egoic means of identifying with or anesthetizing negative emotions or worse - denying their existence through overcompensation and projection - the matriarchal civilization provides for healthy expression of these emotions without trying to change them. Unlike patriarchal civilizations which gravitate to "treating" negative emotions egotistically through deception, superimposing fear, and eschewing accountability, the matriarchal tends to them by acknowledging their existence, honoring self-love, and abiding by the conscience. Respectively, matriarchal societies reflect Infinite Intelligence by embracing its energy of truth, love, and justice - together, Liberty. In doing so, toxicity is transmuted instead of amassed, and love is produced instead of fear.

The matriarchal civilization also succeeds in that it honors the "drops in the lake" metaphor. Unlike patriarchal civilizations which attempt to "manage" their populations through controlling governance, the matriarchal society comprehends that the civilization emerges out of its own collective energy. It sees that a civilization's success or failure is truly the sum of its parts, and that a lake can be only as clean or polluted as the drops of water within it. It understands that there's more to tyranny than simply being the result of a spiritually bankrupt minority who gained power through entitlement, narcissism, and dominance by imposing fear, falsehoods, and injustice. It also understands that there is more to societal collapse than a parasitic, entitled minority within the population that bottom-feeds off tax-payer funded programs. Both cases being relevant to modern day America, they needed a general public with a mass victim mentality willing to go into spiritual debt by remaining docile, ignorant, and/or lacking in self-respect.

In this sense, *the matriarchal civilization has always existed but it has been wildly ignored*. Our current economic, political, and socio-cultural turmoil *is* the byproduct of our collective energy. It reflects the sum of widespread entitlement, narcissism, and dominance plus widespread enabling, narcissistic supply, and docility and the subsequent lack of accountability, human rights, and fairness - all of which a byproducts of mismanaged fear. Here, the matriarchal aspect of our civilization is teaching us that "we all get what we all give." In this, regardless of whether the drops in its lake are pure or not, *the inherent, inescapable, and eternal nature* of matriarchal existence is showing us that, whether we realize it or not, we will always live in its *Spiritual Democracy*, and that during every moment of every day and in every choice behind every action, we all vote with our energy. So, if the majority of us are in spiritual debt, so will be our country. This comes right back to the Laws of Dharma and Karma.

So, we have a choice whether this inherent matriarchal component thrives or not. For it to thrive, it needs to be infused with as much truth, love, and brotherhood as possible. For us to be a part of the solution, we must first earn our own spiritual wealth by being truthful, loving, and accountable to our selves. For us to influence the world as spiritual activists, we must raise others' awareness to truth, love, and brotherhood.

To do this, we must adopt a new consciousness, which is accomplished through mindful and meditative awareness. This awareness allows for us to objectively face our internal suffering by psychoanalyzing ourselves as opposed to denying, amplifying, or projecting its existence. By putting our ego aside and observing this suffering - without judgement and *as it is and for what it is* - we allow for ourselves to *best recognize* these "demons" and learn *how to best tend to them with unconditional love*. This allows for us to truly heal and, as a result, we feel more energetically liberated and healthy as the negative energy of these "demons" is dissolved. Not only do we truly heal in doing so, but we cultivate self-knowledge as a result. This self-knowledge leads to a grounded, inner peace as the "facing of our demons" and learning from them makes us stronger in terms of self-love and self-awareness. With this self-knowledge and lightened state of spirit comes wisdom, and the strength we cultivate allows us to address more of our inner "demons."

The more of us who face and dissolve our demons through mindfulness and meditation, the more we will be comfortable in our own skin as well as this neutral state of awareness. The more we are rooted in this state of awareness, the more liberated we are from the ego. The more we are liberated from the reactivity of the ego, the more we realize our own personal power: we can now be proactive in response to negative thoughts and feelings instead of reactive.

The stabilization in this balanced, neutral awareness eventually unveils a previously unseen, unnoticeable, or disregarded world of perception: the psychic world. There has been much reference to this already. So, why is all this talk about psychic or extrasensory perception important?

Refer back to the symbol of the Ankh for a moment. It was described before how this symbol is considered to be emblematic of a matriarchal civilization, honoring both the "masculine" left-brain and the "feminine" right-brain consciousness as represented by the phallic base and the womb-shaped oval above it, respectively. This makes sense, but why the horizontal line in between?

In the mid-1980s, the US Army and Intelligence Security Command (USAINSCOM) secretly sought to develop programs of spying based on psychic means. This was accomplished by training a select corps of military personnel in a scientifically developed program known as Controlled Remote Viewing (CRV), a tool used to extract information, data, and experiences of the past, present, and *potential* future via extrasensory perception. In order to be successful at remote viewing, its personnel had to develop a working relationship between the conscious and subconscious mind. The information would be received and conveyed by the right-brain (or subconscious mind) as the left had to observe and interpret this subconsciously received data. Incidentally, the two hemispheres tend to not get along initially. The right-brain tends to be symbolic, feeling, surreal, and abstract whereas the left-brain is more rational, logical, realistic, and literal. The more a "language" or mode of communication is established between the two, the more successful the remote viewing practice. Reflecting the interface of this relationship, one of the specific projects was aptly named, "Center Lane."

Considering this, perhaps the middle, horizontal line of the Ankh represents this "center lane." If this is the case, perhaps the civilization of Ancient Egypt wasn't just matriarchal, but one established in extrasensory perception as its keystone. Pragmatically speaking, this is likely the case. I don't why such a symbol would be created - let alone, culturally highlighted - if it weren't.

The Ankh of Ancient Egypt may not be the only emblem of an ancient matriarchal civilization insinuating an emphasis on a left and right brained union perception. Many ethnic Ukrainians like myself are familiar with a symbol associated with our heritage, known as the "Tryzub":

What has been a symbol of national identity in Ukraine for centuries, the origins and precise meaning of this symbol are ambiguous. This ancient, trident-shaped figure is believed to have arisen as a tribal symbol, although the earliest archeological evidence of its specific archetype was found on the seals of the Rurik dynasty (864-879 ca.) with the stylized version above being adopted as the family crest of Volodymyr the Great during the tenth century.

It is commonly believed that this symbol is representative of the Christian trinity, with the middle, tear-drop shape representing a descending dove, or the Holy Spirit. Yet the trident itself was a pre-Christian symbol, often associated with the god Poseidon. Whether the Tryzub emerged as a Christian symbol or one based on an older concept and correlated to Christianity at a later time is a matter of speculation. Yet another, perhaps related, interpretation of this symbol is the divine union of the elements of fire and water manifesting on the physical plane. Still another interpretation of the Tryzub is one which bears the meaning, "Freedom."

What is known is that there existed an matriarchal civilization spanning modern-day Romania, Moldova, and Ukraine known as the Cucuteni-Trypillian Civilization ("Cucuteni" referring to artifacts located in Romania, "Trypillian" to its counterpart in Ukraine) approximately between 4800-3000 BC. Having the largest city-states at the time, with populations as large as 15,000, the settlements of this civilization predate the city-states of Sumer - which they are believed to have traded with - by more than half a millennium.

Derived from the artifacts excavated at these ancient sites, this non-aggressive matriarchal civilization displayed little to no social stratification, had an absence of a political elite, and relied a barter economy.

Whether or not the Tryzub of Ukrainian national identity has its conceptual, rudimentary, or figurative roots in its ancient Trypillian ancestry is pure speculation.

However, considering the Tryzub's design and the various interpretations of its meaning reveals a concept similar - if not, identical - to that of the Ankh.

Like the Ankh's depiction of the union of "masculine" and "feminine" consciousnesses by its phallic base and oval top, the Tryzub may represent these with its two "wings": the left representing the "masculine" left-brain; the right, the "feminine" right-brain. The union of these two "sides" gives rise to divine consciousness, as indicated by the oval centered at the Tryzub's base with its point rising to the top of the emblem itself. This would be compatible to the horizontal line, or "center lane," at the center of the Ankh.

This interpretation of the Tryzub ties together the others previously described. The left and right wings, representing "male" and "female" energies, could be correlated to the masculine or "fiery" awareness of waking consciousness and the fluidity of the feminine, emotional subconsciousness - or that of "water" - respectively. When these two elements merge, just as in male-female sexual intercourse, they give rise to "life." In terms of consciousness, the "child" here is divine awareness or, perhaps, "the Holy Spirit." The energies of truth, love, and justice of divine awareness, as mentioned before, are those of Liberty - or, Freedom.

Still, elements of other cultures - and emblems associated with them - allude to the practice of using meditation to unite right and left brain consciousness in order to connect with an etheric realm. Shinto, a set of spiritual practices indigenous to Japan, means "Way of the Gods." Specifically, the word "Shinto" is derived from the word "shin" meaning "spirit" (or "kami," in Japanese) and "tō," which refers to a philosophical path or study.

Part of the folklore of Shintoism includes a creation-myth involving a male (Izanagi-no-Mikoto) and female (Izanami-no-Mikoto) entity who were called by the gods to help each other create the islands of Japan. This is reminiscent of the masculine and feminine energies thought to be represented by the Ankh and the Tryzub and the foundation behind their respective cultures.

While Shintoism regards everything as containing a spiritual essence, "kami" is considered to be an innate divine or sacred realm, encompassing the existence of gods, spirit figures, angels, and human beings in spirit. Shrines devoted to a high presence of "kami," like many Buddhist temples, often have statues depicting figures practicing meditation.

Shintoism, like the Egyptian and Ukrainian cultures, also has a symbol associated with it. The Torii Gate, pictured below, symbolizes the entrance to sacred space. It represents the transition between the physical, finite world and the infinite world of the gods:

Like the Tryzub, the Torii Gate has a right and left side (depicted as "posts" as opposed to "wings") which bridge across and come together at one end: the top of the gate in this case. Where they meet, a center lane is formed, which is directly above the passageway of the gate. It appears that this symbol represents the access to a sacred realm upon uniting the left and right "sides."

Whether it is remote viewing, meditation, or the bedrock of an ancient matriarchal or extrasensory-based civilization, each gravitates toward recreating the reconciliation and harmony between - up to and including the mergence of - the left and right brain consciousnesses needed to experience the "center lane" of psychic awareness. But where exactly does this center lane lead to which allows us to experience extra-sensory perception?

As mentioned previously, when our souls leave our body, our awareness is no longer partitioned. That is, the right-brained "altered-state" subconsciousness is no longer separated from the left-brained "waking-state" consciousness due to our soul (or energetic body) dissociating from our physical body. When it does so, the right-brain is no longer confined to the brain's right hemisphere and the left-brain is no longer physically localized to the left hemisphere. After physical death, the partitioning that separated the two consciousnesses - or the ego - dissipates and these two consciousnesses merge.

This post-death merging of the subconscious and conscious awareness will be a pleasant experience for some of us. For others, it will not.

If our internal "demons" or "issues" are still present, we will be now be in direct contact with them. This isn't necessarily a "bad thing": by facing our fears and learning from them, we can convert these fears into love. In this sense, "death" will initially be a sort of catharsis. However, if we had been accustomed to overcompensating for and projecting our "demons" - and violating our conscience in process - this mergence of the subconscious and conscious state will be tumultuous and, depending on the frequency and degree to which the conscience was divorced and violated, spiritually agonizing. Here, the soul not only attempts to deflect, project, deny, and denounce its own demons at a very intimate and immediate level, it tries to do the same with its guilty conscience with little success. The inability to harmonize the left-brain with the right, or the conscious with the subconscious, results in a sort of spiritual/mental anguish, commonly known as "hell."

However, the more left and right brain have been reconciled through self-awareness and converting fear into love, the more our spiritual bodies emanate the energies of truth, love, and brotherhood - thus, the more we will personally resonate with Infinite Intelligence.

This harmonization between left and right-brained awareness is the precisely the goal of remote viewing, mindfulness, and meditation: it is to simulate the unification and reconciliation of the subconscious and conscious awareness experienced in post-death. The greater this harmony, and the greater the energies of truth, love, and brotherhood, we more resonate with Infinite Intelligence. The more we resonate with Infinite Intelligence, the more we *resonate with an etheric dimension that allows us to psychically send and receive information as well as communicate with souls who have departed - and it is because this "center lane" bridges the gap between ourselves and the etheric realm referred to as "Heaven."* It is also referred to as "the kingdom of God," "the Force," the Unified Field, or the spirit realm.

This realm of Heaven, of course, is substantially more experiential after our spiritual bodies dissociate from our material ones, yet it can be accessed in our physical form provided our two hemispheres are in communion, our issues have been dissolved, and our remorse has been resolved. So, the more we tend to our "demons" and address our violated consciences with truth, love, and fairness, the smoother the transition into

Heaven will be, whether it be before our "passing" or after. Then, when we are fully aware, the "gates" will open and the "stairway to heaven" will reveal itself.

The more this inner peace and peace of mind is reached, the more we resonate and experience this etheric dimension. Those of us who resonate with this realm will often experience vivid dreams, an enhanced sense of synchronicity, and increased intuition. A deeper connection with this divine dimension can lead to enhanced psychic senses, mediumship ability (since spirits are a part of this realm), and other "miraculous" experiences.

Whether or not regular mindfulness and meditation practice leads to extrasensory perception, its purpose is this: to bring us closer to vibrating with Infinite Intelligence. As the energy in our "drop" becomes increasingly infused with the energy of Heaven, we do more and more to impart this heavenly energy outward to the rest of the lake.

At the very least, mindfulness and meditation can assist the self-psychoanalysis and unconditional self-love needed to dissolve negative energy and our "demons." The more we do so, the more we "lighten" ourselves and love others as a result. Instead of going through life living in fear, anger, frustration, anxiety, and resentfulness, we live in peace, joy, kindness, forgiveness, and love. With this negativity out of the system, we will be less likely spread fear by retaliating, punishing, judging, deceiving, manipulating, condemning, conniving, demeaning, exploiting, and harming others - the modes that are precisely behind the various large-scale systems of corruption that exist today. We will also be more likely to stop enabling such behavior. The less these toxic tactics exist, the sooner we will all be at peace.

And the peace we can realize will be beyond anyone's expectations. The more of us who convert our dark into light and reconcile our right brain with our left, *the more our species will bridge the gap between the physical and spiritual planes. Knowing this, we can literally create our Earth as it is in Heaven. Now, we have the ability to avoid a collective nervous breakdown and make a Heavenly inspired nervous breakthrough.*

But, we live in a Spiritual Democracy. Each and every one of us *needs to choose to do it. We* must *want* it, and we must *will* it. And we must start first by facing our own hell before we get there.

So now, we come full circle - right back exactly where this book started: facing our fears. We need to address our fears, how we've handled them, and transmute them so that our own energies of falsehoods, fear, and injustice are converted to truth, love, and brotherhood - the energy of Infinite Intelligence or, many would call, God.

Then, we can *truly* claim our birthright as "One Nation, Under God. Indivisible. With Liberty and Justice for All."

Only fear is stopping us from becoming the United States of Love; only fear is stopping us from making Heaven a place on Earth.

Notes:

1) Harpur, T. J., Hare, R. D., & Hakstian, A. R. (1989). "Two-factor conceptualization of psychopathy: Construct validity and assessment implications.". *Psychological Assessment*

2) Hare, R. D., & Neumann, C. N. (2006). The PCL-R Assessment of Psychopathy: Development, Structural Properties, and New Directions. In C. Patrick (Ed.), Handbook of Psychopathy (pp. 58-88). New York: Guilford.

3) Julian C. Motzkin, Joseph P. Newman, Kent A. Kiehl, Michael Koenigs. *"Reduced Prefrontal Connectivity in Psychopathy."* Journalof Neuroscience, 2011; 31 (48): 17348-17357 DOI:10.1523 JNEUROSCI.4215-11.2011

4) Kelland, K. *Study finds psychopaths have distinct brain structure.* Reuters 5/8/2012

5) Bradley Hagerty, B. *A Neuroscientist Uncovers Dark Secret.* National Public Radio, 6/30/10

6) Holzel, B., Carmody, J., Vangel, M., Congelton, C., Yerramsetti, S., Gard, T., Lazar, S. *Mindfulness practice leads to increases in regional great matter density.* Psychiatry Research: Neuroimaging Volume 191, Issue 1 , Pages 36-43, 30 January 2011

7) Eileen Luders, Florian Kurth, Emeran A. Mayer, Arthur W. Toga, Katherine L. Narr, Christian Gaser. The Unique Brain Anatomy of Meditation Practitioners: Alterations in Cortical Gyrification. Frontiers in Human Neuroscience, 2012; 6 DOI: 10.3389/fnhum2012.00034

8) Milholland, C. *Gaps Between Pay Of CEOs and Average Workers Is Huge And Getting Wider* KPBS, September 5, 2011

9) *Adding up the Government's Total Bailout Tab,* New York Times, July 24, 2011

10) Opensecrets.org, Lobbying Database. Figures are by the Center forResponsivePolitics, based on data from the Senate Office of Public Records. Data for the most recent year was downloaded on July 24, 2012.

11) http://www.wthr.com/story/17798210/tax-loophole-costs-billions

12) Dinan, S. *IRS Told Employees to Ignore Potential Fraud in Program Used by Immigrants.* Washington Times, August 8, 2012

13) Ryan, J. *Audit Finds $16 Muffins atJustice Department Conferences,* ABC News, September 20, 2011

14) *Is not joining Facebook a sign you're a psychopath? Some employers and psychologists say staying away from social media is 'suspicious'* UK Daily Mail, August 6, 2012

15) Bamford, J. *The NSA Is Building the Country's Biggest Spy Center (Watch What You Say)"* http: / wired.com, March 15, 2012

16) Johnson, R. Even Congress Wants To Know What The NSA Is Doing With This $2 Billion Utah Spy Center. Businessinsider.com, April 4, 2012

17) Bamford, J. *Shady Companies With Ties to Israel Wiretap the U.S. for the NSA.* http: //wired.com April 3, 2012

18) Coast to Coast AM, "Chemtrails and Weather." August 21, 2012